ORGANISATIONAL SEMIOTICS FOR BUSINESS INFORMATICS

Drawing meaningful conclusions from organisational data is challenging, and theoretical frameworks can often illuminate information in fresh and useful ways. This book is one of the first to demonstrate how organisational semiotics can be applied to business informatics and information systems.

Semiotics, a long-established discipline of signs, offers a rich philosophical and theoretical foundation for understanding information systems. This book demonstrates how applying the framework of semiotics to an organisation can provide insights into its communication needs and, as a result, enhance the design of its information systems. The authors demonstrate how organisations collect, process, represent, store and consume information through a complex system that is aligned to support its objectives and enhance performance.

Organisational Semiotics for Business Informatics clearly introduces the basic principles and describes a set of methods and techniques rooted in organisational semiotics. These have been applied to business applications and demonstrated through real-life case studies. This ground-breaking book has the potential to transform the theoretical understanding of information systems into the basis of a scientific discipline.

Kecheng Liu is Director of the Informatics Research Centre, Henley Business School at Reading, UK. He is a leading figure in Organisational Semiotics who has carried out extensive research into information systems and business informatics over the past 20 years.

Weizi Li is a lecturer in business informatics at the Informatics Research Centre, University of Reading, UK. Since completing her PhD in applied semiotics in systems architecture for digital hospitals, her research has focused on co-design methodology for business and IT systems.

In this elegant book, Kecheng Liu and Weizi Li provide a matured perspective and distil their considerable research base arrived at over many years. They achieve the considerable feat of a very clear rendering of semiotics, then show its application in researching and improving business informatics practice. The accelerating digitization we live with requires semiotics tools for its study; this intervention is timely and important.' Professor Leslie Willcocks, Department of Management, London School of Economics and Political Science, UK

'This deeply academic book provides the means to understand the complexities and difficulties of language and communications in Requirements Engineering which have so often resulted in challenged or failed information systems projects. It complements many previous socio-technical approaches to requirements capture and provides the foundation for understanding why, how and when they work. The final three chapters provide excellent examples of Organisational Semiotics applied to the real world, through a wide range of valuable case studies and contextual analyses.' Richard J Self, Senior Lecturer in Analytics and Governance, University of Derby, UK

'This book considers a highly important issue of business-IT alignment from the viewpoint of organisational semiotics. The author demonstrates quite rare deep understanding of differences between traditional computer science and business informatics. The book contains full coverage of fundamental principles of semiotics blended with practical aspects of requirements engineering and organisational modelling. It makes this source very useful during scientific research and design of information systems for various groups of readers: PhD students, scholars, business analysts and IT professionals.' Eduard Babkin, Professor, National Research University "Higher School of Economics", Nizhny Novgorod, Russia

ORGANISATIONAL SEMIOTICS FOR BUSINESS INFORMATICS

Kecheng Liu and Weizi Li

Routledge
Taylor & Francis Group
LONDON AND NEW YORK

First published 2015
by Routledge
2 Park Square, Milton Park, Abingdon, Oxon OX14 4RN

And by Routledge
711 Third Avenue, New York, NY 10017

Routledge is an imprint of the Taylor & Francis Group, an informa business

British Library Cataloguing in Publication Data
A catalogue record for this book is available from the British Library

Library of Congress Cataloging in Publication Data
Liu, Kecheng, 1957–
Organisational semiotics and business informatics/Kecheng Liu and Weizi Li.
pages cm
Includes bibliographical references and index.
1. Information technology—Management. 2. Management information systems. 3. Semiotics. 4. Knowledge management. I. Li, Weizi. II. Title.
HD30.2.L583 2015
658.4′038014—dc23
2014020055

ISBN: 978-0-415-82355-5 (hbk)
ISBN: 978-0-415-82356-2 (pbk)
ISBN: 978-0-203-55097-7 (ebk)

Typeset in Bembo Std
by Swales & Willis Ltd, Exeter, Devon, UK

CONTENTS

FIGURES

TABLES

BOXES

PREFACE

Information is a key resource in an organisation, alongside other long recognised resources such as natural and material resources, human resources and capital resources (including buildings, technology and physical infrastructure). There are many differences between information resources and other resources. Most of other types of resources are physical and tangible, while information is most probably not. In many cases, information is a description of other types of resources, and is a description of the activities that involve using or converting other types of resources from one form to another. The importance of information can be recognised by people when they make decisions and manage or use other types of resources. In a way, the importance of information is often seen from the activities that involve the use or conversion of other types of resources. We have some degree of confidence when we come to talk about other types of resources in, for example, how to measure the value of a piece of machinery, what properties a building has and how a person might respond in a car crash. But when it comes to information, we have little confidence in talking about the value of information to a decision, how information would be best managed to support human users, or the behaviour of information in a certain event or a context.

Informatics is a subject of study that focuses on the properties and functions of information, and on how information can be effectively managed and utilised, mostly with the aid of technology. Informatics in general deals with the structure, behaviour and functions of information to its users. It spans across several stages of the information lifecycle, such as the collection, storage, processing, accessing, presentation and utilisation of information. Informatics may be seen as being related to information science, information-processing, information systems, information technology, software engineering, computer science, computing applications and information management. Among these, some emphases are on technical aspects or the means of information-processing, while others are more focused on the use of information or the effect of information-processing.

Informatics research by the team in Reading, UK, of which the authors are part, places an emphasis on information and the effective use of information in business and scientific contexts. An organisation is seen as an information system in which information is processed and utilised as a key resource to achieve the organisation's goals and objectives. The work reflected in this book is rooted in Kecheng Liu's PhD and was further developed especially when Weizi Li joined the organisational semiotics (OS) research team in Reading.

Professor Ronald Stamper's early work laid the foundation for OS when he worked in the London School of Economics in the 1980s and then transferred to the Business School of the University of Twente, Netherlands, joined there by Kecheng Liu. In his book on 'Information', Professor Stamper proposed a semiotic framework for information management and, using the semiotic framework, explored the nature, characteristics and functions of information in organisational settings. His early project at the time was called LEGOL and aimed to deliver a set of legally oriented techniques for requirements specification. It soon grew into a major research undertaking into Methods for Eliciting, Analysing and Specifying Users' Requirements (MEASUR). Over the years, the programme further expanded into a set of methods to deal with all aspects of information systems.

In the early 1980s, Professor Ronald Stamper's team started to pioneer a series of methodological and practical investigations into information and information systems. OS becomes a philosophical and theoretical foundation for the methods and techniques developed within MEASUR. The methods and techniques of MEASUR enable users to understand and articulate the business problem under study and its context, to capture the semantics and intentions of users in requirements models, and also to implement technical information systems that are flexible and adaptable to organisational change. In the meantime, MEASUR has made significant contributions to the development of OS and has promoted OS into a discipline.

The first ground-breaking event to mark the birth of the discipline of OS was the workshop in Twente in 1995. Approximately a dozen of researchers from the backgrounds of information systems, management studies, computing, philosophy, language and communication from different parts of the world attended this event. Demands for, as well as issues and challenges in, information management were identified, and a research agenda was drawn up. However, it took another 4 years before the second workshop was organised, when colleagues met again in Twente to continue the pursuit.

The third workshop took place in 2000 in Stafford, UK, where Kecheng Liu had taken his first teaching post in the UK. Support for this workshop was received from UK's Engineering and Physical Science Research Council (EPSRC). Another notable milestone came in 2001 when, supported by the International Federation for Information Processing (IFIP), Working Group 8.1 sponsored a working conference entitled 'Organisational Semiotics – Evolving a Science of Information

Systems'. Since then, OS has gradually become a recognised subject of study, and the research community has started to emerge and meet regularly.

In 2009, the workshop for Organisational Semiotics was renamed as the International Conference on Informatics and Semiotics in Organisations (ICISO). These regular events have provided opportunities for academic scholars and industrial practitioners to publish their work and contribute to the advance of the discipline. In the recent years, both Kecheng Liu and Weizi Li have been active in serving the OS community and promoting OS research.

Since Kecheng Liu's early book on semiotics in information systems engineering in 2000, this book is still one of the few exploring the benefits of semiotics in relation to information, its features and functions, and information management in business organisations. This book introduces OS in a gentle and systematic manner. After outlining the basic principles of OS and its relevance to information management and systems, the book presents the methods for requirements analysis and modelling, and techniques for the design and implementation of technical systems. Finally, the last part of the book demonstrates the application of these methods and techniques through a number of case studies.

This book can be an essential text for undergraduate as well as postgraduate students. For example, in previous years, much of the content of this book has been used in Reading and other places for Bachelors programmes in information systems, information technology, and business information management, and for Masters programmes in business information management, information systems, software engineering, business informatics, and information systems analysis and design. Many researchers and PhD students, as well as industrial practitioners, have also used much of the content as a research text or a reference. With its substantial reworking, refinement and further examples, this book will be even better suited to all these audiences.

It is very pleasing to note that semiotics and its importance have been increasingly recognised by many scholars. The subject has been picked up by and incorporated into many teaching and research programmes in informatics, information systems, business and management, and human communication. Semiotics in relation to these applications has been taught in quite a few UK, European and other universities, on both undergraduate and postgraduate courses; examples include Indiana (USA), Washington (USA), Aarhus (Denmark), Tartu (Estonia), Campinas (Brazil), Twente (the Netherlands), Beijing Institute of Technology (China), Beijing Jiaotong University (China), Cardiff (UK) and of course Reading. Adding this work on OS to the currently not-so-thick portfolio of teaching texts will certainly enhance its value to semiotics applied to business informatics.

ACKNOWLEDGEMENTS

There are several people we would like to thank. First, we are deeply indebted to Ronald Stamper, a mentor and a true hero, who introduced us to this fascinating semiotic perspective on information systems. Many colleagues have made significant contributions and greatly influenced the area of organisational semiotics. In particular, we would like to mention a few who have played key roles in the community and in OS research but have sadly recently passed away: Peter Andersen was a close colleague whose books and papers served as important references in the field; Henk Gezendam was one of the key authors of quite a few inspiring works; and Rene Jorna was another associate who will stay in our memory for a very long time.

We would like to acknowledge our colleagues in the Informatics Research Centre (IRC), with whom many discussions have taken place, joint projects have been conducted, and courses have been developed and delivered. Past and current PhD students in the IRC must receive our appreciation for their effort in applying some of the work described in this text; their experiments, validation, feedback and critiques have been extremely useful during the writing of the book. Our students, in particular those on the postgraduate programmes of business information management, information systems, informatics, and business technology consulting, must share some of the credit too. Much of the book's content has been taught on these courses in the past 10 years, and every year students' feedback and assessments have led to a continued improvement of the material.

Finally, Kecheng Liu wishes to express his profound gratitude to his wife, Dr Lily Sun, for her ever-lasting understanding, sacrifice and support. Without that, many things, including this book, would not have become possible.

Permissions have been granted by the publishers for the use of our early materials; acknowledgements are due to Cambridge University Press for most of Part 1 of the book; IGI Global for Chapter 11; and *Systems, Signs & Actions* for Chapter 12.

1

INTRODUCTION

Information and information systems

What is information? Many people have attempted to provide definitions, but most of these are incomplete. A typical explanation is that information is processed data that has meanings for its users. But then questions arise in terms of what 'meaning' is. If *information* is to the study of information as *object* is to physics, and there are many laws by which we can study objects, then what are the laws by which we can study *information*? What is the study of information anyway?

What can be said here is that information is not a simple, primitive notion. Devlin (1991) compares the difficulties faced by a man in the Iron Age in answering the question 'What is iron?' and for a man in today's Information Age when asked the question 'What is information?' To point the Iron Age man towards various artefacts made of iron would not be enough for him to answer the question 'What is iron?'; similarly, demonstrating some of the properties of information is not enough to answer the question 'What is information?' People can feel the possession of information, and can create and use information. They gather it, store it, process it, transmit it, use it and even sell it and buy it. It seems our lives depend on it, yet it is so hard to tell what exactly it is.

In order to understand the nature of information, we may have to uncover some fundamental and primitive notions with which the question can be investigated and explained. The concept of a sign is one such primitive notion that serves our purposes here. All information is 'carried' by signs of one kind or another. Information-processing and communication in an organisation are realised by creating, passing and utilising signs. Therefore, understanding signs should contribute to our understanding of information and information systems (Stamper 1992).

What are information systems? One answer could be that computer systems can process and manage information. But, in recent years, it has become more likely that people will tell you that computer systems plus associated business processes, people (i.e. users) and the organisation are seen as information systems. From a slightly different angle, the study of information systems focuses on how to build information systems and how to make an organisation become an effective system in using information and managing the activities of such systems.

This study of, or inquiry into, information systems is an active area to which other research and industrial communities have paid much attention. There has been much discussion on its pluralistic and interdisciplinary nature, and its foundations. An increasing number of researchers and practitioners are defining information systems as social interaction systems. Social and organisational infrastructures, human activities and business processes are considered to be part of information systems. Information systems in this definition can produce messages, communicate, create information, and define and alter meanings.

The UK Academy for Information Systems provides the following definition of the domain of information systems (UKAIS 2014: 379): 'the means by which people and organisations, utilising technologies, gather, process, store, use and disseminate information'. Ray Paul (2010) offers the following: 'Information systems is information technology in use'. Many authors emphasise the importance of studying information systems in this postmodern society, as well as their interdisciplinary nature. For example, Avison and Nandhakumar (1995) suggest that information systems encompass a wide range of disciplinary areas such as information theory, semiotics, organisation theory and sociology, computer science, engineering and perhaps more.

Business informatics

Computer science, although not as old as physics or other sciences, is recognised as a fairly established scientific discipline. Information systems, software engineering and computer engineering are other disciplines that emerged afterwards and are recognised by the world's largest educational and scientific computing society (Association for Computing Machinery [ACM] 2013).

The word 'informatics' came from the French word 'informatique'. For many, informatics is more or less a synonym of computer science and its related disciplines recognised by ACM, with some reference to the human and organisational context. This places a great deal of emphasis on the methodologies, means, technologies and tools with which information is processed and managed. The definition of informatics from the Informatics Research Centre (IRC 2013; www.irc.reading.ac.uk) emphasises different aspects by stating that informatics is 'the study of the creation, management and utilisation of information in scientific and economic activities'. Business informatics aims to relate informatics to a business context and to investigate how information resources can be effectively managed and utilised to add value to an organisation.

As an illustration, Table 1.1 summarises distinctive differences in the objectives of study between technical subjects such as computer science and information technology (IT) compared with business informatics. This table shows that the technically

TABLE 1.1 Difference in study objectives

Computer science/information technology	*Business informatics*
Format	Content
Syntactics	Semantics
Supply	Demand
Technologically driven	Business pull
Cause	Effect
Cost	Value

oriented subjects focus on the format and syntactics by which information is organised and represented, while business information is more concerned with getting the right information content and right semantics of information. The technical studies focus on the supply of technical means and are motivated by technological development, whereas the attention of business informatics is on addressing the demand that arises from business. IT and the like are drawn towards the causes of problems and consider how to invest in technology spending and how to make it cost-effective; conversely, business informatics centres on how to achieve an optimal effect of technology and maximise value. Both approaches are important, but perhaps the perspective of business informatics makes the focus of study more closely relevant to business motivations once the technologies have become available.

Issues and challenges in information systems

Information-processing and information services have become a major industry that plays a significant role in the current era of the digital economy. Even as early as in the 1970s, Porat (1977), based on an analysis of various sources, suggested that in developed countries such as the USA and Western European countries, approximately 50 per cent or even more of the labour force was engaged in information work. The International Labour Organization (ILO 2006) reports how the rise of IT has brought about a transformation of the workforce on a global scale.

Box 1.1 Techno-economic paradigms

The notion of the change of 'techno-economic paradigms' developed by Freeman (1991) and Perez (2009) is invaluable in understanding the link between the diffusion of ITs on the one hand, and growth and employment on the other. The change of 'techno-economic paradigm' approach incorporates and stresses both the direct and indirect effects of It.

The process of the innovation and diffusion of new ITs that took off in the 2000s constitutes a radical transformation in the means of production, distribution and

TABLE 1.2 Global developments in ICT, 2001–2013

	2001	*2007*	*2010*	*2013*
Mobile phone subscription	15%	50%	75%	96.2%
Individual using the Internet	8%	20%	30%	38.8%
Fixed telephone subscription	17%	19%	17%	29.5%
Mobile-broadband subscription	0%	4%	11%	16.5%
Fixed broadband subscription	1%	5%	8%	9.8%

Source: ITU World Telecommunication/ICT indicators database

exchange (Table 1.2). It has already profoundly affected international trade and investment, the movement of capital and labour, and many work processes and products. It has also accelerated the shift towards services and their outsourcing internationally. The rapid spread, ongoing development and pervasiveness of this flow of innovation is driving a massive reconfiguration of world production and distribution, as well as of the management systems of enterprises and public agencies – with major consequences for employment patterns (ILO 2006).

Measuring the overall economic impact of ITs has, however, proved controversial. For many years, economists were troubled by the 'Solow productivity paradox', named after the economist who pointed out that computers were everywhere, but that no impact was visible in terms of productivity statistics (cited in Brynjolfsson 1993). Economic history suggests that major technological shifts take years to spread widely enough to clearly affect aggregate economic performance. The pace and reach of diffusion of ITs is unprecedented, but economies and societies are still at an early stage in learning how to make full use of their potential (ILO 2006). Numerous studies have reported large company budgets being set aside for IT and huge amounts being spent on systems development projects, yet with only a low economic return from the high investment.

Strassmann (1990, 2004) argues that there is no guarantee that large investment in IT will lead to high business performance or an increase in revenue: 'no relationship between expenses for computers and business profitability' (Straussman 1990) on any usual accounting basis across an industry. Some companies use IT well, but others balance this positive effect with poor returns on IT investment. Many surveys in industry exhibit evidence that a considerable number of information systems developed at great cost fail to satisfy users or have to be modified before they become acceptable. According to an analysis put forward by the US General Accounting Office in the late 1980s, among a group of US federal software projects totalling US$6.2 million, less than 2 per cent of software products were used as delivered and more than half (including those not delivered) were not used. The situation has not improved since.

A recent example is the failure of the computer system upgrade in the UK National Health Service (NHS). The National Programme for IT in the NHS was an ambitious £11.4 billion programme of investment designed to reform how the NHS in England used information to improve services and patient care (House of

Commons 2011). The programme was launched in 2002 with the aim of creating a fully integrated electronic care records system, which was expected to cost around £7 billion in total. The original objective was to ensure that every NHS patient had an individual electronic care record that could be rapidly transmitted between different parts of the NHS in order to make accurate patient records available to NHS staff at all times. However, the programme was abandoned in 2011 with the cost having reached £10 billion. A report by the influential Public Accounts Committee concluded that the programme ended up becoming one of the 'worst and most expensive contracting fiascos' in public sector history (BBC 2013).

Similarly, in 1997, Advanced Technical Strategy Inc. published their study 'The Software Development Crisis' on the Internet, as quoted in Box 1.2 (Boustred 1997). In this figure, the 'shameful numbers' show that a majority of projects cost nearly twice their original budgets.

Box 1.2 Shameful numbers

- 31.1% of projects are cancelled before they are ever completed
- 52.7% of projects cost 189% of their original estimate
- 16.2% of software projects are completed on time and on budget
    - In larger companies, only 9% of projects come in on time and on budget with approximately 42% of the originally proposed features and functions
    - In small companies, 78.4% of software projects are deployed with at least 74.2% of their original features and functions

Bloch *et al.* (2012), in conjunction with Oxford University, published a study on a total of 5,400 large-scale IT projects (projects with an initial budget of greater than $15 million) and found that the well-known problems with IT project management are persisting. Some key findings are quoted below from the report:

- 17 per cent of large IT projects go so badly that they can threaten the very existence of the company.
- On average, large IT projects run 45 percent over budget and 7 percent over time, while delivering 56 percent less value than predicted.

According to another report (Handler 2013), customer acceptance figures show that more than two-thirds of software products are never used or never completed. One of main reasons for these failures is inappropriate studies on users' requirements that lead to incorrect systems analysis and design. Studies have been continued and similar outcomes have been reported, albeit with some slight improvements. Based on a recent report from Handler (2013), 24 per cent of IT projects are viewed as less successful or even worse (Figure 1.1). Figure 1.2 shows the reasons why IT projects fail. It suggests that the mismatch of functionality between what is required and what is delivered is the main reason for the failure of IT projects.

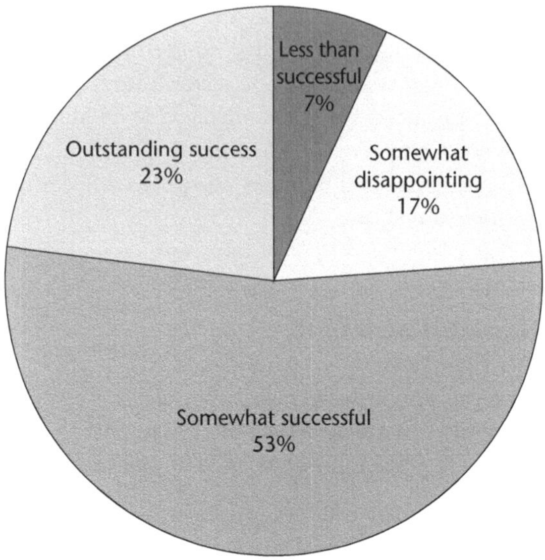

FIGURE 1.1 Customer perception of IT project success (Handler 2013)

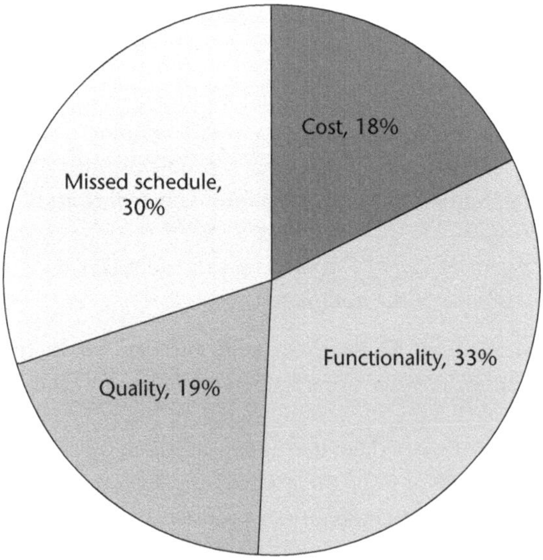

FIGURE 1.2 Reasons for IT projects being less than successful (Handler 2013)

In determining the success of an IT project, the social, cultural and organisational aspects, as opposed to technology itself, play a decisive role. 'A computer is worth only what it can fetch in an auction', Franke (1987) wrote. 'It has value only if surrounded by appropriate policy, strategy, methods for monitoring results, project control, talented and committed people, sound relationships and well-designed information systems.' These information systems are composed of organisational infrastructure, business processes and technological systems. An organisation with an improperly designed bureaucracy and unprepared culture will not guarantee that the possession of more information will improve the quality of management; on the contrary, the quality of management will suffer from being overloaded with irrelevant information (Ackoff 1967). As Lee (1988) points out:

> certainly, this (information) technology has done much to improve bureaucratic efficiency. On the other hand, we claim, it has not helped at all in the management of bureaucratic complexity. Indeed, it has aggravated the problem by obscuring bureaucratic rules and procedures in the form of computer codes. (For instance, many have experienced the frustrations of trying to rectify a computer-generated billing error).

Two other problems are observed in systems developments. One is the long lead-time between the commencement of the projects and the systems becoming available. The commencement stage may be to study the business strategy of a given organisation and to conduct information systems planning, followed by business analysis, systems design, systems implementation and so on. Many systems development projects have taken too long in reaching fruition, hence the immediate risk arises that during the development processes – that users may wish to change the requirements they specified when the projects began. If development methodologies do not allow for the incorporation of modified requirements, the products may after the long lead-time hardly satisfy the users' current, possibly updated, needs.

Another problem observed in practice is related to systems analysis, particularly to the documentation of the analysis. The application of most development methodologies produces huge volumes of documentation. These documents are supposed to be addressed to the technical personnel involved in the development projects. Because the primary purpose of the analysis documents is usually to function as a formal basis for the next stage, i.e. systems design, the deliverables from analyses are often directed particularly to the systems designers in the development teams. The business users, who may actually be the owners of the systems, are not considered as recipients of the information analysis products.

As a result, the analysis products are presented in some artificial languages that are specially invented by and for the systems development communities. Syntactic elements such as the technical terms and jargon of the methods used and the technical disciplines receive more attention than does how to make users understood effectively. The large volume of documentation may contain a great many design symbols and special notations. Each project has to define the meanings of the terms used in the information system in a *data dictionary*. The products of analysis may then be very 'precise' and convenient for the next step, that is, systems design; they may even be automatically translated into a database schema by a computer-added software engineering tool. Nevertheless, these documents are too difficult for the system's owners to understand, and therefore achieving the users' participation is hard.

The users need above all to check the meanings incorporated into the specifications so that the results of the analysis can be verified. However, in most of the conventional methodologies, documentation creates barriers to rather than facilities for the requirements analysis. Voluminous documentation builds up psychological difficulties; in addition, many complicated technicalities have to be learnt through undergoing intensive training. Every time users want to understand a fragment of the representation, the data dictionaries have to be consulted. And even with the help of data dictionaries, users are still unlikely to be able to make an adequate check on the meanings of words. The risk arising from such a situation is that users' requirements may be wrongly understood by the analysts; however, some false but syntactically self-consistent representations may be produced as foundations for systems development. In such cases, it is unwise to expect satisfactory information systems to be produced based on these models of requirements.

As a solution, it is suggested that a method with an emphasis on semantics is needed. The possibilities of preserving and clarifying meanings in requirements analysis should be considered to be the most important criterion. Therefore, a correct requirements analysis can only be guaranteed if users can validate and verify an information systems model that can be technically implemented. Ideally, this model should be a by-product of the business analysis.

Organisational semiotics and the related methods for its analysis introduced in this book may offer us a useful perspective and a set of effective tools to deal with some of the issues and challenges.

How to use this book

One of the motivations behind this book is to examine the relevant issues in information systems development and to provide an insight from a semiotic point of view for information systems in the context of the organisation. Key contributions of this book are the introduction of an organisational semiotics approach that consists of a set of methods and techniques for information systems development, and the application of these methods and techniques in the context of the organisation; in addition, there are a number of case studies to illustrate the use of the methods.

The methods were initially developed by the Methods for Eliciting, Analysing and Specifying Users' Requirements (MEASUR) research team. This team has now grown to a community with colleagues in many countries, and the MEASUR methods have been applied and further developed in many research and industrial situations. Few systematic accounts of MEASUR can, however, be found. This book aims to fill this gap between the many MEASUR articles, technical papers, research reports and project documentations that have been produced.

The book is divided into two parts. Part I (Chapters 2–8) focuses on a discussion of semiotics, the semiotic framework for information systems, and the semiotic methods for information systems analysis. Part II (Chapters 9–13) emphasises the application of the methods. It describes how the semiotic methods are used in systems analysis, design and implementation in real-life projects relating to information systems.

Chapter 2 discusses the fundamental concepts and principles of signs, semiosis and semiotics, as well as their relevance in various domains including computing, engineering and the organisation. Chapter 3 examines different philosophical paradigms and then introduces a semiotic framework for information systems. This semiotic framework represents a radical subjective view of the social world, organisations and information systems. It serves as philosophical and methodological guidance for the development and formulation of the semiotic methods to be discussed later in the book. In Chapter 4, the principles of semiotics in requirements engineering are presented, with a focus on knowledge representation of the requirements. The basic notions of knowledge representation and information analysis are explored, and basic considerations relating to those methods are discussed. An overview of the semiotic methods for information systems MEASUR is then presented. MEASUR comprises a set of methods covering all stages and aspects of planning, developing and maintaining an information system. Key methods such as the problem articulation method (PAM), semantic analysis method and norm analysis method are discussed in detail in other chapters.

Chapters 5–8 study aspects of three layers of the semiotic framework: the *semantic*, *pragmatic* and *social* aspects. The reason for such a careful investigation of these aspects is that they are more relevant than the other three aspects (*physical*, *empirical* and *syntactic*) as far as information systems analysis and design is concerned. For example, physical and empirical issues can be important in designing and implementing a computer network, and syntactic issues can be highly relevant in programming and implementing a database. The tasks of systems analysis and design are primarily concerned with capturing requirements, studying business knowledge and representing knowledge at the semantic, pragmatic and social levels.

Before the semiotic methods are discussed, Chapter 5 explores the method for business infrastructure analysis. A semiotic diagnosis is presented based on the semiotic framework. The PAM is introduced in detail to demonstrate how to decompose and analyse complicated business problems in an infrastructural analysis. After explicating knowledge relating to infrastructure analysis in the business domain, Chapter 6 begins to tackle the issues at the semantic level of organisational modelling. The method of semantic analysis, a key method in MEASUR, is presented and discussed here. Chapter 7 tackles the next layer of the semiotic framework: pragmatics and communication. It also examines other approaches before looking at norm analysis. Finally in this part, we come to the social layer in Chapter 8, to emphasise the purposes that any technical system would ultimately serve in an organisation. It is argued that an effective modelling method should enable the analysis of all these semantic, pragmatic and social issues, and it demonstrates that such semiotic methods are best capable of this.

Part II of the book (Chapters 9–13) deals with using the methods of organisational semiotics in information systems development. Chapter 9 shows strategic systems planning for informal, formal and technical systems in an organisation, as well as substantive, communication and control activities. It also displays the use of the PAM in system planning through a case study. Chapter 10 shows the co-design of business and technical systems. A framework tackling infrastructural, organisational and operational co-design is presented, followed by a case study on organisational co-design for healthcare pathway management. Chapter 11 shows the application of semiotic diagnosis in strategic planning for police organisations. Chapter 12 exhibits the application of the semiotic approach to the re-engineering process with a focus on requirements recovery. Finally, Chapter 13 discusses information systems and business in the digital age, with a focus on supply chains, customer relationships and value chain management.

Questions and exercises

1. With reference to the definition of informatics in this book, identify the key concerns or issues to be studied in computer science, IT and informatics. Consider and justify the statement that, unlike computer science and IT, informatics focuses on the content of information and on how information can bring maximum value to the scientific and practical undertaking where information is used.
2. What are causes of the challenges and 'shameful figures' seen in information systems projects? In contrast to other scientific and engineering disciplines, it seems that information systems is still a young and emerging discipline in the making. Is the lack of a rigorous and well-tested scientific foundation one of the key reasons for the challenges and shameful figures encountered? Ensure your answer includes justification and supporting evidence.
3. If we regard business informatics as about studying the effective use of information as a resource in business applications, what are your motivations for studying business informatics?

PART I
Organisational semiotics

2

UNDERSTANDING SIGN AND SEMIOTICS

The word 'semiotics' comes from the Greek for 'observation of signs'. Charles Sanders Peirce (1839–1914), who was primarily a logician, as well as being competent in mathematics and many other branches of science including astronomy, chemistry, physics, geology and meteorology, was a founder of semiotics as the 'formal doctrine of signs'. At almost the same time, Ferdinand de Saussure (1857–1913) founded semiology, a European school of semiotics. Semiology aims to discover 'what constitutes signs and what laws govern them' (Saussure, cited in Hawkes 1977: 123), with a slight emphasis on social psychology and general psychology. Semiotics covers the whole cycle of signs from their creation and processing to their use, with a greater emphasis on the effect of signs. Although sometimes in literature no clear distinction is made between semiotics and semiology, it is the former which will be the theme of study in this book.

There are three distinct fields of semiotics – syntactics (or syntax), semantics and pragmatics – which ultimately go back to Peirce (cf. Lyons 1977). Morris (1938) made semiotics more generally familiar as a science of signs, making many important contributions, largely from a behavioural standpoint. According to Morris, pragmatics deals with the origin, uses and effects of signs within the behaviour in which they occur. Semantics deals with the signification of signs in all modes of signifying; syntax deals with the combination of signs without regard to their specific signification or their relation to the behaviour in which they occur.

Signs

In Chapter 1, we assumed that a sign is primitive, and that understanding signs will help with understanding information. Moreover, the notion of signs is essential in semiotics. So what is a sign?

Anything can be a sign, if it denotes, signifies or represents something. We can readily agree that the following are examples of signs:

- A watch is a sign; it represents time.
- A national flag is a sign; it represents a country.
- A 'no smoking' notice is a sign; it represents a warning.
- A set of traffic lights is a sign; its represents a legal force that tells us when to go and when to stop.
- Clouds, and their colour, density and shape, can be a sign, as they may tell us how likely it is to rain.

From these examples, we can see that a sign can be natural or artificial, simple or complex, and hard or easy to interpret.

A less serious explanation, but one that reveals exactly the essence of what a sign is the following:

- Anything that one could use to lie with is a sign.

A more serious version of definition is as follows:

- Anything that stands to someone for something else in some respect or capacity is a sign. Every phrase in this last definition is important.
- First of all, we indeed mean 'anything', if it stands for something else.
- Second, when a thing (e.g. A) represents something else (e.g. B), such a representation is meaningful to someone (e.g. C) who understands it and interprets it. Such an interpretation requires prior knowledge; hence the subjectivity in the processing of the sign must be recognised.
- Third, a sign acts as a sign only in a certain respect or capacity. For example, if we asked someone 'Is a pen a sign?', most people would hesitate because the immediate intuitive response would be that a pen is a tool instead of a sign. But there may be a case where someone carries a very expensive pen and shows it off. In such a case, the pen may in this capacity be taken as a sign of being wealthy.

There are three categories of signs (Peirce 1958a): icon, index and symbol.

An *icon* is a sign that resembles the signified object. An iconic sign represents its object mainly by its similarity, and signifies by virtue of metaphor. Icons can also be verbal by making words onomatopoeic. Examples of such signs are photographs, images, portraits, diagrams and maps.

An *indexical* sign is inherently connected in some way to the signified object. An index is normally instructive and signifies by virtue of metonymy. Examples of such signs are smoke signifying fire, a knock on the door indicating someone waiting there, footprints suggesting a person or an animal's presence, and pain in the stomach indicating a disease. A sign of this kind can be used as a part to represent the whole.

The third type of sign is a *symbol*, whose relationship with its signified object is 'arbitrary' or purely conventional. It signifies by virtue of an arbitrary norm that may be rooted in a societal or cultural convention. Examples of such signs are the three colours of traffic signals, which are based on conventions, and the different sounds of a siren indicating the different types of vehicle (e.g. a fire engine or ambulance).

The three categories of signs are not separate and distinct: a complex sign may be a mixture of several kinds.

A primary purpose why human beings create and use signs is communication, unless a sign is purely for primitive use. To be able to use signs properly, one needs to understand the relationships between the signs and things they refer to (i.e. the signified). For the three categories of sign, the degree of connection between the signifier and the signified is different.

Indexical signs have existential or causal relationships with the signified. Iconic signs such as photographs are physically forced to correspond to the objects they represent. However, as discussed in Fiske (1990), there are varying degrees of arbitrary elements with even an iconic sign. A portrait is less iconic or more arbitrary than a photograph; a cartoon is more arbitrary than a portrait. But even with a photograph, the cameraman can take a picture of a different part of an object from a different angle and with different lighting to incorporate some arbitrary elements. Therefore, convention – the cultural norms in a society – is necessary for understanding any sign, however iconic or indexical it is (Fiske 1990: 53).

Norms play a variety of important roles in communication and signification. They can be as formal as being the rules to define the relationship between signs and the signified, and to govern how the signs should be used. Think about English grammar in forming singular and plural nouns. There are probably more informal norms that one can learn from experience, for example the meaning of zooming into some football action and playing it in slow motion on television (is it for a highlight or for showing a mistake?). What is the significance of a sudden start of music in a romantic movie, and what norms enable us to know that there is a significance here? Convention is the social dimension of signs. It is the agreement among users on the appropriate uses of and responses to a sign. One has to understand and to follow social and cultural norms when a sign is created and used, otherwise it will be only private and thus does not function as a sign of communication.

Sense-making through semiosis

A sign is usually used to express or communicate something. Therefore, a sign itself can be seen as a process in which sense-making is essential. This sign process or sense-making process is called *semiosis* (Peirce 1958a).

Semiosis is a process of understanding involving something as a sign to some organism. In his book, Nauta (1972) describes semiosis as a sign-process exercise of 'mediated-taking-account-of'. The mediators are *sign vehicles*; the taking-account-of are the *interpreters*; and what is taken account of are *designata*. These three elements function in every sign process or semiosis. The sign vehicle is the 'something that is a sign to an organism' (i.e. to the interpreter). The sign vehicle is defined as a particular event or object, such as a sound or a mark, that functions as a sign. Thus, a sign vehicle is a special kind of stimulus. In its function as a sign, the sign vehicle refers to something else, the *denotatum*. The denotatum also has a special effect on the attitude of the interpreter, and this alteration of the inner state of the interpreter is called *interpretant*.

Figure 2.1 illustrates the basic concepts involved in semiosis and the relationships between them. Semiosis is the sign-mediated process by which a knowing subject gives meaning to what is taken to be an event or actuality. Formulated in terms of the three universal categories, it is the universal process in which a *First*, a presentation (which could be any quality, any thing or any idea) functions as a representamen or sign in being applied to a *Second*. The *Second* is an object or referent, or actuality, acknowledged through the intermediary of a meaning-mediating *Third* (Kolkman 1993). The notion of an interpretant is richer and broader than interpretation. The effect, the interpretant, also includes feelings and action, or updates of one's view or knowledge base. An interpretant can be in turn treated as a sign in another (higher order) process of semiosis.

Every sign involves a 'signifier' – the material form of the sign – and a 'signified' – the object, action, event or concept it represents. Note that semiosis itself is a process of sense-making in which there will always be three aspects: a sign as a signifier, an object to be signified and an interpretant, or the effect that is achieved on the reader or the user of the sign. The example in Figure 2.1 can illustrate these three elements:

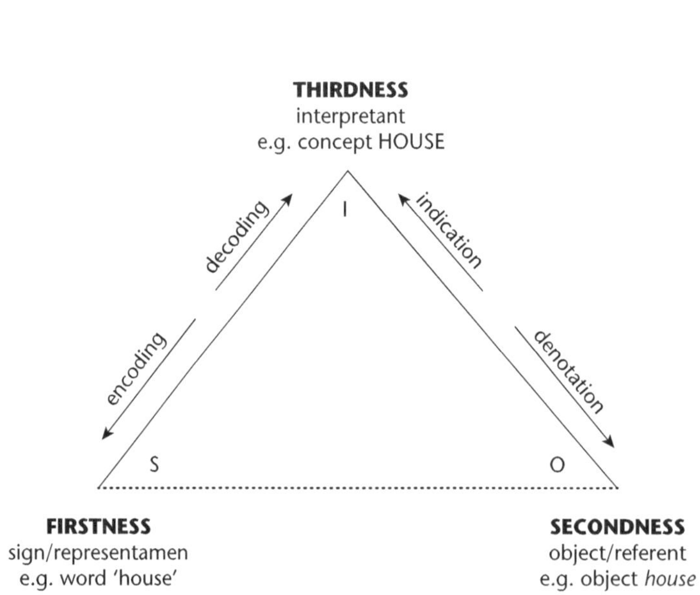

FIGURE 2.1 Semiosis as a process of sense-making

- *the sign*, which is considered as a signifier/vehicle/representamen: the written word 'house' or a drawing of a house;
- *the object*, which can be called signified/described/represented: the type of object of house, or the category of house;
- *the interpretant*: the effect of the sign on someone who reads and interprets it. This leads to a process and result of sense-making using knowledge, for example an impression or an interpretation from seeing or reading the sign. This impression or interpretation will depend on this reader's personal experience and prior knowledge.

The relationships between the signifier and the signified may not be fixed and may differ depending on the sign users' knowledge and experience and the context, culture and language. For example, the word 'slim', although the spelling is the same in both languages, means *cleaver* in Dutch but *thin* in English.

The dotted line in Figure 2.1 between the sign/representamen and object/reference signifies that the mapping between them is not fixed: a sign may mean a different object to a different person involved in the sign process, and therefore the effect or interpretant can be different. This subjectivity is essential in every semiosis.

The labels along the top edges of the semiosis triangle indicate that movements also take place between Firstness and Thirdness (i.e. encoding and decoding) and between Secondness and Thirdness (i.e. denotation and indication).

Characteristics of semiosis

Four characteristics can be used to describe semiosis. First, it is universal. It is applicable to any type of sign-processing activity. It explains the mechanism for both creating and using a sign. Second, semiosis is a process capable of identifying anything present according a specific criterion or a norm. The process of representation can be recursive: a sign can be seen as an object in another sign process, just as an interpretant and an object can be a sign. This will lead to its third characteristic, which is the possibility of making anything not present identifiable. Finally, semiosis is subject dependent. It is closely related to the agent who is involved in the semiosis. The agent can be an individual, a group or a social community with certain knowledge and obeying certain norms. The process of semiosis is always partial in its representation of the object and subjective in its interpretation, depending on the viewpoint of the interpretant and the knowledge and ability that the agent possesses.

Semiosis as an inference process

Semiosis can be seen as the building of structures of experience via signs. Thinking will involve using signs and inferring an object from its sign. That inference, the effect of the sign, is the interpretant (Cunningham 1992). Traditional accounts of inference usually suggest two processes: deduction and induction. However, Peirce proposed three irreducible, distinct modes of inference in semiosis for understanding and learning, the additional one in the Peircean logic system being abduction. The logic of abduction (the *Firstness*) and deduction (the *Secondness*) contribute to our qualitative or conceptual understanding of phenomena, while the logic of induction (the *Thirdness*) adds quantitative details to the qualitative or conceptual knowledge (Yu 1994).

The three types of inference are explained below with examples to illustrate the differences between them (Gust and Kühnberger, 2008).

Deduction: In the case of deduction, one tries to make a conclusion or to find a result on the basis of an observed fact by applying a rule or axiom. For example:

All human are mortal	(Axiom)
Socrates is a human	(Fact/premise)
Therefore, it follows that Socrates is mortal	(Conclusion)

Remarks: a conclusion is derived from given axioms (knowledge) and facts (observations).

Induction is related to the generation of a general rule of the basis of a fact and conclusion. For example:

Socrates is a human	(Background knowledge)
Socrates, and many others, are mortal	(Observation/example)
Therefore, I generalise that all humans are mortal	(Generalisation)

Remarks: a general rule (axiom) is derived from background knowledge and observations.

Abduction in Peirce's theory is the process of forming a hypothesis that explains the given observations (see Peirce 1958a). For example:

All humans are mortal	(Theory)
Socrates is a mortal	(Observation)
Therefore, Socrates must have been a human	(Hypothesis/diagnosis)

Remarks: A premise/hypothesis is derived from a known axiom (theory) and some observation.

In the three types of reasoning, *deduction* draws logical consequences from premises. This kind of reasoning does not lead to the discovery of new knowledge, because the conclusion has already been embedded in the premise (Peirce 1958a).

Inductive reasoning is based on the generality and law of large numbers of cases. Induction generates empirical laws but not theoretical laws because the conclusion one reaches from research with a large number of samples is merely probably (and never certainly) true. Finally, *abduction* works to look for a pattern in a phenomenon and suggest a hypothesis. The objective of abduction is to generate hypotheses and further to determine which hypothesis or proposition to test, not which one to adopt or assert. To achieve a comprehensive enquiry, one should apply abduction, deduction and induction together. Abduction and deduction are the conceptual understanding of a phenomenon, and induction is its quantitative verification. In short, abduction creates, deduction explicates, and induction verifies (Yu 1994).

Abduction and semiosis

Abduction, as the first core concept, constitutes, according to Peirce (1958a), the first stage of any scientific investigation and of all interpretative processes (Box 2.1). The basis for abduction comprises the signs of a certain number of observations. Therefore, abduction is associated with the process of semiosis. When new signs are observed, abduction can be a relevant strategy (i.e. an interpretation process) to start from surprising facts (objects) or from few details and, using them, to try to find a tentative hypothesis or interpretant.

Box 2.1 The interpretive process of abduction (Everaert-Desmedt 2011)

Deduction and induction were studied in depth by the classical philosophers, but no logician before Peirce had recognised the importance or the specific character of this third form of reasoning, which Peirce called abduction. Nonetheless, it is a form of reasoning that happens to be used in the most mundane circumstances as well as in scientific research.

The interpretive process of abduction (or process of deductive hypothesis) can be described in four stages:

1. We encounter a curious fact that is unexplainable according to our previous knowledge; in other words, this fact startles us in our daily habits and prejudices. In the case of scientific research, the fact is not accounted for by any existing theory.
2. We formulate a hypothesis that may explain the fact. Our reasoning is grounded in firstness, in that the hypothesis, which springs to mind with instinctive force, is suggested by the fact. Indeed, there is an analogy between the fact and the possible consequences of applying the hypothesis.

(Continued)

(Continued)

3. Next we apply the hypothesis deductively, and we infer the consequences that follow from it. We adopt an attitude in life that matches the hypothesis. In scientific research, this is a matter of rigorously determining which tests might allow us to disprove the hypothesis if need be (to prove it is false or does not match the facts). While a single experiment can invalidate a hypothesis, it would take an infinite series of experiments to confirm it.
4. By using a kind of induction, or making generalizations based on a number of positive test results, we conclude that the results verify the hypothesis, at least provisionally, until there is proof to the contrary.

Take an example of abduction from everyday conversation:

1. The startling event: Someone says, 'It's cold in here', when the conversation had nothing to do with air temperatures. Let us say that we are in a room with an open window, that I am the listener, and am near the open window.
2. The explanatory hypothesis: I refer to a rule that is part of the commonly shared store of knowledge about things cultural and practical. It is less cold in a room when the window is closed. I have already been in similar situations, and when a room is judged to be cold, one closes the window. Immediately I establish a connection between my previous knowledge and what the speaker actually said, and come up with the hypothesis that the speaker would like me to close the window.
3. Deduction: I take the consequence of the hypothesis as a prediction, and I act accordingly: I close the window.
4. Induction: The speaker makes no objection when I close the window; in fact he thanks me. This result confirms my hypothesis.

Abduction is an argument that appeals to Firstness in order to formulate a rule (or more precisely, a hypothesis, and therefore a possible rule). This may be followed by a deduction in which the hypothesis will be applied to solve a problem and offer an explanation to a phenomenon, tentatively, with some known caveat or uncertainty. In a typical process of theoretical enquiry, this may be further followed by induction, in which inductive reasoning is carried out to generate some credible conclusions that are usually rules (or knowledge), but often with constraints attached or a state of being conditional. It can therefore be seen that such a theoretical enquiry or knowledge discovery process has a high degree of similarity to semiosis.

Semiotics applied in various domains

'Semiotics could be anywhere', yet 'it can be hard to offer a simple definition which is of much [practical] use', as the excellent book of *Semiotics for Beginners* (Chandler 2007) describes.

Semiotics is a study of signs. Semiotics is 'concerned with everything that can be taken as a sign' (Eco 1976: 7). Interest in a sign in semiotics can be approximately categorised as forms and structure, substance and meaning, and functions and effects. These can be put under the headings of syntactics, semantics and pragmatics. A sign in semiotics is far more than what we refer to in our everyday speech; instead, it is anything that stands for something else, such as a mark, image, gesture, musical sound, object or event, and the relationship between any of these. The subjects of study for semiotics are all kinds of signs: verbal language, pictures, literature, motion pictures, theatre, body language and more.

Semiotics has been a discipline actively attended to by scientists of linguistics, media studies, educational science, anthropology and the philosophy of language. Semiotics as a whole or some of its branches have influenced many of these studies and led to much domain-related semiotics.

Computer semiotics

Computing, including the development and use of computer systems, is a field in which semiotics has shown great relevance. Computer semiotics, as defined by Peter Andersen (1997), studies the special nature of computer-based signs and how they function. It is an emerging discipline that guides people in the design and development of computer systems.

In Andersen's map of computer semiotics (Figure 2.2), the perspective of viewing *the signs as systems* occupies the centre. In addition, there are three main branches: the psychological view of signs-as-knowledge, the sociological view of signs as behaviour, and the aesthetic view of signs as artefacts. In the 'signs-as-systems' perspective, the individual is considered to be a creator, interpreter and referent of signs, or a user who make use of a semiotic product from others. In the signs-as-knowledge perspective, the individual is considered as an assemblage of parts: a person's biological ability and psychological mechanisms will enable them to learn, so the use of signs is a processing of understanding and learning. Signs, particularly languages, can serve as a means of describing, expressing, designing and constructing both social and computer-based systems. Winograd and Flores (1987) also advocate the same approach and illustrate how the development of information systems can be started from social reality as the natural foundation.

Another related area is computational semiotics (Gudwin and Queiroz 2005, 2007), which refers to the attempt to incorporate semiosis into a computational (or computing) process. The fundamental assumption in this approach is that all computational systems are semiotic systems. This enables the construction of autonomous systems that are able to perform intelligent behaviours such as perception, modelling, value judgement and action generation.

Applications of semiotics and its methods and techniques can be found in many other areas, such as computational linguistics, information systems, computer-supported collaborative work, knowledge engineering and artificial intelligence

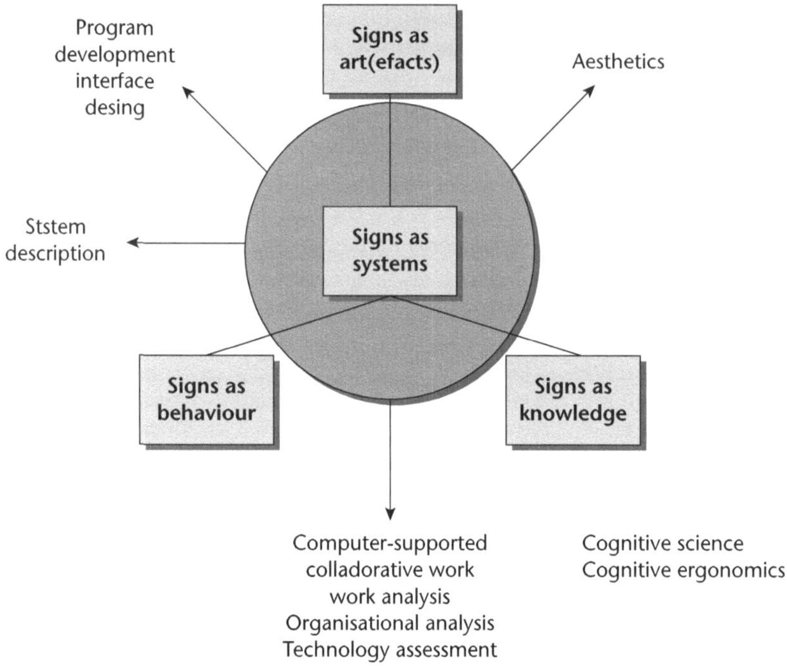

FIGURE 2.2 Map of computer semiotics (after Anderson 1997)

(see, for example, Benyon 1994; Beynon-Davies 2009; Cunningham 1992; Fiske, 1990; Gonzales 1997; Klein 1996; Liu and Dix 1997).

Semiotic engineering

Semiotic engineering is the process of engendering messages in an appropriate code – that is, with an emphasis on message expression – so that the targets for content interpretation can be met (Souza 1993). The issue of semiotic engineering is to identify semiotic principles that will make a better systems design. Semiotic theory, as a discipline devoted to the study of signs and how they are used in communication – a crucial process in intellectual activity (Souza 2005) – provides constitutive principles for producing signs. One of the hallmarks of semiotic theories of communication is to account for innovation and the creative uses of language and numerous other sign systems (Eco 1976).

Two main theoretical aspects support semiotic engineering: the communication process-oriented and the unlimited semiosis perspectives. Eco identifies the process-oriented theory of sign production as a branch of semiotics theory that accounts for phenomena related to communication. The theory of sign production identifies four parameters for a classification of the modes of production of signs: the physical labour performed by the agent, the token:type ratio of the sign, the type of continuum selected for expression, and the mode and complexity of articulation. These parameters provide a process-oriented insight for semiotic engineering.

On the other hand, semiosis as the process of semiotic activity provides a generative process for semiotic engineering. The basic concepts, sign, interpretant and object, involved in semiosis and the relationships between these concepts can be viewed as showing how the designer of a sign might view the process of engendering messages in an appropriate way. In semiotic engineering, the object is known to the designer, who creates a sign that is meant to lead to a successful interpretant, suitably matching the object.

Specifically, semiotics engineering supports information systems design and evaluation by crystallising the production of signs and the communication process. On one hand, it has the ability to integrate the perspective of back-end and front-end development activities, and to let users know and enjoy the benefits of all the intellectual efforts that eventually crystallise into software artefacts. On the other hand, it has the ability to frame the users' experience within increasingly broader contexts of communication – from a basic user–system dialogue to contemporary user-in-cyberspace activity (Souza 2006).

Human–computer interaction (HCI) is an important field of application of semiotic engineering. First presented as a semiotics approach to user interface design (Souza 1993), semiotic engineering has evolved into a theory of HCI. Semiotics is important because HCI involves signification and meaning-related processes that take place in both computer systems and human minds. Like all other intellectual products, the artefacts of HCI are communicated as signs in a particular kind of discourse that we must be able to interpret, learn, use and adapt to various contexts of need and opportunity. Thus, the semiotic engineering of HCI is about the principles, the materials, the processes, the effects and the possibilities for producing a meaningful interactive computer system discourse. Souza (1993) suggests four guidelines as an initial framework for semiotic engineering in HCI:

- *Guideline 1*: User interface language designers should produce signs they recognise as existing codified expressions or the intended contents.
- *Guideline 2*: User interface language designers should try to select expressions that are recognised as a token of an established type of expression system that accounts for the intended contents (ratio facilis).
- *Guideline 3*: User interface signs referring to domain objects and to computer-modelled solutions for problems should be heteromaterial, whereas the representation of the input/output elements should be homomaterial and subject to direct manipulation.
- *Guideline 4*: User interface language designers should always resort to expressions derived from a recognisably codified (rule-based) system.

These guidelines converge to the goal of getting the message across at the interface level, and apply to both textual (Scott and Souza 1990) and non-textual interaction (Norman 1991). Furthermore, a space for the creation of signs in semiotics engineering (Figure 2.3) is proposed according to the above guidelines. This space model points out an optimal resource space for the selection or creation of all expressions of user interface languages, whose dimensions are defined by the physical labour needed to produce the expression (from Guideline 1), the token:type ratio (i.e. the popularity ratio, from Guideline 2) and the level of articulation and regularity of the expressive system (i.e. grammaticalised – explained by the book authors, from Guideline 4).

The other semiotic engineering approach applied in HCI derives from Barr *et al.* (2004), who propose a highly structured model of user interface metaphor based on the semiotic process (Figure 2.3).

Applications of semiotic engineering can also be found in areas such as interactive systems, extensible applications and software development (see, for example, Barbosa and Souza 2001; Prates and Souza 2000; Souza 1997; Souza and Barbosa 2001).

Semiotics in organisations

Organisational semiotics is one of the branches of semiotics particularly related to business and organisations. As manifested in a workshop that was attended by many of those working in various areas of the application of semiotics (Organisational Semiotics Workshop 1995), 'Organisational Semiotics is the study of organisations using the concepts and methods of semiotics'. This study of semiotics is based on the fundamental observation that all organised behaviour is affected by people's communication and interpretation of signs, both individually and in groups.

The functions of creating, reproducing, transmitting, transforming, preserving and manipulating signs have always been performed with the aid of various

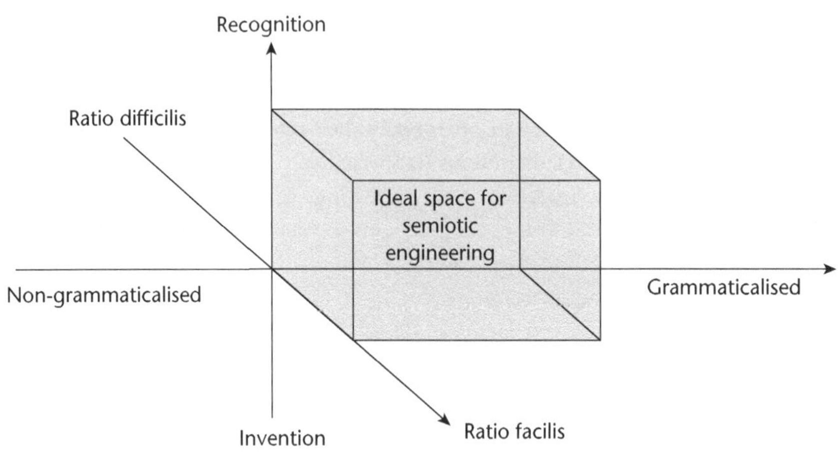

FIGURE 2.3 Space for the creation of signs in semiotic engineering (Barr *et al.* 2004)

technologies. Semiotics, as 'the doctrine of signs', draws from many disciplines to throw light on the ways in which people use signs for all kinds of purposes. The scope of organisational semiotics includes both public and private organisations, and concerns their inner workings and their interrelations with the environment and with one another. The aims of this study are to find new and insightful ways of analysing, describing and explaining organisational structure and behaviour. The results of this work will in valuable ways relate to and augment current theories about organisations that are based in many disciplines such as economics, social theory, social psychology, anthropology, history, law and information systems.

Specific problem domains being addressed by people working in organisational semiotics include aspects of such fields as marketing, human resource management, business law and business ethics, the historical development and future evolution of the organs of government, religion, politics, justice, social care and healthcare, as well as private and public businesses. The study is not confined to information expressed in speech, writing or graphics, but takes account of the semiological aspects of the products and productive resources of organisations, including the architectural forms that they inhabit. It is relevant to the conservation and changing of organisational structure and behaviour. Although the subject is wide and touches on many other specialist branches of semiotics (e.g. education, law, architecture, media, etc.), it only overlaps with them where they are concerned with matters of organisation in their areas.

Semiotics has been also applied to information systems work. During the last decade, information systems research has grown dramatically to embrace the insights of several philosophical traditions, with semiotics as one of these contributing to information systems research. It has been recognised that, within the research community, there are at least two major camps: realists and constructivists. For realists, recognising that the natural language is the ultimate meta-language, their tasks are to devise effective, formal languages as a means of modelling the structure and behaviour of organisations, and to improve the semantics preserved in the models. Constructivists, on the other hand, consider that language is not only a medium of expression, but also an active force shaping the way the mind functions. By using language, one is engaged in a social process of sense-making and reality construction. Efforts have been made through the study of signs and language to facilitate communication between adherents to alternative philosophical traditions in information systems research.

Questions and exercises

1. Of the three types of signs (iconic, indexical and symbolic), some are more intuitive than others. Can you explain the reasons for this?
2. In information representation (e.g. computer interface design), why should we, as far as possible, use intuitive signs? Illustrate the benefits of such a usage of signs with examples from commercial software applications.

3. Why is semiosis a process of sense-making? In such a process, how do a sign, an object and an interpretant work together? Use examples to elaborate the process of semiosis.
4. Of the three types of reasoning, only abduction generates knowledge, while deduction applies knowledge and induction verifies knowledge. Can you find examples in your daily work or life to support such a proposition?
5. What are key elements in determining the quality of information?

3

THE ORGANISATIONAL SEMIOTICS FRAMEWORK FOR BUSINESS INFORMATICS

The semiotics of Stamper (1973), based on the work of Peirce (1958a), Morris (1938, 1946) and others, along with 'information theory' (Shannon and Weaver 1949), has evolved into a set of semiotic theories and methods that are particularly relevant to studying business problems in organisations. Organisational semiotics is such an emerging paradigm that guides their research and practical application in organised activities, business informatics and information systems (Feng *et al.* 2009; Liu *et al.* 2013). The organisational semiotics framework (Stamper *et al.* 1988) highlights the key principles of organisational semiotics that have developed over the years.

Stamper's organisational semiotics, as for any other methodological approach, has its own philosophical foundation. It has accepted and adapted a radical, subjectivist stance as the fundamental principle. In this chapter, the discussion will focus first on major philosophical paradigms and next on the subjectivist paradigm for Stamper's organisational semiotics. The organisational semiotics framework (Stamper *et al.* 1988) will then be examined in detail.

Philosophical paradigms

A paradigm is a set of the most fundamental assumptions adopted by a professional community that allows its members to share similar perceptions and engage in commonly shared practices. Scientific achievements recognised in the particular community and research traditions educate its members to commit to the same rules and standards for scientific practice (Kuhn 1962). The adoption of a certain paradigm will determine the way of exploring the world; it will guide the development of the research theory and method in the first place, as well as determine the adoption of a certain theory and method in the scientific enquiry. The usual considerations on scientific paradigms may be complemented by considering a set of presuppositions as paradigmatic; thus, they fundamentally relate the discussion to philosophy.

Objectivist paradigm

A predominant philosophical position is the objectivist paradigm, which assumes that there is a subject-independent world – some objective reality. Objectivism in its rigorous forms regards the universe as being made up of self-existent entities. The main tenets of objectivism are threefold (Mishra 1982):

- The entities (facts, objects) under study in logics, mathematics and the physical sciences are not mental in any usual or proper meaning of the word mental.
- The existence and nature of these entities are not in any sense qualified by their capacity of being known.
- The degree of unity, consistency or relatedness subsisting between entities is a matter to be empirically ascertained.

In this stance, the human mind is treated as a 'blank sheet' on which all the knowledge that it later comes to acquire is 'written' by the external world. Individuals are passively receiving similar ideas. They will arrive at a 'natural' consensus, which is dictated by the external world. Because human perceptions are seen as a kind of mirror image of the world onto the mind, it is believed in this paradigm that if one makes the investigation carefully enough, one will arrive at the same picture of the world as everyone else. Natural sciences presuppose that there is a body of knowledge that is universally true. The task of scientists is to continuously discover the unknown part of the world and to perfect the knowledge. Sufficient education will enable a person to know the right way of learning and to be able to deduce new knowledge, so that person should reach the same conclusion as anyone else based on what is known to them.

These basic assumptions may be justified in some limited circumstances if the area of study is of a mechanical nature, regardless of human impact. The objectivist position urges us to apply models and methods derived from the natural sciences to the study of human affairs. The social world is treated as if it were some natural world composed of billiard balls (see, for example, Burrell and Morgan 1979; Hirschheim and Klein 1989).

However, a quick observation of daily operations will tell us a different story. In our social affairs, different opinions are always involved. The notion of true universal knowledge seems not to work as it is supposed to by the objectivist. Differences in political and economic interest and cultural background lead to diversified judgements instead of a common conclusion on basis of the 'objective truth'. Reaching a consensus, for example about a management decision, normally requires much effort in terms of discussion, clarification and negotiation, although members of the management team live in the same physical world. This is because of the subjectivity of knowledge, experience and perception.

This objectivist position leads to a set of basic beliefs in the fields of language and language use, communication and information systems. Hirschheim and Klein (1989) illustrate that there are different paradigms of information systems development, which they term functionalism, radical structuralism, social relativism and neohumanism, and these can be placed in a coordinate system (Figure 3.1).

In his criticism, Lyytinen (1987) characterises the objectivist position in systems analysis and development by examining the following four objectivist principles:

1. *Correspondence*: There is a fixed, immutable entity-structure in an enterprise. The description of the problem domain is a representation of reality that has a correspondence between the words and entities and relationships. The problem with this principle arises when dealing with 'soft entities', such as 'legal person', 'loan', 'customer', 'order' and so on. Many disputes in legal cases have been caused by the ambiguous meanings given to such 'soft entities'.
2. *Objectivity*: This principle suggests that the statements or observations of a problem domain are independent of an observer because observations made by anyone should be the same. According to this principle, a sentence such as 'The marketing director believes that the sales have dropped by 10 per cent' is meaningless because someone's belief suggests that this may not be a fact, which is beyond the scope of discussion. The objectivist position tends to ignore the contextual information associated with the observations. Modalities, purposes and intentions are filtered out from the statements.
3. *The excluded middle*: This principle is rooted in one of fundamental theories of formal logic – bivalence – which says that every sentence, statement or proposition is either true or false. (For more on the definition of *bivalence*, see the glossary in Hacck 1978.) However, social organisations are not built up on the basis of a set of axioms, and they do not always function following a finite

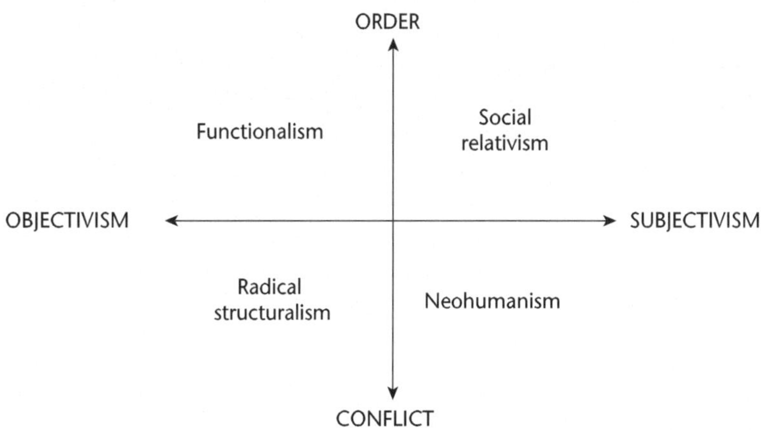

FIGURE 3.1 Different paradigms for information systems studies (Hirschheim and Klein 1989)

number of logical rules. Despite a general applicability of norms, there are exceptional situations when one is allowed to violate a rule (Holy and Stuchlik 1983; Lee 1988; Ryu and Lee 1993). For example, a police car may disobey traffic signals in an emergency situation. Norms do provide standards of conduct, but more often than not deviance of behaviour occurs in society (Gibbs 1981) due to differences in standards and beliefs. Because of these differences, behaviour considered 'right' or 'wrong' based on one standard may be judged to be neutral based on other standards.

4. *Language neutrality*: This assumes a descriptive role of language. A language is seen as a means of representation and not a means of construction of a world.

These objectivist principles are not suitable for studying problems in social settings and may lead to harmful and even dangerous consequences if they are adopted in business informatics, such as in the areas of information analysis and systems development.

Subjectivist paradigm

In daily business practices and legal and other practical affairs, consensus continually breaks down as individuals see the world differently from each other. This acknowledgement gave rise to the idea of putting the focus on subjectivism in order to investigate whether this doctrine would provide a more proper basis for studying the types of problems in social domains.

Whereas objectivism assumes a single reality and explains differences of ideas as aberrations, subjectivism treats the different ideas of individuals as starting points for a shared reality. In its radical forms, it turns away from pretended absolutes and origins, from fixed principles and closed systems. Subjectivism emphasises the abilities of individuals, their freedom to choose courses of action and the moral responsibility for their choice, as well as the uncertainty, novelty and strife these bring about. Importance is assigned to the affective and cognitive behaviour of people as well as to their cognition. Reality in this stance is experience and is found within sensible flux. It is not ready-made but found in a making-process, unfinished and growing in all places where individuals pursue their ends.

The subjectivist paradigm rejects the appropriateness of methods of natural science for studying the social world and seeks to understand the basis of human life by delving into the depth of individuals' subjective experiences. The social world is studied by pursuing an understanding of the way in which members of society create, modify and interpret the worlds to which they belong.

Table 3.1 summarises and compares the typical objectivist and subjectivist positions in some key concepts related to information systems work. The subjectivist position has an increasing influence in studies of communication and information systems. One of the key influences is that the role of language is seen as not only descriptive, but also constructive. The using of language is the performing of actions. A social world can be created, altered, twisted and moved by the use of language. For

TABLE 3.1 Objectivist and subjectivist views of key concepts of business informatics

Concept	*Objectivist view*	*Subjectivist view*
Reality	Objectively given, the same for everyone and composed of entities, their properties and relationships	Created subjectively and socially, with subtle differences between groups of knowing agents
Data	A means of representing the truth about reality	A means of indicating intentions and coordinating actions
Truth	The correct correspondence between some real entity	A consensus reached (temporarily) as a basis for coordinated action
Meaning	A relationship between a sign and some real entity	A relationship between a sign and some pattern of action established as a norm within a group
Information system	A kind of 'plumbing' system through which data flow	A semiological system, mainly informal but supplemented by formalised messages
Role of the analyst	To specify the truth, data, structure and functions of the system needed by the users	To assist users to articulate their problems, discover their information requirements and evolve a systemic solution

example, performative utterances such as 'I do' (. . . take this woman to be my lawful wedded wife) – as uttered in the course of the marriage ceremony – and 'I name this ship the *Queen Elizabeth*' can create new states of affairs even without any physical action being involved (Austin 1980). All speech acts (Searle 1969) will in proper circumstances have the effect of constructing or altering the world, for example by creating an obligation or by changing a legal relationship in business affairs.

Radical subjective paradigm

Stamper's organisational semiotics adopts a radical subjectivist paradigm (Stamper *et al.* 1988). In this paradigm, reality is seen as a social construct achieved through the behaviour of the agents. People in this world share certain patterns of behaviour that are governed by a system of norms. As people argue, communicate, negotiate and interact with each other, the world is constantly changing. This changing world will, in turn, set up new values, habits and beliefs as norms. When one is trying to understand concepts such as knowledge, truth, language and meaning, agents and actions should be taken as the starting point. This position can be formulated in terms of the following two axioms, on which the major part of the research body is based:

1. There is no knowledge without a knower.
2. There is no knowing without action.

These two axioms suggest that, in information analysis, systems modelling or knowledge representation, subjectivity is crucial at two levels. The first level is that of the information analyst or knowledge engineer who produces the model or the representation. He or she must be responsible for what is produced. Subjectivity at the second level is about the content within the model or presentation. Each piece of information or knowledge in the model must be explicitly referred to the agent who knows it or has constructed it, and is responsible for it. Knowing something or being able to do something only becomes a valid piece of knowledge when it is referred to the agent.

For example, in a business domain, to *enrol* a *student* into a *course* is part of business function of a university. When this part is modelled, the axioms require that, at the content level, the model must contain an explicit link to who will perform the function of enrolling (e.g. the agent); therefore, it is possible to talk about ownership and responsibility, and who will follow the norms or exercise the norms relevant to the enrolment. The notion of a universal truth therefore becomes irrelevant in this case. Given the norms accepted in an organisation, exercising, evaluating and judging an action or a piece of knowledge becomes the responsibility of the agent. The concept of responsibility becomes as vital as the notion of truth in classical logic.

Social constructivism

Social constructivism emphasises the importance of culture and context in understanding what occurs in society and constructing knowledge based on this understanding (Derry 1999; Kim 2001; McMahon 1997). This perspective is closely associated with many contemporary theories, most notably the developmental theories of Vygotsky and Bruner, and Bandura's social cognitive theory (Bandura 2001).

The assumptions underlying social constructivism are based on specific assumptions about reality, knowledge and learning. To understand and apply models of instruction that are rooted in the perspectives of social constructivists, it is important to know the premises that underlie them:

- *Reality*: Social constructivists believe that reality is constructed through human activity. The members of a society together invent the properties of the world (Kukla 2000). For the social constructivist, reality cannot be discovered as it does not exist prior to its social invention.
- *Knowledge*: To social constructivists, knowledge is also a human product and is socially and culturally constructed (Ernest 1999; Gredler 1997; Prawat and Floden 1994). Individuals create meaning through their interactions with each other and with the environment in which they live.
- *Learning*: Social constructivists view learning as a social process. It does not take place only within an individual, nor is it a passive development of behaviours that are shaped by external forces (McMahon 1997). Meaningful learning occurs when individuals are engaged in social activities.

Intersubjectivity of social meanings

Intersubjectivity is a shared understanding between individuals whose interaction is based on common interests and assumptions that form the ground for their communication (Rogoff 1990). Communications and interactions entail socially agreed-upon ideas of the world and the social patterns and rules of language use (Ernest 1999). The construction of social meanings therefore involves intersubjectivity between individuals. Social meanings and knowledge are shaped and evolve through negotiation within the communicating groups (Gredler, 1997; Prawat and Floden 1994). Any personal meanings shaped through these experiences are affected by the intersubjectivity of the community to which the people belong.

Intersubjectivity not only provides the grounds for communication, but also supports people to extend their understanding of new information and activities among the group members (Engeström 1987; Rogoff 1990). Knowledge is derived from interactions between people and their environments, and resides within cultures (McMahon 1997; Shunk 2000). The construction of knowledge is also influenced by the intersubjectivity formed by cultural and historical factors in the community (Gredler 1997; Prawat and Floden 1994). When the members of the community are aware of their intersubjective meanings, it is easier for them to understand any new information and activities that arise in the community.

Actualism

Actualism is a view in contemporary philosophy (Heil 2013; Tomberlin 1998). Actualism claims that everything there exists or is actual (including everything that can in any sense be said to be). Putting it in another way, actualism denies that there is any kind of being beyond actual existence; to be is to exist, and to exist is to be actual. Actualism therefore stands in total contrast to possibilism, which holds the position that there are merely possible objects and that not all objects are actual.

Stamper's radical subjectivism shares much with the ontology of actualism in that agents' action is central to knowledge. Only the agents' behaviour constitutes the fundamentals of any knowledge. In such an ontology, agents have a duty to justify and respond to any criticism of their adopted system of thoughts. The knowable reality for the agents demands a rigorous testing of their knowledge; in the meantime, this reality enables them to extend their knowable reality.

The organisational semiotics framework

Traditionally, the divisions of semiotics have been *syntactics*, *semantics* and *pragmatics*, which deal with the structures, meanings and usage of signs, respectively. To these, Stamper (1973) has added another three. *Physics*, as a separate branch concerned with the physical aspects of signs at the level of signals and marks, has been further added to the taxonomy of semiotics. It gives a handle to deal with the factors governing the economics of signs that has become important in business contexts. *Empirics* has been introduced as another branch to study the statistical properties of signs when different physical media and devices are used. At the other end of the spectrum, Stamper adds another layer of the *social world*, where the effects of the use of signs in human affairs are studied. All these branches of semiotics are organised into a semiotic framework (Figure 3.2).

Issues relating to the three upper layers of the semiotic framework are concerned with the use of signs, how signs function in communicating meanings and intentions, and what the social consequences of the use of signs are. Studies of issues in the lower three layers will answer questions on how signs are structured and used in language, how signs are organised and transmitted, what physical properties signs have and so on.

Physics

A sign in a physical form is a phenomenon. It can be a sign in motion, which is normally termed a 'signal'; alternatively, it can be static, in which case it is a 'mark'. The physical properties of a sign can be its shape, size, contrast, intensity, speed of movement, acceleration, loudness, source, destination and so on, depending on the type of the sign. Such physical properties can be studied using methods borrowed from physics and engineering. Other related questions can also be investigated, such as the material that makes up the sign carrier, and the energy carried or consumed by the signal.

The direct relevance to communication and information systems of knowing such physical properties is that people can design physical devices for storage, transmission and representation. From the physical point of view, there are in databases collections of physical tokens that can be stored and moved around for input,

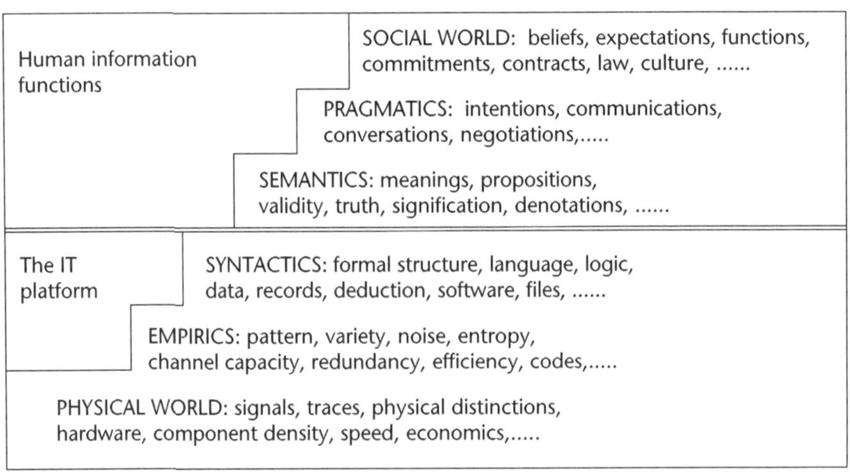

FIGURE 3.2 The organisational semiotics framework (adapted from Stamper 1973)

output and display. For an information system or a communication network to function properly at this level, one has to get the right RAM or disk storage and the right cable connections between personal computers and stations.

The word 'information' has many different common-sense usages. In the physical area, it simply means a collection of tokens, as when we talk of the information in a database amounting to x megabytes, for example. We might, in a practical way, talk of a signal, such as flash of light, 'meaning' that there is a mark such as a transparent area on a film. Models of information systems at the physical level describe the range of *physical tokens* (signals or marks) available as input to or output from various physical components, and they model the cause-and-effect relationships between them, their energy and their material requirements. For example, when developing information systems, we model the locations and telecom links between sites, the volumes of information in terms of the number of characters per unit of time that they generate and the volumes they store, in order to discover the capacity of the channels and storage devices needed.

Empirics

As a branch of semiotics, empirics studies the statistical properties of signs, in which the object of study is a collection of signals or marks. Questions for study at this level relate to the effect of coding, entropy measurement, optimal signal transmission, channel capacity and so on. Information from the angle of empirics can be viewed as a stream of signals that must be transported from one location to another, regardless of what they mean. For example, if binary coding is used for communication between sites, we could have the following coding:

a = 00001

b =00011

c = 00101

d = 00110

In such communications, coding is carried out at the sending end, and decoding at the receiving end. The coding and decoding procedures aim to achieve an optimal transmission of information through noisy channels with high accuracy at a rate close to the channel's maximum capacity. There will be always some necessary measures associated with a communication process: imposing a structure of a block of messages before transmission, transmitting some additional messages to describe the structure, and then processing the structure at the receiving end. To get more out of the channel, more elaborate checks, calling for the transmission and storage of larger blocks of signals subjected to more complex processing, are necessary. Information should be coded with the minimum number of 'carrier signals' for efficiency of coding and transmission. The word 'meaning' in this context means the equivalence of codes.

Syntactics

When there is a satisfactory range of physical tokens that provide a reliable way of encoding diversity of use, the physical representation of signs and their statistical properties are covered by *physics* and *empirics*. We can then focus on the complex structures of a language regardless of the actual expression in specific terminal tokens. We can define a syntax using the names of syntactic categories and production rules, but we are indifferent to the rules representing the terminal characters.

Syntactics is concerned with rules for composing complex signs from simple ones. Information can be coded following a certain structure: a complex sign, a word, a mathematical expression or a sentence can be composed of some more basic parts according to the rules. For a formal language, terminal symbols (or vocabulary) are fundamentals of sign construction as far as syntactics is concerned. The rules for generating and parsing formal expressions allow us to measure the complexity of a single formula and a sign system. When a formula can be produced or parsed in two or more ways, we have an instance of *syntactic ambiguity*, another semiological phenomenon in the syntactic domain. A formula or an expression carries a piece of information. The meaning of the information at this syntactic level can be studied using the transformation rules. Two sets of formulae have the same meaning (i.e. they paraphrase each other) if each can be deduced from the other. The meaning of one includes the meaning of the other if it allows the other to be deduced from it.

The rules for combining these parts are called grammar. Grammars of a natural language teach people how to construct grammatically correct sentences, but they do not say how to express semantic meanings. However, if we want to express ourselves precisely, following the grammar is one of the conditions for this.

Semantics

The meaning or semantics of a sign is normally considered to be the relationship between a sign and what it refers to: a sign denotes a denotatum. This is its referential meaning. Under this definition of meaning, a 'reality' has to be assumed so that signs can be mapped onto objects in that 'reality'. For example, the sign 'table' represents a kind of object with certain properties, such as having legs and a flat surface. This way of treating meaning is reasonable if the problems are simple, the boundaries of signs and 'reality' are clear and a shared consensus, for example, on the properties of objects, has been established. Meaning is then a logic function mapping words to reality.

But in most social affairs, this is not the case: there is no agreed unique 'reality', and a consensus does not stay there forever. People strive for clarification and consensus. Once a consensus has been established, it is soon subject to question, criticism or modification. The use of signs and languages can clarify ideas and can also alter or construct the world. Meaning in this respect is more appropriately seen as a relationship between a sign and behaviour. A sign has its behaviour, sign-behaviour,

behaviour in which signs occur (Morris 1946). The meaning of a sign relates to the response the sign elicits in a given social setting. It signifies any and all phases of the sign-process (the status of being a sign, the interpretant, the fact of denoting the significatum), and frequently suggests mental and valuational processes as well (Morris 1946). This is what Stamper calls the behavioural meaning (Stamper 1973). Meaning in this sense is a result of the use of signs, and is constructed, constantly tested and repaired through the use of signs.

At the semantic level of the use of language, meaning acts as the operational link between signs and practical affairs. People use signs or a language in communication. To enable one person to understand another, there must be some norms governing the use of signs that are established and shared in a language community. These rules regulate people's behaviour in using signs, producing sentences. Norm-confirming uses of signs are acceptable to and understood by the members of the same language community, so that the expected effects on the audience can be produced. The ultimate goal of using signs is to produce effects on the audience, and furthermore to change states of practical affairs, but the intentional and social effects are embodied in a sentence. In a sense, they are implied in the sentence and are an extensional aspect of such a sentence. What is first reflected in the sentence is the meaning at the semantic level, which is accommodated by propositions. The sentence can be examined for its validity, signification and correspondence to the business world.

However, meaning can be only understood if the context in which the sentence is uttered is taken into account. A word, as well as a sentence, can mean anything. The 'literal meaning' of a sentence, as described by Searle (1979: 117), is the meaning that is independent of any context whatsoever. One can well imagine how difficult it would be to establish such literal meanings. Winograd and Flores (1987) show with the following example that it is impossible to establish a context-independent basis for circumscribing the literal use of a term even as seemingly simple as 'water':

A: Is there any water in the refrigerator?

B: Yes.

A: Where? I don't see it.

B: In the cells of the eggplant.

Andersen's example of conversations in a car repair shop (Andersen 1991) illustrates that background information is often necessary to understand the meaning of words, phrases and fragmented sentences. Meaning is highly dependent on the process of using these, dependent on the behaviour of the agents.

A sign's functions in the three upper layers of the semiotic framework, the *semantic, pragmatic* and *social* levels, are concerned with interaction with humans. In a broad sense, they all directly relate to the use and effect of signs. Talking about functions, when people employ a sign or utter a sentence, the first object is to express a meaning. The next goal is to convey a certain intention. The ultimate goal is to produce effects at the social level, such as to set up an obligation or alter a state of affairs. Fulfilment of the objective at each of the former levels is the basis for the latter. For example, someone may tell another person, 'You are stepping on my toes.' The meaning of this sentence is not difficult to understand – the intention is to inform the addressee that he has done something wrong. But the effect of the sentence does not stop there: the speaker is trying to change the situation of being stepped on, and is perhaps pushing the addressee to feel obliged to apologise.

Pragmatics

When a sign has a meaning, it can be used intentionally for certain purposes, such as communication. *Pragmatics*, in such a case of the purposeful use of signs, is a branch of semiotics concerned with the relationships between signs and the behaviour of agents. Within a social community, there exist common knowledge and shared assumptions. These basic assumptions serve as a minimum basis for communication. However, differences in personal experiences, values and expectations can create difficulties in understanding. As soon as there is a problem in understanding, people have to come back to the minimum basis, and from there they can expand their common knowledge and reach their new agreement. Dik (1989) calls the personal possession of knowledge and experience 'pragmatic information'.

A process of verbal communication between two people can be modelled like this: The speaker and hearer each have their own pragmatic information base. The speaker's pragmatic information base allows them to form an utterance with an expectation that the hearer will understand both the semantic meaning and the speaker's intention. For example, by saying 'I'm hungry', the hearer will then interpret the sentence, using their pragmatic information, understanding that the speaker is actually saying, 'It's time for lunch, let's go to the cafeteria.'

If two participants in a conversation are from the same cultural community, they have a large amount of shared pragmatic information. In this case, they can each assume the pragmatic information of the other. Knowing the pragmatic information of the opposite side can shorten the route of conversation and improve its efficiency. On the other hand, an incorrect assumption of the pragmatic information of the opposite side can mislead the conversation. Therefore, it is important for speakers to know what assumptions they share with hearers before communicating. Dik (1989) suggests that the speaker should start from shared information and proceed from there to estimated non-shared information in order to have this added to, or substituted for, pieces of the hearer's information. The shared or non-shared pragmatic information is determined mainly by cultural differences.

Apart from the shared knowledge, the context in which the communication takes place is important for the pragmatic effects. The following elements can be considered in the context: speaker, hearer, intention, purpose, theme, time, location and psychological states of the speaker and hearer, such as intentions, desires, beliefs and so on.

The relative positions of the speaker and hearer, as discussed in Searle and Vanderveken (1985), are also an important aspect of the context. For example, suppose there are two different relative positions of the speaker and hearer: in one, the speaker has an authority over the hearer, and in the other case, the two are peers. An utterance of the sentence 'Leave the room' produces different pragmatic effects. In the former case it may be an order, while in the latter it may be a request. The speaker has an intention when starting the conversation by uttering the speech act. Words such as 'report', 'inform', 'announce', 'declare', 'suggest', 'propose', 'require', 'order', 'allow', 'permit', 'enquire', 'suppose', 'assume', 'hypothesise' and 'apologise', either as verbs or as other forms, can characterise intentions. When speakers use such words in their utterances, one can know their intention in terms of whether they want either to report their observation or to require something. But in an actual conversation, these words may not need to be used for speakers still to be able to express their intention. In such cases, analysing the intention by means of formal modelling is difficult. However, it is always possible for hearers to grasp the speaker's intention by applying their pragmatic information with intuition in an informal way. Some techniques for capturing intentions will be found in Chapter 7, where the semiotic method for systems analysis is presented.

The purpose of the conversation is set up by the speaker and is related to the speaker's intention. Speakers can conduct a series of speech acts to pursue their purpose, which may be clearly stated by them or hidden. For example, if the speaker 'suggests' something to the hearer, the speaker's purpose of carrying the conversation may not be simply to 'suggest' but to persuade the hearer to join them in some action. Such a purpose is difficult to detect from the beginning of the conversation but may become clear to the hearer as the conversation develops further. The hearer's perception of the purpose can change in the course of the conversation. In this example, at the beginning of the conversation, the hearer may understand it as merely 'suggest'. But as soon as the hearer changes their perception of the speaker's purpose, they may interpret 'suggest' as 'persuade'.

The purposes of communications are difficult to model by formal means. However, we can understand the underlying mechanism by studying social and cultural norms at the social level. Functional grammar (Dik 1978, 1989) provides an elaborated method of handling the pragmatic functions of sentence constituents such as theme, tail, topicality and focality. The analysis of these constituents is useful to establish a view on the functions of a sentence in relation to the wider communicative setting in which the sentence is being uttered. It can help us to obtain a continuous picture of the flow of communication.

Time and location are also important aspects in studying communication effects. The effects of communication acts cannot be studied in isolation: they have to be related to any surrounding communication phenomena, time and location being aspects of the context that are indispensable for understanding.

The social level

When a conversation takes place between two or more people, a change will be caused at the social level. A conversation can be seen as a proper chain of speech acts. It begins with the speaker expressing some intention in an illocutionary act. As soon as the speech act is addressed to the addressee, an obligation is usually already built up for the addressee to respond regardless of the content of the conversion. For example, if a person simply says 'Good morning' to a small group of colleagues as a social convention, there is an immediate obligation on individuals of the group to acknowledge the greeting. If someone did not do so, the speaker might not feel at ease.

In a social setting, norms or social conventions govern people's behaviour. Communication must follow a certain pattern. Any deviance from the normative patterns may be unexpected, which may either require an excuse or otherwise be regarded as unacceptable. For example, an 'invitation' can lead to either 'acknowledge but not accept' or 'accept'. The obligations are established on both sides by the speaker and the addressee. As soon as the invitation is issued, the speaker must be prepared to be able to entertain the guest. If the invitee accepts, they have actually made a promise to the inviting person that they will fulfil their obligation, that is, they will go to the party or dinner at the agreed time. Meanwhile, the inviting person has committed to receiving the guest. The interpretation of the communication acts, in a given circumstance, produces social consequences.

The process of performing communication acts is sometimes a complex process of invoking, violating and altering social norms. Consciously or otherwise, people interact with each other and make interpretations according to norms, while they sometimes deviate from the normatives in their own interest. As Stamper (1973) remarks, for man, a social animal, the norms are a biological necessity.

Norms have long been classified into several categories: perceptual, cognitive, evaluative and behavioural. Perceptual norms are implicitly agreed ways of seeing the world. With these norms, words can be assigned meanings that enable people to use them as labels for the happenings around them. People can code the message picked up by their eyes and ears in a way that is useful to other people. Cognitive norms are the standardised beliefs and knowledge possessed by a group. These norms ensure that the members of the group acquire the knowledge and expectations about the world that have been accumulated by other members of the cultural group. Evaluative norms direct the group towards common ends. They provide a framework of valuation by which people's behaviour can be assessed. Behaviour norms govern people to behave in an appropriate manner in a given cultural setting.

The nature of a group to which people belong can vary from just a cultural group, an informal meeting group or a gang formed in the street, to a business establishment or a government organisation. Accordingly, various degrees of formality of norms can be found. For a casual, informal group, the norms are very often informal, while in case of a highly formalised group, for example an administrative department of government or business organisation, most of the norms are formal. In addition, there is a horizon of norms that are explicit or implicit. Table 3.2 shows examples of these types of norms.

TABLE 3.2 Types of norms

	Formal	*Informal*
Explicit	Officially documented norms, e.g. laws, legislation and organisational regulations	Non-official but agreed vocally, e.g. everyone sharing this big office will buy the coffee supply in turn
Implicit	Not applicable	Habit or convention are never vocally mentioned but people follow; e.g. Club members wear formal dress when attending their monthly meetings

An example of semiotic analysis

At a strategic level, semiotics can guide people to understand how an organisation works as an information system. Operationally, it can also help people to analyse how to make a simple communication process such as a telephone conversion successful. Here, a simplistic example of a telephone conversation is used to illustrate how a simple semantic analysis can be conducted to diagnose possible problems in communication. A successful telephone communication is determined by the factors in six semiotic aspects.

- *At the physical level,* the telephones must be connected by a phone line through the telephone service provider.
- *At the empirical level,* the voice signals will be converted into electronic (or optical) signals and transmitted between the two telephones.

These two levels are the technical infrastructure that is provided by the telephone companies. They are normally not the concern of the users.

- *At the syntactic level,* the two people involved in the telephone conversation must follow the same grammatical rules, that is, speak the same language.
- *At the semantic level,* the words, the technical and non-technical terms, and the things referred to in the conversation must be understood by the two people. The sentences and the contents of the conversation must make sense to both of them.
- *At the pragmatic level,* there is a concern relating to the intention (of the caller), and there may be 'silent' messages beneath the surface. For example, if person A calls person B and says, 'I'm interested in your goods but the price is a bit too high', A's intention will be to ask whether B can lower the price a bit.
- *At the social level,* social commitments and obligations can be often created or discharged as the result of a conversation. Following the above example, if B answers, 'You'll get a 10 per cent discount if you buy ten or more of the PCs', there will be an obligation on B to give the discount if A does buy ten or more PCs.

A communication, from the caller's point of view, can be said to be successful only if their messages are understood by the listener, their intentions are learned by the listener and social purposes are met.

Questions and exercises

1. Information is a complex notion, and many popular definitions have not been able to fully describe the nature and characteristics of information. Explore how the concept of information can be discussed in terms of the six aspects of the semiotic framework.
2. Consider the website of a supermarket that provides online shopping. Using the semiotic framework to conduct a semiotic diagnosis, assess the effectiveness of the supermarket's e-commerce website from a customer's point of view.
3. If the senior management board is to assess the e-commerce website, would their perspective differ from that of a customer? What may be the differences, and why?
4. Using your own words and possibly relating to your own experience, explain the issues for consideration, as suggested in the semiotic framework, that are encountered during the design of an information system.

4

REQUIREMENTS ENGINEERING IN INFORMATION SYSTEMS DEVELOPMENT

The development of an information system normally goes through several stages, and this whole process is termed a systems development 'lifecycle'. There are various definitions of a systems development lifecycle (see, for example, Avison and Fitzgerald 2006; Carmel and Becker 1995; Hedman and Lind 2009). Many researchers have been engaged in bettering the methods for each of the phases in a lifecycle. Some of the methods are aimed at one of the phases, while others are claimed to be useful for more than one of them. A great deal of attention has recently been paid to the analysis and specification of users' requirements. This is because, by examining the sources of difficulty for large systems projects, the incorrect code is a relatively insignificant factor, dwarfed by incorrect functional specifications and (even more significantly) incorrect requirements (Chakraborty *et al.* 2012; Nuseibeh and Easterbrook 2000).

There are many ways to phase activities in systems development. Some models may be excessively simple while others are extremely elaborate. In general, activities of systems development can be grouped under several headings, as illustrated in Figure 4.1:

- *preliminary investigation*, mainly including understanding the business organisation (e.g. its vision, strategy and objectives), the business domain and the scope of business that the information systems will support;
- *requirements analysis*, including business requirements and systems requirements;
- *systems design*, including business processes and systems, as well as technical systems;
- *systems acquisition*, through in-house development or the acquisition of off-the-shelf systems;
- *implementation and maintenance*, which may include testing, acceptance, systems and data migration, regular maintenance and upgrades.

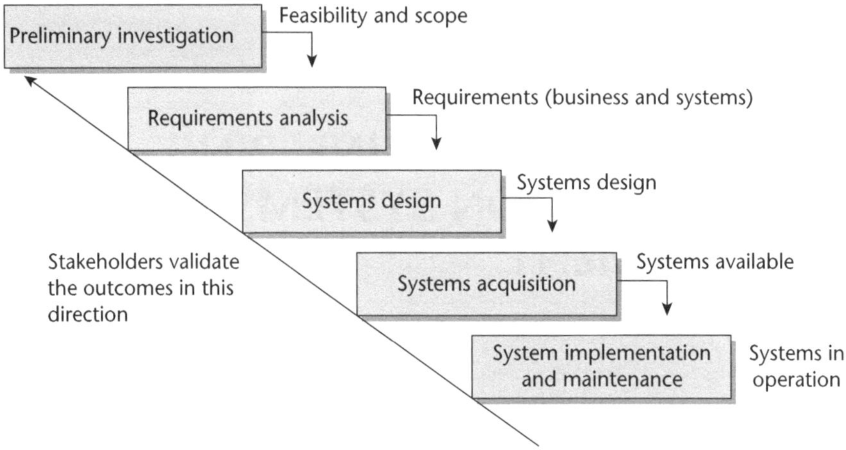

FIGURE 4.1 The information systems development lifecycle

Requirements engineering

Requirements engineering is the process of eliciting individual stakeholder requirements and needs, and developing them into detailed, agreed requirements that are documented and specified in such a way that they can serve as the basis for all other systems development activities (Pohl 2010).

There is a common misconception that requirements engineering is just a single phase that is carried out and completed at the outset of systems development (Hull *et al.* 2005). However, requirements are in fact essential to every stage of systems development as well as communications within the organisation. As seen in the information systems development lifecycle, requirements engineering influences the requirements across all aspects of the information systems development lifecycle, including the stakeholders, systems design, systems acquisition, implementation and validation.

For example, a good set of stakeholder requirements can provide a concise, non-technical description of what is being developed at a level that is accessible to senior management. These descriptions can serve as a basis for a further identification of systems requirements. Similarly, the systems requirements can form an excellent technical summary of a development project. Another role that requirements can play in an organisation is to act as a means of communicating within a information systems project team and even between projects. With good requirements management, hearing the voice of users and customers becomes a matter of clear lines of communication throughout the development process.

Requirements engineering normally involves a group of participants and covers a range of activities. These participants are called stakeholders, and they all have an interest in the systems development. The stakeholders are the concerned parties who are either involved in the systems development, are the owners of the system or are its users (there is a large body of literature on stakeholder analysis; see, for example, Kolkman 1995). The process of requirements engineering carried out by the parties concerned is characterised by the following activities (after Kotonya and Sommerville 1998):

- *Requirements elicitation*: The information requirements and systems requirements are uncovered through consultation with stakeholders and from systems documents, domain knowledge and market studies. Other names for this process are requirements acquisition and requirements discovery.
- *Requirements analysis and negotiation*: The requirements are analysed in detail, and different stakeholders negotiate to decide which requirements are to be accepted. Stakeholders may have different requirements in terms of information and systems functions, and conflicts may exist over these requirements. There are also possible ambiguities in the requirements captured. The negotiation and analysis allows a clarification of the meaning of the requirements. It also provides opportunities for stakeholders to decide on the set of agreed requirements for the system.
- *Requirements documentation*: The agreed requirements are documented with an appropriate level of detail. The requirements document should be understandable by all the stakeholders so that they can all check and validate the requirements (the objective of the next activity).
- *Requirements validation*: The requirements must be checked for consistency and completeness. To achieve this, it is highly beneficial for all the stakeholders to take part in the validation. The involvement of the stakeholders can boost the quality of the requirements and hence improve the quality of the system. (This may, however, be difficult to achieve with many methods because of the technical complexity embedded in the presentation of the requirements.)

As shown in Figure 4.2, requirements engineering is not a straightforward process, and different stages will have direct or indirect impacts on each other. For example, the result of the requirements validation will lead to a refinement of the requirements documentation or further activities related to eliciting, analysing and negotiating the requirements. Several iterations are normally required before a set of requirements can be produced with reasonable accuracy and confidence.

Semiotics in requirements engineering

An organisation can be seen as an information system in which people and technical systems employ signs and behave in an organised manner to achieve goals and requirements. The requirements should cover all aspects of sign communication in achieving technical functions and human activities. It is therefore essential to cover the requirements of sign communication across the physical, empirical, syntactic, semantic, pragmatic and social levels during requirements engineering.

At the physical level, requirements engineering deals with the hardware issues of information systems. It includes requirements, driven by technological change, for

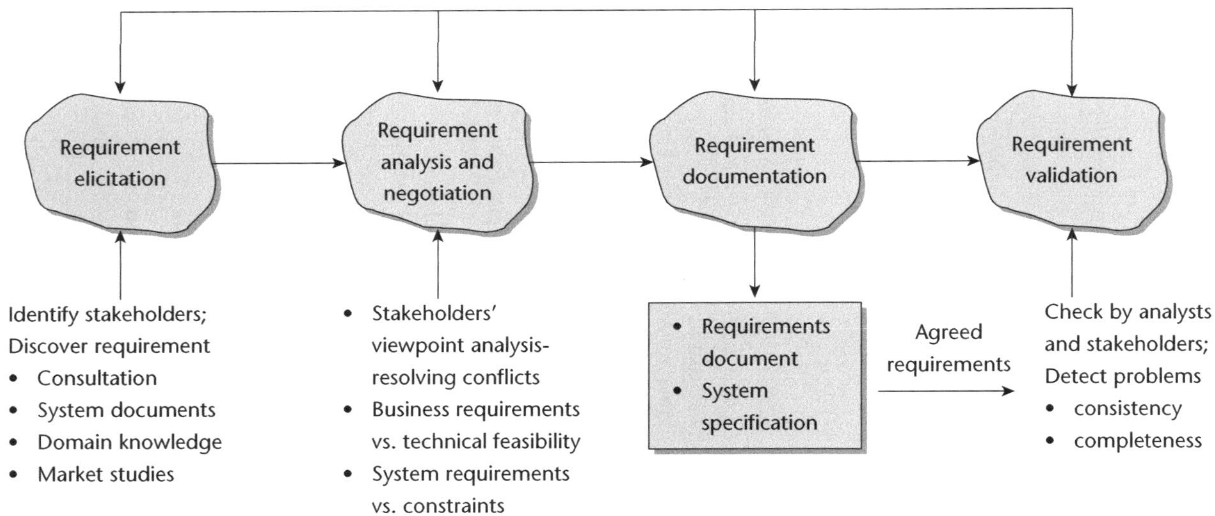

FIGURE 4.2 The requirements engineering process

improvements in the physical properties of signs, where issues relating to the costs and efficiency of information systems are rooted. Communication channels and their capacities are considerations in requirements engineering at the level of empirics, where variety, statistical uncertainty, message volumes and evolving communication networks drive the requirements. Requirements engineering at a syntactic level is associated with formal languages, logic, models, software, record syntax and database structures. It has been further driven towards the distributed syntactic structures for distributed computing with abilities to build reliable structures in complex globalisation.

Requirements engineering at the first three levels is mainly concerned with efficiency issues and computer-based systems. These are important of course, but they are quite inadequate for understanding organisations as information systems. Therefore, requirements engineering is indispensable in human information-handling functions.

Requirements at the semantic level consider how meanings are made, maintained and used in communications in organisations. Requirements engineering at the semantic level explains the relationships between signs and human behaviours. It also emphasises the interpretation of changes and requirements in terms of what stakeholders value and perceive. Requirements engineering at the pragmatic level investigates how information systems support negotiations across cultural boundaries, conducting commercial relationships in the context of changing laws, more sophisticated relationships with customers and suppliers, and pragmatic norms. Requirements engineering at the social level considers the impact of information technology (IT) on organisational change. It also investigates the role of technology as an embodiment of norms and the effects that this has on the maintenance and adaptation of IT systems.

Requirements engineering as semiosis

Requirements engineering is a process of semiosis, as illustrated in Figure 4.3. Processes of semiosis are able to guide requirements engineering from actual requirements (objects) mapped to signs (descriptions and modes). All these will lead to an agreed understanding in the business domain, specifically in terms of the following:

- *Requirements specification – sign*: This considers the formal properties of symbols as they relate to how words and conceptual notations are used to form requirements statements and models. Requirements specification provides a route into determining how a shared semiosis between systems engineers and stakeholders starts.
- *Actual requirement – object*: Mapping from the problem domain/actual requirements (which refers to the 'objects' in semiosis) to the requirements specification (which refers to the 'signs' of the expected requirements specification) will facilitate understanding at the semantic level.
- *Agreed understanding – interpretant*: Like semiosis, requirements engineering is context-dependent. It is closely related to the organisation with certain knowledge (interpretant) and obeying certain norms. A systems engineer and stakeholder, for

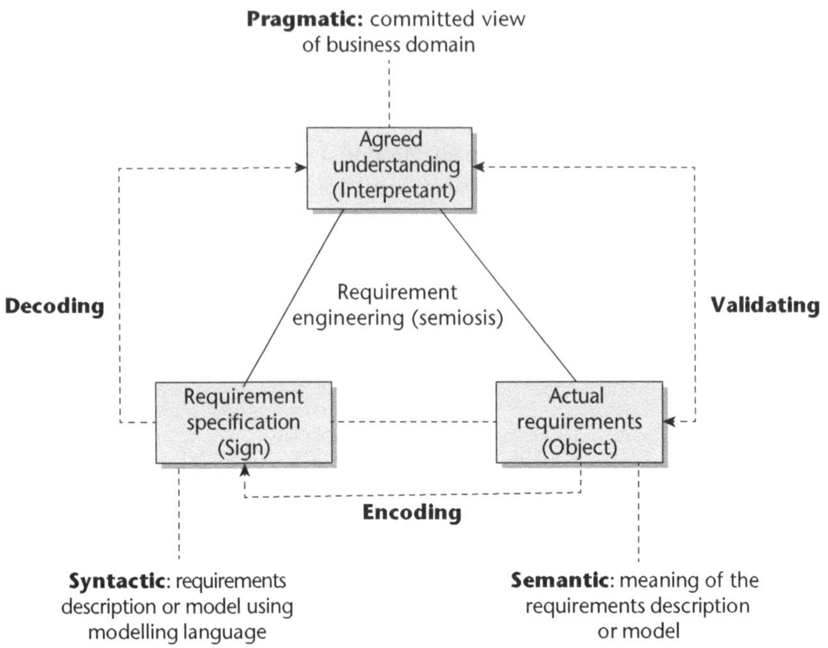

FIGURE 4.3 Requirements engineering as semiosis (adapted from Liu and Benfell 2011)

example, would review a requirements and systems specification that contained various models or codes (syntactics) and would derive a meaning (semantics) for each model. Effective requirements engineering can only be achieved when a consensus is reached between systems engineers and stakeholders through the contextual interpretation (pragmatics) of the requirements specifications.

Therefore, semiosis between different stakeholders is important to achieve effective requirements engineering in terms of the following aspects:

- *Syntactics*: an agreement made between the systems analysts, developers and stakeholders relating to the structure and modelling language of the requirements specifications.
- *Semantics*: a dynamic recursive agreement relating to the meaning of elements and models when constructing the requirements specification.
- *Pragmatics*: a context-aware interpretation of the effect of the requirements description using specific criteria or negotiation/communication norms.

Critical role of requirements engineering

Ultimately, an exercise of requirements engineering addresses two issues. First, it is concerned with understanding the business itself and the business needs. Second, it is about how these needs can be met by providing an organisational and technical system. So the information analysis deals with both understanding the problem and producing a solution. Proper requirements engineering will enable systems developers to ensure that they address the right problem and answer the right questions. It should then deliver the right information requirements on which a systems solution can be designed. Therefore, information analysis is extremely important in the development of information systems.

Empirical studies have on many occasions shown that an information systems project has not addressed the right questions because the requirements were wrongly understood. Evidence also shows that an error in the requirements engineering can be incredibly expensive. Figure 4.4 summarises these findings and shows the orders of magnitude of the cost of errors encountered at the major phases of an information systems lifecycle. Figure 4.4 shows that the activities in the analysis and design phases have an effect on the relevant phases on the realisation side of the diagram. For example, the quality of the requirements analysis affects the running of the business. The design of an IT systems solution influences the running of the IT system. Similarly, the construction and delivery of an IT system determines the installation and overall result of the system's implementation in the business organisation. An error during the analysis of requirements can cost considerably more than an error of coding in the construction phase. Therefore, an adaptation of a proper method and a careful analysis of information requirements are important because they deal with the activities of the first phase in the systems analysis and design process.

Fundamentals of requirements representation

Any method of information analysis must adopt fundamental assumptions in relation to four aspects, which one should always examine: the ontological position, epistemological position, social context and presentation (Hirschheim *et al.* 1995):

- *The ontological position* is concerned with questions of the nature of reality or of what is being studied. Is there an objective reality that is independent of anyone? How does the world come to exist? What constitutes the application

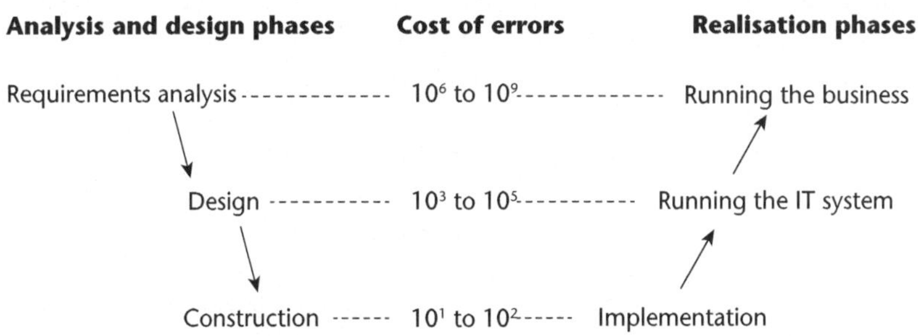

FIGURE 4.4 The cost of errors at different phases of information systems development (after Liu *et al.* 1994)

domain that is being studied and modelled? Is the object system (or the application domain) being studied defined, created and sustained by physical components, operations, roles, decisions, social actions, speech acts or something else? These are typical questions concerning ontological assumptions.

- *The epistemological position* explains how people to come to understand the world and how they acquire knowledge about the application domain. Is there an objective truth? How do we justify the knowledge acquired about the application domain? How do we define the validity of knowledge, and how do we prove it? The epistemological position that a method adopts is to a large extent determined by its ontological position.
- The assumption related to the *social context* determines first of all how to see the relationship between information and action. Information is created and processed by people and will serve people in their decision-making and actions. The value, relevance and validity of information are all related to the social context in which information is used. Second, a proper information analysis exercise can only be carried out if the people involved use the same language and have a substantial common understanding of the problem domain.
- Finally, the assumption related to *presentation* determines the type of information to be presented and the form of presentation. For example, some methods present information in a way that is close to the use of natural language, while the relational data model recommends normalised data entities (i.e. tables). The efficiency of presentation is also part of this concern.

In addition, a sound method of information analysis must meet these criteria and be the following:

- *Adequate*: A method of information analysis normally includes an identification of the information requirements, followed by an elicitation and specification of the requirements. Techniques for defining the scope of the application domain for analysis should be available. In many cases, the prospective users of an information system may not know exactly what they want. The information requirements are difficult to know beforehand. The method should therefore assist those involved in the analysis to elicit the requirements systematically as the requirements specification develops.
- *Instructive*: A method should not be like a cooking recipe; instead, it should provide guidelines and allow creativity. However, it should also provide clear step-by-step instructions on how to perform the analysis.
- *Capable of capturing rich business semantics*: An information model should reflect the patterns of behaviour and rules of the business domain, which explicates the meaning of the application domain – the business semantics. The business semantics should be clearly expressed and this, and not the technical design issues (such as data formats for storage), should be treated as the focus of the modelling.
- *Rigorous*: An information model resulting from an analysis should be precise in representing meaning. It should not lend itself to ambiguous interpretation.

- *Easy for verifying or falsifying the validity of the information model*: An information analysis is often a process involving a group of people with multiple roles and perspectives. The prospective users, who are stakeholders, will normally have to approve the results of the analysis based on the outcome of validation of the information model. A sound model should allow users to understand it without having to go through a lengthy training process in order to make sense of the model, comment on, critique and finally approve or disapprove the model. Many methods in fact discourage users from checking the analysis because of complicated syntactical notations, technical jargon and implementation-related issues, and the users therefore have to approve the analysis without really understanding the information model, so that they often become committed to a particular computer system .

These fundamental issues and criteria can be useful in evaluating and selecting methods of information analysis for systems development or other purposes.

Knowledge representation as a foundation for representing requirements

Requirements engineering, especially in the representation of requirements, shares many fundamental concepts and principles with knowledge representation. Similarities are found in the techniques and methods the two use. They both address how people understand the world and how they represent their understanding. The meaning of the symbols and languages used in modelling is a central issue for both.

'All men by nature desire to know,' said Aristotle in his book *Metaphysics*. As agents experience the flux of the world in which they act, their faculty of sensation enables them to feel and observe the affairs around them. Their memory helps them to accumulate these observations, and from these they learn about the world and know what they can act upon in given circumstances. Many philosophers and scientists, such as psychologists and linguists, have been preoccupied with the study of knowledge. As computer scientists have joined in the enquiry, new perspectives of study have suddenly been widened.

Knowledge representation has become one of the most important areas of study because it is directly related to the exploitation of human knowledge by means of artificial intelligence, (deductive) databases and other computer-supported methods. Each theory of knowledge (epistemology) presupposes a semantic theory, otherwise knowledge cannot be captured and represented with any language or sign system. Knowledge representation is about meanings that are relationships between signs and the other things for which they stand. In many ways, it shares the same concepts and principles as information analysis.

Expressive adequacy and notional efficiency

A formal language or method for knowledge representation is devised with the intention of encoding knowledge and describing practical affairs. The notion of expressive adequacy questions whether a method is capable of describing all the types of information that are needed in knowledge representation. A few crucial elements have to be taken into consideration when a formal language or method is developed. Knowledge or belief can be subjective. This subjectivity must be possibly expressed in a knowledge model. General knowledge and belief (e.g. human knowledge about the universe) can evolve or change; knowledge about particular events is more dynamic. Therefore, it is important that the temporality of knowledge be expressed in a knowledge model.

In a given circumstance, knowledge can help the agent to make decisions. The decision-making process can be quite complex, involving knowledge about the past, and predictions and hypotheses about the future. Modalities (typified by auxiliary verbs in English such as 'must', 'could', 'may', 'shall', etc.) will be needed in this kind of reasoning process.

The notational efficiency of a language of representation concerns the syntactic usage of the language. An important question regarding efficiency is how easily the language can be understood and worked with. This is often referred to as *conceptual efficiency*. Another consideration is *computational efficiency*.

Types of knowledge

Ryle (1949) distinguishes two types of knowledge: *declarative* and *procedural*. The former type of knowledge is about *knowing what*, while the latter is about *knowing how*. Declarative knowledge is theory oriented. It consists of an explicit description of the relationships between concepts. These relationships can be definitional dependencies in terms of concepts, and functional dependencies between quantities. This type of knowledge can be conveniently represented in many representation methods, for example semantic networks and frames. Procedural knowledge is practice oriented. It often consists of a set of prescriptions for actions in relation to certain types of conditions. These are referred to as *situation-action rules* or *production rules*. Rule-based systems are a typical example of a suitable representation approach for this type of knowledge. Winograd (1975) summarises the arguments in the declarative/procedural controversy as follows:

- *Economy*: Procedures specify knowledge by saying how it is used, and every use requires a different procedure. A declarative approach requires only a single copy for all uses.
- *Modularity*: Procedures bind knowledge and control together in a single package. By keeping them separate, a declarative approach makes it easier to update and generalise the knowledge base.
- *Exception handling*: Procedures can do anything, and problems that are not covered by the formal theory can often be handled by an *ad hoc* piece of code. A declarative approach may find difficulty with exceptions that were not anticipated by the theory.

These three arguments are important considerations for anyone who develops a method of knowledge representation. Fortunately, the advantages and disadvantages of the two strategies for representation are recognised by the artificial intelligence community. Many of the methods developed so far can also be characterised as being more suited to one type of strategy than another. But since the declarative/procedural controversy arose over the role of procedural knowledge in intelligence in the late 1970s (cf. Winograd 1975), many developers have tried to cope with both types of knowledge in their methods, because both are needed.

Knowledge representation approaches

In knowledge representation, knowledge relates to 'any kind of belief that a rational person might hold'; therefore, the exercise may be more suitably named conceptual modelling (Way 1991). Conceptual modelling deals with questions about the 'knowledge' or beliefs that are held by some agents. These beliefs are concerned with the status of universals, abstract ideas and concepts, which are supposed to be reflected in a model.

Typical examples

There are some well-recognised typical approaches to knowledge representation, such as the logic approach, semantic networks, frames, rule-based methods and conceptual graphs. The book by Ringland and Duce (1988) offers an overview of these typical approaches and some of the research issues.

Logic approach

The logic approach is mainly based on first-order logic, although other types of non-classical logic, for example modal logic, also have a role to play here. The system of logic involves what are known as definite Horn clauses, which are essential rules of the form:

A if B_1 and B_2 and . . . B_n

This has exactly one conclusion, A, but zero or more conditions B. Propositions are basic elements and can be further translated into several predicates. Propositions have truth values that are determined by a certain interpretation function. That is to say, any proposition must be TRUE or FALSE under the interpretation, which sets up a correspondence between the symbols of the language and the objects or values in some domain. The predicates can be connected with connectives [e.g. $\wedge$ (and), $\vee$ (or), $\neg$ (not) and $\rightarrow$ (implies)] and quantifiers [i.e. $\exists$ (existential quantifier) and $\forall$ (universal quantifier)].

Thus, for the piece of 'knowledge':

John gives a book to Mary

the constituent concepts can be first identified as 'John', 'Mary', 'book' and 'give'. A decent representation can be obtained as follows:[1]

giving(e)	e is a giving 'event'
agent(e, John)	John was the giver
recip(e, Mary)	Mary was the recipient
$\exists$b, book(b) $\wedge$ object(e, b)	A book is the object of giving
time(e, T)	the giving was at time T
$\forall$e, y, t, x giving(e) $\wedge$ recip(e, y) $\wedge$ time(e, t) $\wedge$ object(e, x) $\rightarrow$ ($\forall$t1, t1>t $\rightarrow$ owns(y, x, t1))	if y was the recipient of x at time t, he becomes the owner for all time after this.

Semantic networks

Semantic networks are designed as a means of describing the concepts behind word meanings and the ways in which such meanings interact. A network is a net or graph of nodes joined by links. The nodes in a semantic network usually represent concepts (e.g. BOOK, GREEN) and the links (or labelled directed arcs) usually represent relations (e.g. a book IS COLOURED green). Semantic networks may be loosely related to predicate calculus by following the substitution: *nodes and relations* replace terms by *labelled directed arcs.*

Frames

Frames are ways of grouping information in terms of a record of 'slots' and 'fillers'. The record can be thought of as a node in a network, with a special slot filled with the name of the object that the node stands for, and the other slots filled with the values of various common attributes associated with such an object. This approach can be conveniently suitable for representing knowledge about structure domains or structured knowledge. The intuition behind the frames is that the human brain is less concerned with strictly defining the properties that entities must have in order to be considered as exemplars of some category, and more concerned with the salient properties associated with objects that are typical of their class.

Conceptual graphs

Charles Peirce proposed several methods for producing conceptual graphs. He suggested that a graph can be used as a consistent system of representation, founded upon a simple and easily intelligible basic idea. It can iconically represent facts, concepts and relationships (cf. Peirce 1958a, 1977). Graphs have recently been used for developing many methods of knowledge representation, for example semantic networks (cf. Brachman 1979; Randal 1988), conceptual dependency graphs (Schank

1972, 1975), knowledge graphs (Hoede 1986; Smit 1991) and conceptual graphs (Sowa 1984). Methods involving graphs generally claim to capture some deeper cognitive properties compared with syntactic structures. Many studies in this area have tried to discover some basic concepts and types of relations so that the meanings of words can be described by 'case relations' (i.e. semantic relation primitives linking verbs to some other structures and elements). For example, Schank (1972) has identified a set of primitive actions, states and 'conceptual cases'. Knowledge expressed in natural language can be represented by employing these primitives.

Conceptual graphs were devised by Sowa (1984) as a language of knowledge representation based on philosophy, psychology and linguistics. Knowledge in the form of a conceptual graph is highly structured as a result of modelling specialised facts that can be subjected to generalised reasoning. In the graphs, concept nodes represent entities, attributes, states and events, and relation nodes represent how the concepts are interconnected. A concept is drawn as a box, a conceptual relation as a circle; an arc with an arrow links a box to a circle (Figure 4.5).

This can also be expressed in linear form, in which case the boxes can be represented by square brackets, and the circles by rounded parentheses. The equivalent expression in linear form for Figure 4.5 is therefore:

[concept_1] → (relation) → [concept_2]

The reading of the expression in either form can be: the *relation* of *concept1* is *concept2*. Sometimes, however, the reading of an expression can sound grammatically awkward.

Consider the following example:

[Vehicle] → (part) → [Trailer]

The reading of this – 'A part of a vehicle is a trailer' – can be simplified as 'a vehicle with a trailer'. These readings are helpful mnemonics and not linguistic rules for mapping the graphs into English-language sentences. Conceptual graphs are finite, connected, bipartite graphs. Conceptual relations may have any number of arcs, but most of the common ones are dyadic. Some are monadic, such as the *past tense maker* (PAST) or the *negation* (NEG); others are triadic, for example *between* (BETW); and there are any other number of other arcs.

The primitives of the conceptual graphs are *concept types*, *concepts* and *conceptual relations*. The *concept types* represent classes of entity, attribute, action, state and event. Examples of such concepts are *cat*, *animal*, *arrive*, *attribute*, *big*, *cat*, *command*, *colour*, *justice*, *love* and *warm*. Any conceptual graph system may have

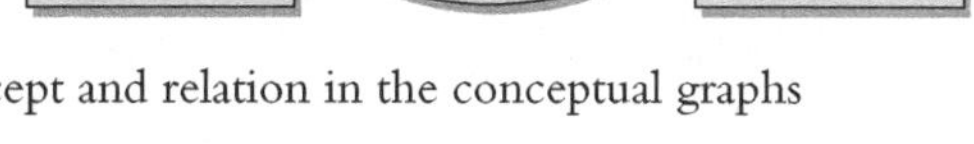

FIGURE 4.5 Concept and relation in the conceptual graphs

a set of types as a basis. This set of concept types is organised using a relation _ defined over the set. The concept types can be partially ordered according to the super-type and sub-type relations. For example, consider the concept types PHYSICAL-OBJECT, ANIMAL, MAMMAL and CAT; these can be arranged as in following order:

CAT _ MAMMAL _ ANIMAL _ PHYSICAL-OBJECT

which means that a cat is a kind of mammal, every mammal is a kind of animal and so on: CAT is said to be a sub-type of MAMMAL, mammal a super-type of CAT. The type hierarchy is not a tree-like structure but a lattice structure. This can be seen from organisation of the following concept types:

ELEPHANT _ MAMMAL

ELEPHANT _ WILD-ANIMAL

RATTLESNAKE _ WILD-ANIMAL

TIGER _ MAMMAL

TIGER _ WILD-ANIMAL

Concepts are instances of concept types. For example, the concept 'the mammal known as Clyde' can be written in the conceptual graphs of Polovina and Heaton (1992) as:

[Mammal: Clyde]

A concept that appears without an individual referent corresponds to a generic referent. Such generic concepts could be denoted as *[<Type_Label>:*]*. Writing *[<Type_Label>]* is merely a convenient shorthand. Generic concepts may take up an individual referent (Clyde, for example, would have a particular trunk). A unique number referent can suffice to make a concept distinct. Thus, the generic concept *[Trunk]* might become *[Trunk:#1234]* in respect to *[Mammal:Clyde]*. The following would then be produced:

[Mammal: Clyde] → (part) → [Trunk: #1234]

Conceptual relations are links between concepts, and they indicate the *role* that each concept (or percept, in terms of referent) plays. Typical examples of conceptual relations found in the dictionary in Sowa (1984) are *agent*, *cause*, *duration*, *experiencer*, *instrument*, *location*, *negation*, *part*, *past*, *point-in-time* and *successor*. Figure 4.6 shows an example of how the propositional attitude *think* is handled in a conceptual graph. Other information on contexts, such as negation, tense, modality and propositional attitudes, can also be incorporated in this way.

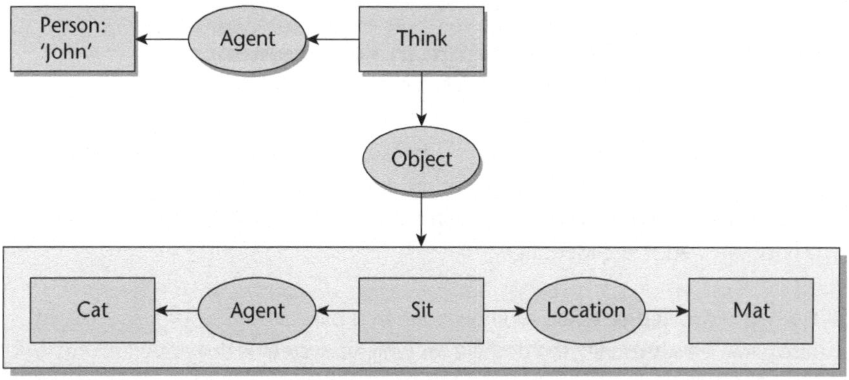

FIGURE 4.6 An example of a conceptual graph (Jackman and Pavelin 1988)

Managing requirements

Requirements can be all kinds of knowledge that emerge during requirements engineering or more generally while working with requirements. Knowledge about requirements may consist of the implicit or explicit information that is created and used during the elicitation, analysis and representation of requirements for developing information systems.

However, a considerable amount of requirements knowledge, such as the rationale behind decisions or domain assumptions, is tacit and remains in people's heads. For example, aspects of the system that may seem trivial, such as the individual's experience in accessing the system, the individual's accessibility and usability, or the localisation of a specific mobile device, might not be explicitly captured and discussed during requirements engineering. Therefore, it is important to identify, access, externalise and share all types of requirements knowledge from and to all stakeholders, including analysts, developers and users.

Identifying implicit requirements knowledge is a complex task. In projects that evolve over a long period of time, or which reuse existing frameworks and libraries, for example a recovery project for legacy system requirements (see Chapter 13), information related to requirements remains 'unknown' or undocumented for 'historical reasons'. Moreover, requirements engineering tasks are often based on assumptions and presuppositions. Customers assume that developers know the domain, while developers assume that customers will tell them about everything that should be implemented – a vicious circle.

In addition, identifying requirements from documents and artefacts is not a trivial task. The various stakeholders might have a different understanding of what is relevant knowledge on requirements, where it should be documented, with what level of detail and how. As a result, requirements can easily become scattered across different sources, including requirements documents, emails, websites, marketing brochures, contractual documents and technical documentation. Thus, identifying requirements is also about identifying which types of information can be captured and found where (Box 4.1).

Box 4.1 Types of knowledge in requirements engineering (Maalej and Thurimella 2013: 7)

Requirements knowledge is diverse, because requirements affect different engineering activities (including design and implementation) and because requirements engineering involves different stakeholders. Five types of requirements knowledge are identified.

Domain knowledge refers to knowledge in a particular area or a specialised discipline. This is usually the domain for which a system is developed. Domain knowledge includes a vocabulary, standards in the domain (e.g. telecommunication or banking standards) and business rules (i.e. domain constraints, standards, and regulations to be satisfied when designing or using the system).

Engineering knowledge includes requirements "content", such as the requirements specifications, dependencies between requirements, as well as other artefacts needed to understand and implement the requirements such as models, test cases, or system architecture, also informal notes and personal comments annotating artefacts like models, requirements, or plans.

Management knowledge includes quality measures, templates, and properties of requirements such as status, priority, and stakeholder preferences. Moreover, emerging requirements-related issues, decisions, and action items are part of this knowledge. For example, during a requirement review, open issues, decisions, and action items on requirements might be identified, discussed, and planned.

Collaboration knowledge includes information about people, their interactions, discussions, argumentation chains, and presuppositions. Discussions include information exchanged or shared between different stakeholders on various problems related to requirements. They may also include requirements rationale or reasoning behind the requirements, a crucial piece of knowledge to understand and implement requirements especially when people leave the projects.

Practice knowledge includes information on tools, methods, and processes to be used for a particular situation while engineering and managing requirements. Organisation or vendor guidelines include information on how to perform requirements engineering activities or how to use a tool

Approaches and methods for information systems development

Approaches for information systems development provide guidelines, methods and techniques to follow for completing every activity in the systems development lifecycle. There are some famous approaches that have been widely used in systems development processes. For example, the unified process has been developed as a set of activities that a team performs to transform a set of customer requirements into a software system. It is a generic process framework that people can customise by adding and removing activities based on the particular needs of and available resources for a project.

The best-known and extensively documented refinement of the unified process is the rational unified process, which is a specialised version of the unified process. Another form of implementation is the agile unified process, which is a simplified version of the rational unified process (Waters 2008). It describes a simple, easy to understand approach to developing business application software using agile techniques and concepts. The agile unified process applies agile techniques, including test-driven development, agile modelling, agile change management and data refactoring, to improve productivity.

Frameworks and methodologies have always been regarded as fundamentals for information systems. Many authors offer comprehensive reviews and critiques of frameworks and methodologies for information systems (see, for example, Avison and Fitzgerald 2006; Hirschheim *et al.* 1995; Iivari *et al.* 1998; Olle *et al.* 1991). An elaborated analysis and comparison of some methodologies and models for information systems can be found in Hirschheim *et al.* (1995), where methodologies and models are evaluated against around fifty criteria that are grouped into technical, usage, economic and behavioural aspects. It is suggested that there are four paradigms – functionalism, social relativism, radical structuralism and neohumanism (Hirschheim *et al.* 1995; Hirschheim and Klein 1989) – and each information systems development approach may be based on one of the paradigms.

Goguen (1992) has described two cultures in information systems development and requirements engineering: the 'dry' and the 'wet'. Bickerton and Siddiqi (1993) classify some thirty methods for systems development and requirements engineering in a framework in which two of the important considerations are whether the methods are 'hard' or 'soft' in character. More studies and comparisons of methodologies for developing information systems can be found in the literature.

There are confusions in the concepts and theories of information systems, which actually contribute to the difficulties of developing and selecting a suitable methodology. The FRISCO (FRamework of Information System COncepts) task group of the International Federation for Information Processing (IFIP) WG 8.1[2] has set up as its goal the removal of such confusions in concepts and theories (Falkenberg *et al.* 1998). The following passage (quoted from Falkenberg *et al.* 1990: 2) manifests dissatisfaction about information systems development:

> There is a growing concern within IFIP WG 8.1 about the present situation, where too many fuzzy or ill-defined concepts are used in the information systems area. Scientific as well as practice-related communication is severely distorted and hampered, due to this fuzziness and due to the frequent situation that different communication partners associate different meanings with one and the same term. There is no commonly accepted conceptual reference and terminology, to be applied for defining or explaining existing or new concepts for information systems.

A great deal of effort has been put into studies on information systems. One of the purposes of this is that criticism and suggestions regarding the methods can be identified, and improvements can be made. There are, however, some problems in many of the these studies. One of the problems is that the majority of commercially available methods for information systems development are 'dry' or 'hard' in nature; social and organisational aspects tend to be ignored. However, as noted in the preface of Galliers (1987), 'few would argue that the study of information and the need to treat the development of information systems from the perspectives of *social* as opposed to technical systems remains as crucial today as it was when Stamper first published his book in 1973'.[3]

Motivated by these same reasons, many people have put much effort in bringing about workable theories and methods for the development of information systems, enabling both social and technical systems to be handled (see, for example, Checkland 1981; Lyytinen and Lehtinen 1986; Mumford and Weir 1979; Stowell 1995).

Organisational semiotics in information systems development

Information systems development is an area in which organisational semiotics has been applied. MEASUR – Methods for Eliciting, Analysing and Specifying Users' Requirements – is a research programme that was initiated by Ronald Stamper in the 1970s. This research programme then led to a set of methods and techniques for information systems, first published in the late 1980s and continuing to evolve ever since (Liu *et al.* 2001, 2002, 2013; Stamper 1987; Stamper 1992).

Organisational semiotics has been applied to information systems with the aim of achieving a more rigorous and scientific treatment of information. The central lesson from the semiotics of information in organisations is revealing. IT industries deal with the problems of the physical aspects of signs (e.g. hardware) and economics (e.g. transmission, storage and manipulation by software). All of these are vitally necessary, but they are not sufficient. We must, however, realise that managers in an organisation may not want to think about the movements and manipulations of signs and signals; they want to know what the messages mean and what people are trying to do with them. Business users want to know the effects of using messages and information (i.e. communication in the business context): how the use of information changes what people believe or expect, or what they agree to do. Unless the use of information changes people's attitudes in such ways, it never delivers any value. IT industries, with all their tools and techniques, have precious little to do with the meanings of signs (information of various kinds), the intentions behind the messages produced or the interpretations resulting in changes of attitude. These, especially the purposes of the use of information and social issues, are the key interests that MEASUR aims to address.

MEASUR is a set of norm-oriented methods for business systems modelling and requirements specification for developing information systems. The concept underlying MEASUR is that organisations themselves are information systems and the social norm is the appropriate unit of specification. As shown in Figure 4.7, the problem articulation method (PAM), semantic analysis method (SAM) and norm analysis method (NAM) are the three key methods for information systems development. Figure 4.7 summarises the contents of MEASUR and its positioning in the context of semiotics and organisational semiotics.

Problem articulation method

The PAM comprises of a set of techniques (Liu *et al.* 2006; Kolkman 1995) that can be applied at the initial stage of a project for developing information systems. In the initial stage, the information systems development team often feels that the problem to be addressed is vague and not clearly specified; in addition, the organisational context may be complex, with no clearly defined scope of the work but with many entangled aspects. PAM aims to help the user to understand the context and identify issues worthy of attention.

In the case of solving a problem or a project relating to an innovation, the central task will be identified as the focal system. The situation (i.e. the context) in which the problem resides and the envisaged system operates is seen as the infrastructure,

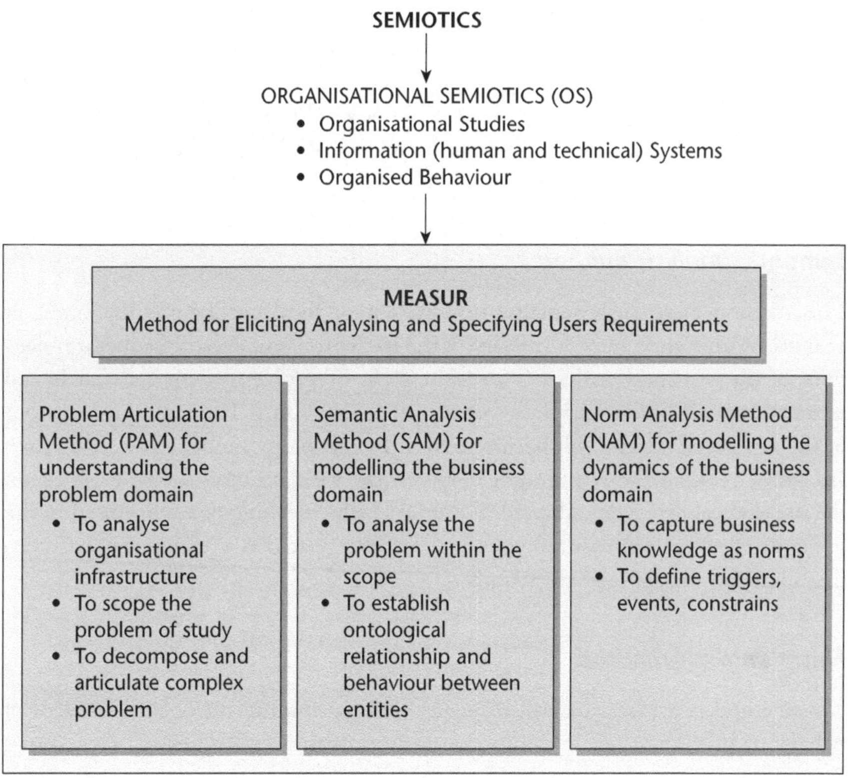

FIGURE 4.7 Architecture of MEASUR using the PAM, SAM and NAM approaches

and will be treated as a composition of many collateral systems. In order to characterise the problem situation, the user of the method will be assisted in defining the unit systems that have a start, an end and affordances that are valued by stakeholders. By using this method, the number of undesirable omissions from the analysis and specification can be reduced. The results can provide a basis for socio-economic analysis, lifecycle management and project control.

Five specific methods fall under the heading of problem articulation:

1. *Unit system definition* is a technique that provides handholds to describe a course of action and list interdependent agents who might take an interest in it.
2. *Stakeholder identification* is a technique that facilitates the identification of the relevant parties (i.e. stakeholders), their involvement in the organisation and how their interests and concerns affect a group's or an organisation's success in delivering the intended results and in maintaining the viability of the product or service.
3. *Collateral analysis* is a technique that assists in structuring a problem situation into a central course of action and surrounding (collateral) activities, and subsequently gives names to each part.
4. *Systems morphology* is a tree-like classification used to clarify three basic functional areas (i.e. substantive, communication and control) of a socio-technical or a business system. Each of these components can in turn be treated as a unit for continued analysis.
5. *Valuation framing* is a technique that can be used to reveal the cultural behaviour of the stakeholders and assess the impact of the innovation (e.g. a course of action or a change) in terms of its benefits and drawbacks.

Semantic analysis method

This method takes an articulated unit system or focal problem as the input of analysis. Within the agreed boundary of the focal problem, one of the major objectives of the semantic analysis is to assist users or problem-owners to elicit and represent their requirements in a formal and precise form. The required functions of the envisaged system will be specified in the ontology model, which describes an agreed view of the responsible agents in the focal business domain. Based on the ontological principles adopted in the SAM, the meaning of a word used in the semantic model to represent the business world is treated as a relationship between the word and the appropriate actions.

Norm analysis method

This method provides a means to specify the dynamics of the agents' patterns of behaviour in the business system. The analysis of the regularities of behaviour is focused on the social, cultural and organisational norms that govern the agents' actions in the business domain. A norm can define the responsibility for an agent occupying a certain incumbency (e.g. a person playing a certain role). A norm specifies conditions in which an action *may* (or *must*, *must not*, etc.) be performed by some agent. The norms can be specified in NORMA, or a pseudo-knowledge representation language, and can further be translated into a programming language for implementation.

Questions and exercises

1. There are differences and similarities between the representation of knowledge and the representation of requirements. Why would the understanding of knowledge representation be useful for requirements representation?
2. Is requirements engineering a typical process of semiosis? If so, how do we understand the sign, object and interpretant, and their relationships, in requirements engineering?
3. In a typical information systems development lifecycle, it seems that an error at an early stage costs much more than one at a later stage. How would you explain this? And what should we learn from this?
4. Find examples of implicit and explicit knowledge in the development of information systems. Discuss how the quality of systems development is affected by the different types of knowledge.

Notes

1 Based on Pavelin, in Ringland and Duce (1988).
2 WG 8.1, part of the International Federation for Information Processing, is one of the Working Groups on Information Systems, and focuses on methodologies and issues in the design and evaluation of information systems.
3 Stamper (1973) began his book with the significant remark that the explosive growth of IT has not been accompanied by a commensurate improvement in the understanding of information. He appeals for an understanding of both machine and human information systems.

5

INFORMATICS IN THE BUSINESS CONTEXT

Business informatics is about information management. The key here is understanding the context, which includes the organisational mission and vision, objectives and other infrastructural aspects. Only when these conditions are met can the requirements be understood and the effective management of information be possible. Infrastructure analysis is an important phase in information systems development projects where the business context is the focus of analysis. This section will describe how the problem articulation method (PAM) in Methods for Eliciting, Analysing and Specifying Users' Requirements (MEASUR) can be used to understand the business context. The discussion of systems analysis, design and implementation will be brief as these will be the main focus of discussion in the following chapters.

Infrastructure analysis

The objectives of an infrastructure analysis are to understand the social, organisational, cultural and technical contexts, to understand the business objectives and strategies in the organisation, and to identify business and technical problems and the feasibility of solving those problems. To achieve these objectives, we can apply the semiotic framework for a semiotic diagnosis, followed by the PAM (Kolkman 1993; Liu et al. 2006, 2011).

Semiotic diagnosis

A semiotic diagnosis examines the organisation as a social system that is constructed through the use of information. The main steps in the diagnosis are same as the layers described in the semiotic framework (see Figure 3.2). The framework links the physical and social worlds through the information mechanisms people use in the organisation, rather than separating the issues into problems for the experts in production engineering and logistics, and problems for the experts in social psychology, industrial relations and organisations. Let us see how each of the levels in the semiotic framework can be used:

- *Physical problems* concern the media for carrying and storing signals. Word of mouth, paper and electronic devices are examples. The diagnosis at this stage will focus, for example, on whether the stocks contain the same information as the inventory, the placement of machines matches the plan, and the production processes are as reported. As far as the informal information system is concerned, the physical locations of the participants are crucial to their communication. Thus, architecture and travel arrangements are important components of the physical aspects of communication. Business issues arise because of the economics of physical resources. Information technology (IT) can often enable us to substitute a cheap medium for an expensive one (email for 'snail-mail'), and it may even allow us to eliminate a number of lorries and a depot full of stock by using information more skilfully.
- *Empirics* is concerned with the problem of the unexpected, the randomness of the entropy that so-called 'information theory' treats as the root of all information. Individuals running organisations have to cope with many different streams of events that are loaded with randomness. Therefore, they organise to turn unpredictable raw materials into uniform products, to give clients a predictable service to cope with their unpredictable problems. They try to keep the plant running smoothly despite randomness in the supply of labour and the functioning of machines, failures of transport systems and the irregularities of demand. They also want to generate diversity and unpredictability in order to innovate, to keep competitors guessing and keep on their toes. Business issues are frequently prompted by considering the management of uncertainty – either overcoming it or generating it. These are not necessarily primarily concerned with information systems, but one should not forget that the ultimate goal of having information systems is to help with the management of uncertainty.
- *Syntactics* is the aspect of semiotics concerned with structure. At one level, it concerns the structure of sentences in a language, but it can be treated much more broadly for this diagnostic purpose. The activities we have to manage are often chaotic, and the issues of interest here are how to impose order and regularity, and hence operate far more efficiently. That is what production engineering is about in the factory, and, by analogy, systems analysis in the office setting. We look for the right kind and degree of formality. Only when we have succeeded in this can we introduce a computer system to provide support.

These three levels are all concerned with efficiency issues. This class of problem can normally be solved using technology. Such problems receive nearly all the attention when classical methods of requirements analysis are used. MEASUR, however, is able not only to draw attention to the next three levels of the framework, but also to provide methods for tackling the problems they raise. They are always information-oriented problems, and they are continually becoming more important:

- *Semantics* concerns meanings. When people from different backgrounds have to work together, they need to understand one another. On a smaller canvas, we can depict semantic problems that organisations constantly encounter – the need to respond to a new technology, a new marketing concept, a social change affecting consumers, a new organisational concept. Effectiveness is a matter of doing the right thing, and that entails a continual search for such new ideas, and these all throw up problems of semantics.
- *Pragmatics* concerns intentional behaviour. Signs are used to indicate intentions. Doing business is largely a matter of getting things done through signs that are both meaningful and charged with intention. The characteristic of an organisation with pragmatic problems is muddle. This is sometimes caused because there is no consensus about goals, the commonly accepted intentions of a team, but sometimes the muddle is caused by misunderstandings related to intentions. Issues in this area have to be resolved at the highest level in strategic planning, but they also have to be resolved at the micro-level in the design of the organisation and its information systems.
- *Social problems* are essentially those related to how people do or should behave, that is, problems of norms and expectations. The culture of the organisation is significant because all information systems are ultimately dependent for any of their capacity to use signs upon the culture in which they are embedded. MEASUR is based on the analysis of the norms of an organisation, so MEASUR takes the social level as the starting point and is ideally suited for elucidating issues in this area.

MEASUR concerns itself with the three upper levels in the semiotic framework, those constituting the human functions. Thus, the use of methods is not constrained by any technical platform on which the human information system stands.

The problem articulation method

Unit system definition

The first task in PAM is to identify the constituent units in a given problem situation (or context) that are to be investigated. Definition of unit system provides the guidance for breaking down a complex problem situation into related unit and sub-unit systems comprising business activities, information and resources. Unit systems can be identified following these principles:

- A unit system consists of a collection of organised activities involving people or automata to achieve a set of objectives.
- A unit system must consume resources and play a contributing role in the problem situation.
- A unit system may consist of sub-unit systems.

The analysis of unit systems provides an effective means to examine the problem situation with the required recourses, activities and subsequent plans of action. However, this analysis does not formally define who are involved in the unit systems and in what capacity they are responsible for the unit systems. A separate analysis for that is carried out at the stage of the stakeholder's identification.

Stakeholder identification

The analysis in PAM recognises the importance of the people and their involvement in the organisation, because their interests and concerns directly affect a group's or an organisation's success in delivering the intended results and in maintaining the viability of the product or service. Stakeholder identification in the PAM facilitates the identification of all the stakeholders for the purpose of identifying their success measures and turning these into the quality goals of the unit. A stakeholder can be described in terms of role and responsibility. The stakeholder may play multiple roles in a context (i.e. unit systems) where he or she fulfils the responsibilities. The value of the stakeholders can be measured in terms of how much the outcomes out of the context are worth to them in relation to gain and loss.

Equation (1) defines the characteristics of the stakeholders within a unit system:

$$\text{UnitSystem} \supset \{\text{Stakeholder, (Role, Responsibility), Value}\} \tag{1}$$

PAM defines a *role* in six categories, each role being responsible for its functions in a unit system:

$$\text{Role} = \text{Actor} \mid \text{Clients} \mid \text{Provider} \mid \text{Facilitator} \mid \text{Governing Body} \mid \text{Bystander}$$

where the following descriptions apply:

- *Actor*: An actor has a direct impact on the course of the action. This role often involves substantive and message-passing activities among the other roles, which operates within the influence of norms.
- *Client*: The client is the user or beneficiary who is the recipient of the consequences or outcomes of the unit system.
- *Provider*: The provider is the developer who is responsible for creating the conditions and resources to facilitate the deliverable of a unit system, for example the supplies and authorisation to enable the functionality and operability of the project.
- *Facilitator*: The facilitator is the initiator and enabler of the system and acts as a focus point for the group in directing the course of the action. Primary responsibilities of the facilitator are to resolve conflicts, ensure continuity and steer the team towards the organisational goal.
- *Governing body*: The governing body determines the strategic aims, high-level objectives and direction of the unit system to keep them under review and ensure they are on track. A governing body may take part in the management

and planning in the unit system. The governing body cannot, however, (a) intervene in the operation of the unit system, or (b) exercise authority over people appointed under the project team who are employed by the unit system.

- *Bystander*: Bystanders exert a participative role in shaping the course of action that provides informal and formal norms by which the system should abide. The bystanders are not usually part of the project itself since they are not directly involved in the direct decision-making of the unit system. However, bystanders will influence the system and its outcome in many ways, determining the course of action or 'core' system.

These roles may affect a unit system with varying impacts. Figure 5.1 shows that the closer the role is to the unit system, the greater the impact of the unit system on it. This impact can be measured as a tangible value by using the valuation-framing technique, which indicates a gain or loss in terms of the unit system from the perspective of each involved stakeholder.

Collateral analysis

Once the unit system, sub-unit systems and corresponding stakeholders have been articulated, a collateral model can be produced. The method of collateral analysis helps in the analysis and articulation of relationships between the unit systems that comprise the large, complex system. PAM takes the central task in an innovation, such as an IT project, as the focal system. The scope of the analysis is the focal system

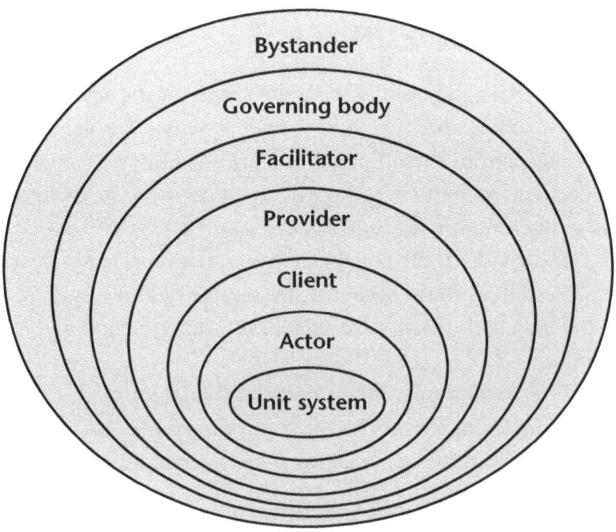

FIGURE 5.1 Stakeholders and their degree of impact on a unit system (adapted from Kolkman 1993)

and the infrastructure in which the focal system resides and operates. Suppose that the proposed IT system has been approved to go ahead; the focal system will then be the new IT system in operation.

But it does not spring out of nothing, and it can only function successfully within the right infrastructure. Collateral analysis forces us to take the total system apart into a number of unit systems around the focal system. These collateral systems are interrelated and form an infrastructure for the focal system (Figure 5.2). This model defines object systems (in rectangles) and service systems (in ellipses). The latter type of system provides services and transform the former from one stage to another. Together, the collateral systems constitute the entire infrastructure that supports the focal system, and this focal system represents the principal goal of the entire problem situation.

The object systems and service systems enable the development of the focal system through four phases: the constructing cycle, the launching cycle, the operating cycle and the back-up cycle. The collateral analysis provides a coherent view of the lifecycle of problem situations and assists in producing the complete requirements specifications that will then be used for the system planning and technical design phases.

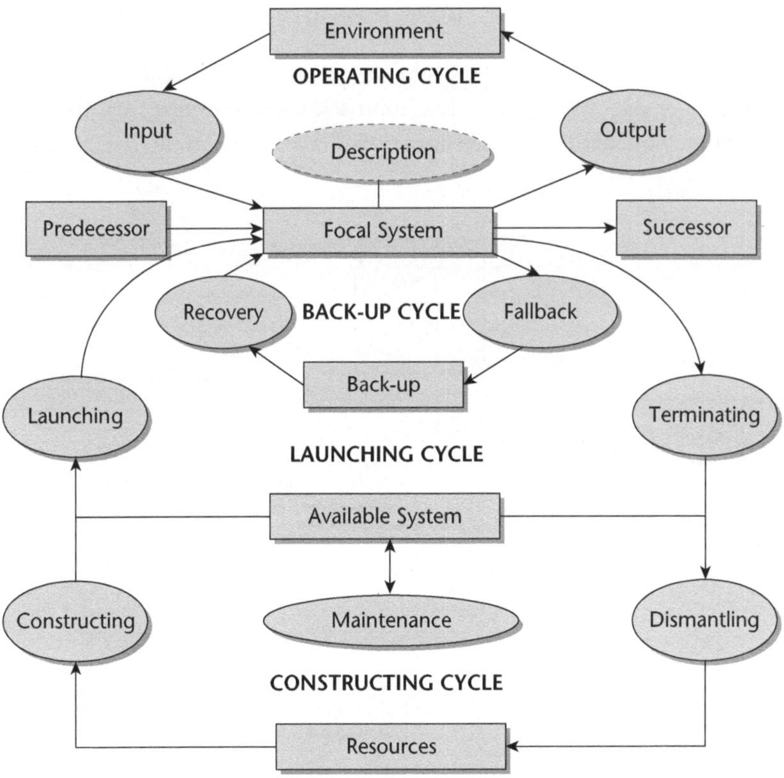

FIGURE 5.2 The collateral structuring model (adapted from Kolkman 1993)

The outcome of the collateral analysis can be documented in a template as described in Figure 5.3 and stored in a repository for future retrieval, which enables the traceability and configuration management of requirements.

The collateral analysis method takes a possibly fuzzy total system and locates its effective boundary in a given environment. This method, which serves as a useful checklist for any innovation, guides people to identify all the collateral systems and organises them into a logical structure. This method can be particularly useful if the social and technological infrastructure is inadequate or is posing problems; similarly, an innovation project may have become a more unexpectedly complex and larger scale operation than expected.

Such a comparison can be made by considering the situation of building a new plant for electronic products in the 'silicon valley' of an economically advanced nation as opposed to placing it in a developing country. In daily life, the lack of a piece of electrical cable, for example, may make it impossible to connect a personal computer to a power supply, which means that the machine will not be able to work in a remote undeveloped area. In order to bring the focal system into operation and sustain the situation, the analysis for planning and management of the innovation project must cover all these collateral systems.

Systems morphology

The method of systems morphology, like that of collateral analysis, looks inward at the structure of each unit system. The approach taken is similar to a 'top-down', structured method, but the focus of attention is radically different. It focuses on the

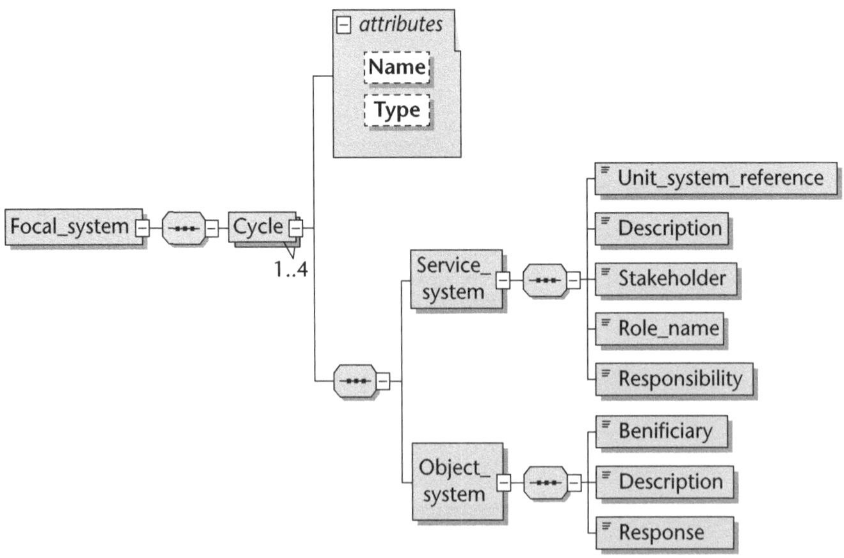

FIGURE 5.3 Schema for the collateral model

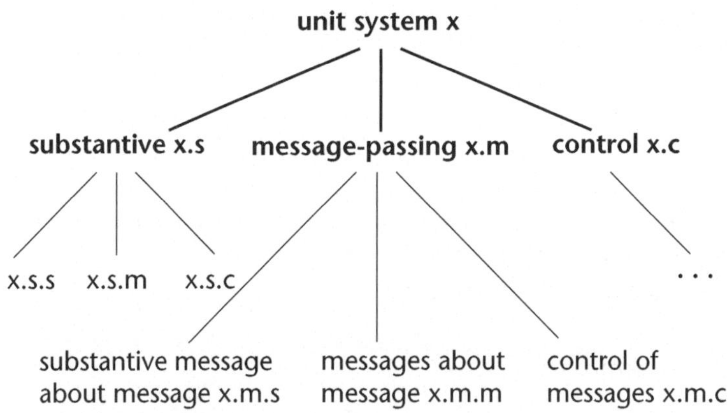

FIGURE 5.4 Systems morphology for analysing unit systems

identification of types of behaviours and norms that govern people's behaviour in a unit system. Each unit system is divided into three sub-systems: the substantive, communication and control sub-systems (Figure 5.4).

The *substantive* behaviour is directly related to the organisational objectives and contributes to the core business of the organisation. The outcomes of activities in this category contribute directly to the attainment of the organisation's business goals. Actions undertaken here will normally result in the creation of value that could be economic or social, and tangible or intangible, depending on the nature of the organisation. There will be norms governing the behaviour of the members in the organisation. For example, if it is in a car manufacturer, the norms will direct the worker on how to produce cars. In a service firm, the norms will direct staff how to provide services.

Communication (message-passing) is the second type of behaviour, which is concerned with signs, the 'input' and 'output' of the communication process. The communication activities involving passing messages from one person to another within the organisation and will enable the members to behave in a coordinated and organised manner so that the first types of actions may be successfully performed. Signs are employed and sent between agents, with meanings agreed by parties involved in the communication to express their intentions. The norms in this category inform, instruct and direct the members about when, where and how to conduct themselves. When people are widely separated in space and time, an informal system is less effective. The effective deployment of all means of communication becomes essential, including formal and informal means and various modes and channels.

The third type of behaviour is related to *control*, which aims to ensure that the first and second categories of activity are properly conducted. Measures of enforcement are an integral part of this control. Within the organisation, the enforcement associated with inducement or punishment is stipulated in the rules and regulations. Between organisations, it may be generated from inter-firm agreements, treaties or contracts. However, the power of enforcement both within and between organisations ultimately rests upon socially established norms that may be underpinned by the law. This control aspect of behaviour within a firm ensures that every relevant agent acts properly in performing the substantive as well as communication tasks. If a member or an agent fails to comply with the rules, organisational control will be imposed on the agent. Sanctions (punishments and rewards), as well as incentives for achieving the organisation's goals, are the necessary means for maintaining social and organisational order.

Valuation-framing

Valuation-framing enables an analysis of the impact of an innovation or project on the relevant stakeholders. It recognises that for any project, such as the introduction of an IT system to a workplace, differences in the stakeholders' perspectives will lead to different perceived values and hence different responses.

After the stakeholders have been identified in the early stages of the problem articulation, the valuation of the impact of the innovation will be calculated from each stakeholder's perspective. Let us imagine that a company is going to initiate a project to develop a computer information system. The stakeholder groups in

TABLE 5.1 Ten aspects for stakeholders in relation to an innovation

Aspects	*Descriptions*
Subsistence	Physical livelihood, existences; e.g. the impact of the new system on job quality and efficiency
Classification	Differentiation of people by sex, age, level of education; e.g. whether the new system will improve equal opportunity for all
Territoriality	Accessibility; e.g. the impact of the new system may lead to an erosion of control, influence or authority
Temporality	Time division, synchronous, asynchronous; e.g. issues of time zone differences
Learning	Sharing knowledge, gaining awareness; e.g. de-skilling or more providing opportunity for learning new skills
Recreation	Fulfilment, joy; e.g. whether the job becomes more interesting or more boring
Protection	Fairness, rights; e.g. granting file rights access to the appropriate groups of people and maintaining the confidentiality of information
Exploitation	An individual's vs. organisation's interests; e.g. cutbacks on operating costs with salary cuts, retrenchment or longer working hours
Association	Grouping, alliances; e.g. the formation of teams to evoke competitiveness and a sense of belonging in employees
Interaction	Interrelations, communications, e.g. fostering collaborative attitudes in the workplace

Source: after Kolkman (1993), Liu *et al.* (2006)

this case will include the owners of the company, the management, the operational staff, the IT department, the clients, suppliers, competitors, bystanders, the general public and so on. These different stakeholders, based on their own values, may react differently to the proposed project. Hall (1959), drawing on work from anthropology and cultural studies, defines ten criteria for an assessment of the gains and losses of each stakeholder in relation to the innovation or change occurring in the social system (Table 5.1).

To enable a complete valuation, the valuation-framing must be applied to each stakeholder in all terms of all ten aspects, as illustrated in Figure 5.5. The management, for example stakeholder C in the figure, may see the proposed IT project, in the aspect of exploitation, as an opportunity for improving productivity, which may be viewed differently by the operational staff.

The outcomes of this analysis signify a tangible value (ranging between –3 and 3) that each a stakeholder has gained if such an innovation takes place in their workforce. Equations (2) and (3) can be used to form a matrix that contains values by performing valuation-framing using the following formulae:

$$C_j = \sum_{i=1}^{10} V_j \qquad (2)$$

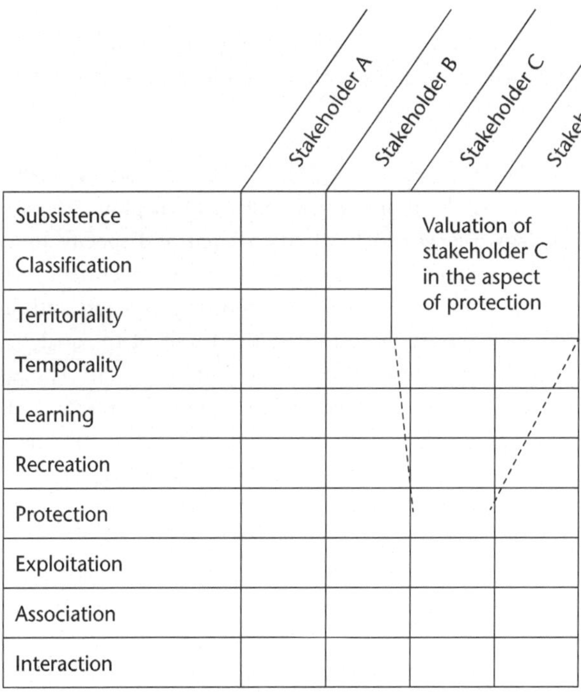

FIGURE 5.5 Valuation-framing for an organisational and context analysis

where C_j is the total value of all the stakeholders affected by the aspect of concern j in an unit system, and:

$$S_i = \sum_{j=1}^{n} V_{ij} \qquad (3)$$

where S_i is the total value of the impact of the aspects of concern as assessed by stakeholder i in an unit system.

The computed values represent a perceived impact of the concerning aspects compared with the involving stakeholders. The result of S_i will then be inputted to Equation (1), assigning the actual values to the specific stakeholders.

Systems analysis, design and implementation

The result of the infrastructure analysis gives us the power to explain the problem situation and to articulate the innovation project to give a better defined and better structured problem. It also generates sufficient terminology to represent all the relevant actions. The major tasks in the further stages of a systems development project will be as follows:

- *requirements analysis*, which includes information analysis and functional analysis;
- *construction*, which includes systems design and implementation;
- *operationalisation*, which includes the use, monitoring and maintenance of the system.

This section briefly describes which MEASUR methods can help in coping with these tasks; details will be found in the following chapters.

The *semantic analysis method* can be used to elicit and specify users' requirements. The first step is to identify the agents in the problem domain. These agents are people in different roles, with different responsibilities and authorities in an organisation. A semantic model, produced as the result of the analysis, will capture the possible actions (or patterns of behaviour) of the agents. These patterns of behaviour are called affordances, actions are afforded by the agents, and the agents are potentially capable of doing so. The affordances depend on the agents, which is called *ontological dependency*. Because the information on which agent is capable of doing what action is the most important item of content of the semantic model, it is also called the *ontology model*.

The *norm analysis method* can then be used to capture the norms (i.e. rules, regulations and conventions) of the situation. These norms act as conditions and constraints; they govern agents' behaviour, normally in a prescriptive manner to decide when certain actions will be performed. Norms, in conjunction with the semantic model, clearly define the roles, functions, responsibilities and authorities of agents.

The knowledge representation language used for semantic modelling and norm specification is called *NORMA* (a language for describing NORMs and Affordances).

A semantic model, produced as the result of a semantic analysis, is not only rich in semantics, but also contains information on, for example, temporal and ontological dependencies between agents and affordances. All these features of the information can be captured in a predefined, uniform data structure in the *semantic temporal database*. This database constitutes the most important foundation for an integrated software environment, *NORMBASE*, which supports semantic analysis and norm analysis, and ultimately produces a computer information system that is based on semiotic principles and MEASUR methods.

Summary

A project to develop an information system may undergo a number of major phases, each of which comprises a range of activities. These activities and phases are not totally sequential. Many of them take place in parallel and may reoccur several times during the project. Table 5.2 shows the major phases and activities, as well as the MEASUR methods that can be used to assist in the activities.

The MEASUR methods can be used in virtually any sequence and may be mixed with other techniques at many points. For example, at the design stage, the entity–attribute relationship method can be used, or at the implementation stage a fourth-general language or an object-oriented language may be adopted. But using the MEASUR methods throughout all the phases may potentially bring great benefits to the entire project. This is because, first, all the methods are consistent with one another and based on the same underlying principles. The result of analysis at an earlier phase always lends itself readily to the MEASUR method in the next phase.

Second, there are software tools developed to assist activities at all stages. The problem articulation tool (PAT) is a computerised analytical facility. Use of the PAT guides users to define all the unit systems, to identify the relationships between the collateral systems and the stakeholders, to assess the organisation's business strategy, and to establish project plans. The PAT can also be used for project management if the plan is constructed with this tool. NORMBASE is the computerised environment that provides support to cover the whole range of systems development activities. It supports the whole process of a semantic analysis, a norm analysis and production of the systems documentation.

TABLE 5.2 MEASUR methods and major systems development activities

Major phases	*Major activities*	*MEASUR methods*
Infrastructure analysis	Business strategy analysis	PAM
	Information planning	PAM/SAM
Requirement analysis	Information analysis	SAM
	Functional analysis	NAM
Construction	Design	NORMABASE
	Implementation	NORMABASE
Audit	Audit	PAM, SAM, NAM

NAM, norm analysis method; PAM, problem articulation method; SAM, semantic analysis method.

Questions and exercises

1. In information systems development, why is an analysis and understanding of the business organisation as the context of the technical system important? What should be analysed and understood in the organisation before focusing on the technical system?
2. What are the major differences in analysing the whole system between collateral analysis and the hierarchical decomposition approach – the process of decomposing a system in a top-down fashion, first into sub-systems, then into functions, and then into modules? When would collateral analysis be more appropriate than hierarchical decomposition?
3. Suppose you are in a project team to design a new customer relationship system in a banking organisation. Conduct a collateral analysis and build a collateral structuring model by identifying components and purposes for all the object systems and servicing systems in the model.
4. Using systems morphology and treating a car manufacturer as the whole system x, identify major activities as examples in each of the three categories (substantive, message-passing and control). Discuss the role of the activities in each category.
5. With reference to valuation-framing, consider the scenario of introducing a new mobile communication device into the business process in a business organisation (e.g. a hotel, a restaurant or a hospital). Illustrate why different stakeholders may respond to such an innovative change in business differently.

6

ORGANISATIONAL MODELLING FOR INFORMATION SYSTEMS

An organisation is an information system that is infinitely rich and complex. One can never exhaustively study a social or business organisation. What is modelled is always a part of it; and what is seen is just a realisation (or an instance) of a pattern of behaviour of some agent. If one wishes to model a business system, one has to focus on the level of the pattern of behaviour. The method of semantic analysis provides a means to do this by devising a canonical formalism with focus on a the responsible agent and his or her repertoire of behaviour. This method covers a range of activities in information modelling, such as requirements elicitation, analysis, specification and representation.

Concepts of organisational modelling

The relationship between behaviour and knowledge works in two directions. In one direction, an agent learns about the world through his actions to gain knowledge so that he gets to know exactly the meanings and boundaries of objects, concepts and relations. On the other side, the behaviour manifests knowledge that the agent possesses. The functions of both sides work at the same time; that is, what the agent knows tells him what to do, and what he does reflects what he knows (partly because what he does may be a kind of trail to learn some new knowledge). Any rational action on the part of the agent is constrained by the repertoire of behaviour and directed by his knowledge of the world. This repertoire of behaviour can be seen as affordances.

Affordances

'Affordance' is the word that Gibson (1968) and the 'direct perception' school of psychologists (cf. Michaels and Carello 1981) use for the behaviour of an organism made available by some combined structure of the organism and its environment. 'The affordances of the environment are what it offers the animal, what it provides or furnishes, either for good or ill', Gibson (1968: 127) writes.

He gives an example to show that if a terrestrial surface is horizontal, flat, sufficiently extended and firm, the surface *affords support*. It is a surface of support. It is stand-on-able, permitting an upright posture for quadrupeds and bipeds. It is therefore walk-on-able and run-over-able. It is not sink-into-able like the surface of a swamp. The properties of the surface, when they were measured as an affordance of support for a species of animal, have to be measured relative to the animal, and not just treated as physical properties. According to ecology, a species of animal is said to utilise or occupy a certain niche in the environment. The natural environment offers many ways of life, and different animals have different ways of life. The niche implies a kind of animal, and the animal implies a kind of niche. Together they constitute the totality of the world.

The theory of affordances can be naturally extended to the social world for studying social behaviour. The society acting as an environment makes many patterns of behaviour possible. People are agents living in a world of flux. This world is socially constructed through the agents' actions, on the basis of what is offered by the physical world itself. The state of being an agent-in-its-environment makes it possible to acquire certain abilities of behaving that might be completely impossible if the agent were separated from the environment. While agents act, they experience the environment and alter it at the same time. Their previous actions build up a possibility of some new type of action. For example, a person's ability to recognise a telephone is socially afforded by the fact that there is an artefact called a telephone. Only if this person has the ability to recognise a telephone can they be taught how to operate it, and will they then be able to make a telephone call.

An agent learns his direct knowledge through detecting *valuable invariants by act-in-relation-to-environment*, both physically and mentally. By knowing the invariants, the value of certain ranges of behaviour are learned. Having sufficient experience in the social environment and knowing enough about the invariants, an agent can know the boundaries of behaviour that are socially acceptable. However, what he learns is only his direct environment, the here-and-now. To be able to know anything beyond the here-and-now, signs must be employed so as to compose propositions and images.

By using signs, another dimension of the world is opened up for the agent, and he can then gain access to that part of the world that is beyond the here-and-now. Signs afford appropriate action at a distance. In particular, they afford coordinated actions between the members of a society. People create signs, assign meanings to them and use them to refer to the future and the past. This ambience, full of man-made signs, is called 'culture' and supports most of our daily social interactions. A natural deduction, which can be socially confirmed, is that different cultures, for example, western or eastern, Christian or Buddhist, provide different affordances, and hence different perceptions of reality.

Ontology and some other fundamental notions

Ontology

Lacey (1976: 206) offers the following explanation about *ontology*. His use of capitals indicates his view that some of these categories are more important than others:

> A central part of metaphysics is *ontology*. This studies BEING, and in particular, nowadays, what there is, for example material objects, minds, PERSONS, UNIVERSALS, numbers, FACTS and so on . . . A particular theory about what exists, or a list of existents, can be called an ontology.

Questions that an ontological theory tries to investigate are fundamental and general. This theory seeks an inventory of kinds of things that exist and asks what can be said about anything that exists, just in so far as it does exist. Can we classify all that exists into different fundamental kinds (categories), in one way or more ways? Is there any hierarchy between kinds of things? Do some depend on others for their existence? These are typical questions concerned in any ontological study, and involve the relations between very general notions, such as, *thing*, *entity*, *object*, *individual*, *universal*, *particular*, *substance* and also *event*, *process* and *state*.

In his paper, Stamper (1985) examines three very different ontologies that have strong influences on studies of information and knowledge. The first recognises only symbol structures; this is the ontology of a relational database language. The second ontology recognises distinct, individual, identifiable objects; this lies behinds predicate logic as its formal semantics is based on set theory. The third ontology assumes that the only thing we can know is our own behaviour in our own environment; this is the ontology that the semantic analysis bases itself on. This ontology assumes that the world known to particular agents comprises only the actions they can perform in their environment.

Agent, dependent and determiner

The agent can be as simple as an individual person or as complex as a cultural group, language community or society. What exists in the world relies on the repertoire of behaviour of the agent. For example, an ink pen may exist in a sense of an *ink pen* in one cultural community, but of an *unknown object* in some other cultural community; a particular sword may exist as a weapon in one society, but as only an ornament in another. In these examples, the existence of the pen and the sword depend on the agents, whose affordances allow them to recognise them, to assign meanings to them, to know their properties.

This leads to the notion of dependency in this ontology: the agents learn abilities; these affordances then enable them to act in ways that determine the shape of the world they inhabit. The affordances the agents have gained are universal invariants that constitute the repertoire of their behaviour and allow them to react recurrently and circumstantially. Every particular action they performs is a realisation of a universal pattern of behaviour. The two main categories of the *construction blocks* of the world are *agent* and *affordance*, but the definitions of agent and affordance are context sensitive. Some simple agent, for example, a person, is ontologically dependent on some other complex agent, say society; in this case, the agent, the person, is an affordance itself. Nevertheless, a criterion for determining whether an affordance can ever be an agent is that an agent must be able to act responsibly. Properties of the agents and affordances are another fundamental class of the *construction blocks*, labelled as *determiners*, which result from complicated measurements of the agents and affordances.

Universal versus particular

Actions of agents should usually be modelled at the universal level concerning the universal patterns of behaviour in knowledge representation and requirements analysis, although in the end they will be recorded in a database at both levels. Loux (1978: 13) reports that Aristotle's definition of the universal is 'that which is of such a nature as to be predicated of many objects'. Frege considers that concepts are the referents of predicate-expressions. Russell (2001: 49) states that 'substantives, adjectives, prepositions, and verbs,' the expressions that serve as predicate-terms, 'stand for universals'.

In the knowledge representation language NORMA, the universals represent invariant patterns of behaviour, or mechanisms. The universals can have realisations that are particular instances. This universal/particular conceptual construct is found in conceptual graphs as well (cf. Sowa 1984). Universals are represented by concept types, while particulars are concepts. However, the representations of both universals and particulars in NORMA are in the same direction because there is no fundamental difference between the universals and the particulars. Both of them represent repertoires of behaviour. The similar treatments of both universals and particulars can be found related to semantic analysis in later sections.

NORMA

NORMA is a knowledge representation language developed in the Methods for Eliciting, Analysing and Specifying Users' Requirements (MEASUR) research programme (Stamper 1992; Stamper *et al.* 1988). A primary function of this language is for conducting semantic analysis. 'NORMA' comes from *norm* and *affordance*, and was devised as a language for specifying norms and affordances as systems analysis and requirements specifications. This section will introduce NORMA in terms of some of its most important concepts and syntax.

Well-formed formula

The focus of systems analysis is the agent in action. No matter how complex the agents are in a social environment, they can be studied by observing their actions and detecting the invariants, that is, their general patterns of behaviour. Two axioms that dominate the basic formulation of the language are:

There is no knowledge without a knower, and

there is no knowing without action.

These axiomatic, philosophical assumptions suggest that the only feasible way to depict any fragment of knowledge is to model the agent and his action at the same time. The meaning of representation of action is only determined if the viewpoint is chosen; therefore, the place of the agent in a knowledge representation model is essential. Following this, a well-formed formula for knowledge representation is derived as always having the following structure:

<knower-term> <behaviour-term>, or

<agent-term> <action-term>

such as Ax, where A is an agent and x stands for a pattern of action, for example person stand.

This well-formed formula forces every piece of knowledge to be tied to the agent who is responsible for it. The knowledge can be about universal patterns of actions or particular instances. In any case, the agent is responsible for possessing the knowledge, performing the action or designating meanings to actions.

Affordance and ontological dependency

Some affordances can be possible only if certain other affordances are available. This kind of dependency is *ontological*, which is taken as an essential theme in representing knowledge. For example, for a person to be able to stumble, he must first walk; for two persons to be separated, they must have a marriage or other relationship that involves being together. In these two examples, *walk* and *marriage* are *ontological antecedents* for *stumble* and *separate*, respectively, which are called *ontological dependants*. These ontological antecedents are more direct extensions of affordances of the agent or agents. An agent with affordances can be seen as a *modified agent*, the affordances being treated as extensions. To represent the above two examples, the following expressions can be obtained:

person walk stumble

where *person walk* is the modified agent that affords *stumble*; and

(person$_1$, person$_2$) marriage separation

where (person$_1$, person$_2$) is a complex agent, the modified agent is *(person$_1$, person$_2$) marriage*, on which a further affordance *separation* is an ontological dependent.

These two expressions have employed a syntactic formula:

Axy

for example person walk stumble; and

(A,B)xy

for example ($person_1$, $person_2$) marriage separation.

In most cases, the analysis of the agent (either a simple one, such as a person, or a complex one, such as a corporate body or an institution) with their behaviour would be a recursive application of this principle of modified agent to obtain the expressions in the well-formed formula.

The affordance can be composite. When an agent is doing one thing, they might also be doing another. For example, when a person stands, they might also speak. Thus,

A(x,y)

where ',' reads as 'while', a restriction; for example, *person (stand, speak)*, meaning: a person stands while speaking.

The agent may do one or another or both of two things at a time. For example, a person either speaks or sings. The syntax for this is:

A(x:y)

where ':' reads as 'or-while', a conflation; for example, *person (speak: sing)* for a person either speaks or sings.

If the agent has an affordance of doing one thing while the other is not experienced, for example a person sits while they are not singing, the following syntax is designed for designating that:

A(x;y)

where ';' reads as 'while-not', an exclusion; for example, *person (sit; sing)* for a person sits while he is not singing.

A composite affordance can be partitioned into several parts. For example, the student council is ontologically the dependant of the university, and the chairperson (the role or incumbency in the office rather than the person) is a part of the student council. The notation in NORMA is defined as follows:

Ax.y

which means *y* is a part of *x*, for example *university student council. chairperson*, the student council is the ontological dependant of the university, and the chairperson (the role or incumbency in the office rather than the person) is a part of the student council.

Semiotic behaviour

Two types of behaviour have to be identified: substantive and semiotic. An agent can perform an action and can also use signs to describe the action (although the using of signs itself is an action). Without involving signs, the agent is confined within their here-and-now environment, for example they stand, walk and move about. If they want to make their actions linked with the past and the future, they must use signs. The abilities to use signs in various ways are called semiotic affordances, while the behaviour directly bringing about a change of a physical or social world is considered substantive.

For example, *marriage* can be considered as a substantive behaviour of the two persons concerned. The associated semiotic behaviour with *marriage* would be announcing the start or the finish of the marriage, for which the production of semiotic entities (signs), such as speeches and documents, would be involved. Such semiotic behaviour can be represented in the following form:

B"Ax"

where *B* is the agent performing the semiotic action, and the text between and including the quotes represents the signs employed by *B* in his behaviour. *Ax* is the meaning or referent of the semiotic action, for example *Mary "John happy"*.

Time

Time is one of the most effective measures to determine the meanings of concepts, actions and events that are expressed in our language. Affordances have an ontological nature that allows them to be placed into the flux of the world in terms of time.

The benefit of using time is exploited in NORMA in many ways. When an agent and an affordance are identified and defined, their existence period must be determined, marked by a *start* and *finish*, for both a universal and a particular. Determining the boundaries in terms of time is the minimum required as a guarantee that the meanings of the words and expressions appearing in an analysis are clear. It is also used as a clue for seeking agreed meanings from different viewpoints. Several operators are defined in NORMA to enable us to describe patterns of behaviour that are related to the *start* and *finish* of the affordances. Two of these operators are *beginning* and *ending*:

Ax<

for example *person stand<*, meaning: a person begins to stand, which may terminate an action of sitting and lead to a start of standing if the *beginning* process is successful.

Ax>

for example *person stand>*, meaning: a person ends standing, which may bring the action of standing to a finish if the *ending* process is successful.

Determiner and identity

Agents and affordances have properties that are invariants of quality and quantity that differentiate one instance from another. This kind of invariant is called a *determiner*.

Typical examples of determiners are individuals' names, addresses, weights and hair colours. To describe the determiners, the following mechanism is devised:

A#x, or *Ax#y*

where the hash sign indicates that what follows is a determiner, for example *person#name*, *person#weight* or *person salary#amount*.

Agents may have many roles to play when they are involved in many actions or relations. For example, a person can be seen as a father, a partner, a manager or a customer depending on the circumstances in which the person is looked at. The role name, essentially serving the same purpose as the other properties discussed above, is also a determiner of individuality. The following expression gives an example:

(person#husband, person#wife)marriage

This describes that a marriage is a joint affordance of two persons, of whom one has a role name *husband* and the other a role name *wife*.

Generic–specific relationship

Agents and affordances can be placed in generic–specific structures according to whether or not they possess shared or different properties. The generic–specific classification is normally determined by norms that may be socially or culturally formed. In some cases, the classification rules can be defined by the parties involved in the particular practical affairs. For example, in a society, there are several specific kinds of legal persons, such as natural persons, corporate bodies and governments. The formula to represent the generic–specific relationships is as follows:

A((b:c:d:e)→ f)

where *b*, *c*, *d*, and *e* are specific affordances of the generic *f*. For example, *society((natural-person:corporate-body:government)→legal person)* means that, in a society, there are several specific kinds of legal persons, such as natural persons, corporate bodies and governments.

The generic–specific structures are contingent on social decisions and are not logically necessary. For example, one may classify a whale into the category of fish or mammal, or both.

Defining authority and responsibility

The notion of *responsibility* is as essential in NORMA, as is the notion of *truth* in classical logic, because in NORMA any recognition of affordances and their existence periods are tied to the agents. Realisations of actions and change of states are all decided by the responsible agents in accordance with the authorities. For example, the commencement and termination of a studentship is authorised by someone who is in a role of student registration officer, and the qualification of enjoying a social security benefit is determined by the particular government office. The responsibility and authority over realising each instance of the affordances are analysed and traced in the analysis. The following way is defined for denoting authority in NORMA:

$A(x@\rightarrow y)$

which means the authority for x is y, for example *nation(law@→* parliament).

Graphic representation – the ontology chart

An old Chinese idiom says 'A picture is worth a thousand words', and NORMA offers a way of graphic representation for this. Agents and affordances are nodes in the graphic representation and are linked by lines. The antecedents are placed on the left of the dependants. In other words, the left–right positioning reflects the ontological dependencies. The example in Figure 6.1 explains how ontological relationships can be represented in graphic form in NORMA.

Society is the root agent in this model, and it has two affordances: *person* and *thing*. Person is an agent, and thing is a normal affordance. Both are ontologically dependent on society, which means both are defined in the context of a certain society. If the society does not exist, the concepts of person and thing become undefined. Therefore, it is the *society* that has affordances of recognising the *person* and *thing* and the other dependants. If the society is seen as a modified agent with the extension of affordances of person and thing, it makes it possible to talk about *owns*. More straightforwardly, a person can own a thing.

In the graphic representation, agents, such as society and person, are placed in ellipses. Role names, that is, owner, seller and buyer, are put in semi-circles. Actions and other kinds of affordances are put in rectangular boxes. Note that the action *sell*

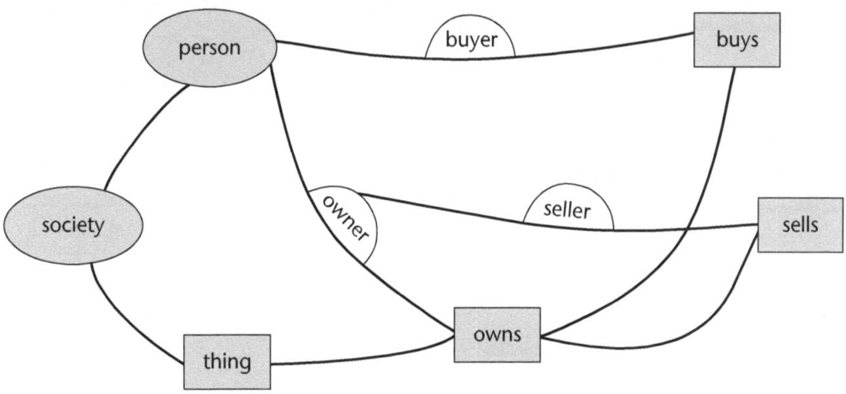

FIGURE 6.1 An illustration of NORMA in graphical form

is ontologically dependent on the *owner* (the role) and on *owns*, and the action *buy* is built upon *person* and *own*. This suggests that selling is only possible for the owner who owns the thing, while selling is for any person. Selling and buying are referred to the affordance *own*. That means that when people are trading, it is the ownership rather than the physical thing itself that is dealt with. In this sense, the representation ontologically reflects the social practice that is dominated by the shared norms in the social context.

The example in Figure 6.2 involves the representation of affordances having generic–specific relationships. The root agent *nation* affords *legal person* within the given social and legal context. Under the generic heading, more specifics can be found: *natural person* and *corporate body*. Within the heading of corporate body, there are more specifics: *company*, *government* and *learned society*. The specific kinds of affordances under a generic heading share some properties; for example, all specific kinds of corporate body have a *management* as part of the organisation. Any natural person can be employed by a corporate body, in which he is called *employee* and the other party is *employer*. The *management* is a part of the corporate body. Therefore, a line with a dot is drawn to indicate the whole–part relationship between them. To be a manager, one is first of all considered as an employee of the corporate body, which is narrated by putting being an *employee* as an ontological antecedent for the *incumbent*. When the analysis is conducted, this constraint is assumed as a norm generally residing in social organisations.

The ontological relationship is considered to be the most fundamental relationship to model in NORMA. All other relationships, such as generic–specific, whole–part, determiners, roles and so on, are treated on basis of the ontological relationship. Therefore, the process of producing a graphic representation in NORMA is called *ontology charting*, and a complete conceptual model represented in NORMA graphic notation is called an *ontology chart*. Figure 6.3 presents some of the syntax notations of NORMA in both textual and graphic form, and briefly summarises some of the discussions in this section.

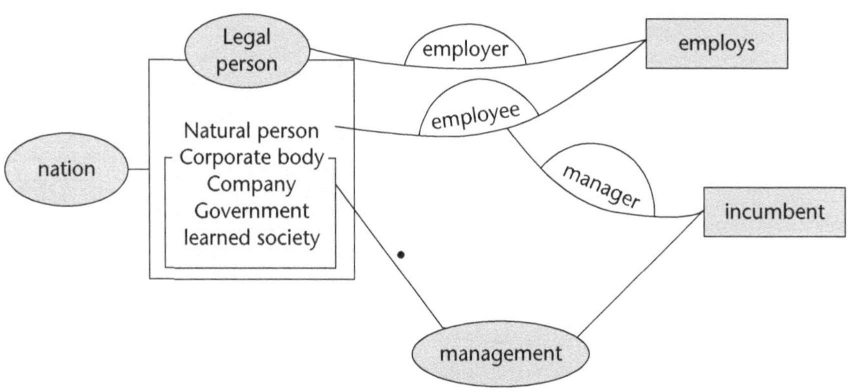

FIGURE 6.2 Another graphical illustration of NORMA

Textual	Graphic	Meaning	Example in graphic representation
Ax	A——x	x is an affordance of A	person —— walk society —— person
Ax.y	A——x ——•——y	y is a part of x; they all are afforded by A	nation —— school ——•—— department
Ax#y	A——x ——#y	A affords x which has a determiner y	society —— person —— #weight
A((a:b:c:d)→f)	A—— [f: a b c d]	a, b, c, d are specifics of f	nation—— [legal person: person corporate body]
(A#x,B#y)z	A (x) —— z B (y) —— z	A with role name x, and B with role name y jointly afford z	(employer) corporate body —— employs person (employee) —— employs

FIGURE 6.3 Part of the NORMA syntax, with examples

The method of semantic analysis

Semantic analysis, rooted in organisational semiotics, is a method for eliciting and specifying user requirements. The method has been applied in many fields such as user requirements for business systems, organisational analysis, legal document design and analysis and the design of computer systems.

The method of semantic analysis can be summarised in a few major phases as schematically presented in Figure 6.4. The first phase is for the people involved to receive a document that is sometimes called a *problem statement or definition*, and for them to understand the problem. The people involved may be a single analyst or, for a large project, often a group of analysts with users' participation. The next phase, *candidate affordance generation*, involves producing a list of vocabulary of semantic units that may possibly be used in the semantic model to describe agents and their patterns of behaviour. The phase of *candidate grouping* will allow a further analysis of the semantic units. Following that is *ontology charting*, in which a complete semantic model is produced. Finally, *norm analysis* will allow the identification of norms and a linking of the norms with each part of the semantic model.

Each of these phases will now be elaborated. A case study of project management will be used to illustrate the whole process of semantic analysis.

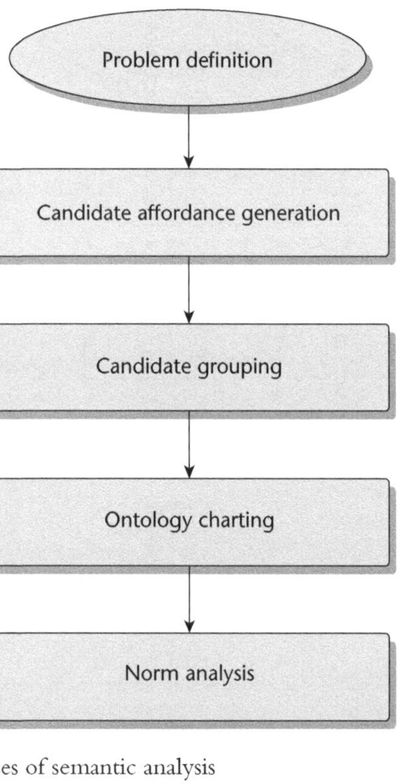

FIGURE 6.4 Major phases of semantic analysis

Understanding the problem domain

A semantic analysis exercise always begins with the phase of *problem definition*. In this phase, the assignment for systems development is given in the form of a written document in which the problem is defined. But the written official definition would normally not be enough to capture a complete picture of the problem. Therefore, thorough investigations have to be carried out by studying the relevant documents. In addition, interviews with potential users of the envisaged system can be carried out to collect supplementary information.

Box 6.1 shows a simplifed version of the *problem statement* of project management, which describes the case study that is going to be used to illustrate how to conduct a semantic analysis. Our task here is to take the problem statement as the main source, supplemented with interviews and observations as necessary, to produce a semantic model using the process of semantic analysis. The result can be used to reflect on the understanding of the problem domain and the practice of project management in the company, which will serve a basis for designing a computer system for project management.

Box 6.1 The problem statement: the project management system

In the company, departments are responsible for projects. Each department and each project has a budget.

An employee works in a department but can be assigned to several projects. A project does not belong to a single department. Work activities are charged at an hourly rate that depends on the function of the employee.

The total time that an employee spends on a project is accounted for at the hourly rate, and the total cost of the project is computed for project management purposes.

The problem is basically introduced in the problem statement, so by reading it the analyst can gain an overview of the problem. However, the problem statement is sometimes too vague and the requirements may be fuzzy. In this case, more information about the problem must be gathered, usually by collecting relevant documents and conducting interviews with the problem-owners. The documents and interviews, as important supplements to the formal definition, can help the analyst to understand better the words and expressions found in the problem statement.

Generating candidate affordances

The second phase, *candidate affordance generation*, involves studying the collected papers and notes, and singling out the semantic units, for example nouns, noun-phrases, verbs, verb-phrases and prepositions, that may indicate possible agents, affordances and other relationships.

In this phase, semantic units are identified from the problem definition, as listed in Figure 6.5. Every word in the problem definition is in principle useful in the analysis; therefore, one has to be careful if a word is going to be ignored. Even an article, a preposition or an auxiliary verb might suggest some additional information on a concept, a relationship or an intention, although nouns and verbs are more likely to suggest concepts of agent and affordance. The words and phrases that form the semantic units are singled out as candidate affordances, and these will contain complete concepts. It should be noted that some words will be left out, but that does not mean they will not be included in the model. Some words are taken in different forms, for example from the plural form of a noun to the singular form.

Candidate grouping

The phase of *candidate grouping* consists of a few small steps. First, the semantic candidates are categorised as agents or affordances. The affordances themselves can then be further classified into universal action types, determiners, role names and so on. The specific affordances should be grouped into generic families. The dependants will be connected to the antecedents. The work in this step can be seen as a preparation the next phase.

In this phase, the functions of the listed semantic units are first studied by labelling them as agents, affordances, role names and determiners. They are also classified according to universal–particular and generic–specific relationships. As shown in Table 6.1, these semantic units are not only classified; at the same time, additional information for explaining the functions is also noted, which will be useful for the

TABLE 6.1 Candidate grouping (I)

company	agent
department	agent, a part of a company
responsible for	affordance (a department)
project	affordance
budget	affordance
amount	determiner of budget (required to add to quantity a budget)
employee	role name (of a person who works in a company)
work	affordance
assigned to	affordance
belong to	affordance (of department and project)
activity	affordance (of employee)
charged	affordance
hourly rate	determiner (of function or activity?)
depend on	affordance (of function?)
function	determiner (of employee)
total time	a derived value as determiner, will not appear in the model
spend	affordance (of employee and project)
imputed to	complex action governed by rules, will capture as norms
total cost	a derived value as determiner, will not appear in the model
computed	complex action governed by rules, will capture as norms

next step in constructing the complete ontology chart. Table 6.1 shows that the functions of some semantic units are not certain at this stage. For example, the *hourly rate* is noted as 'determiner (of *function* or *activity?*)', showing an uncertainty over which the antecedent the semantic unit *hourly rate* will be. Will it be *function* or *activity*? A few more affordances may be added to the list in Table 6.1, as they are needed for a more sound representation of the underlying ontologies.

Finally, sketches of piecemeal ontological structures will be conceived at this stage (see Figure 6.6).

These unconnected pieces of ontology charts help us to see better the effect of grouping the semantic units. We can start with the 'easier' pieces; for example, an *organisation* and a *person* jointly afford the dependency *employ*, in which the *organisation* plays the role of *employer* and the *person* plays the role of *employee*. Additional information may be added at this time, such as categorising the employee as permanent staff and contractor, with the justification that this information is relevant in this project management system.

Company	Charged	Department	Hourly rate
Responsible for	Depend on	Project	Function
Budget	Total time	Employee	Spend
Work	Imputed to	Assigned to	Total cost
Belong to	Computed	Activity	

FIGURE 6.5 Candidate affordances

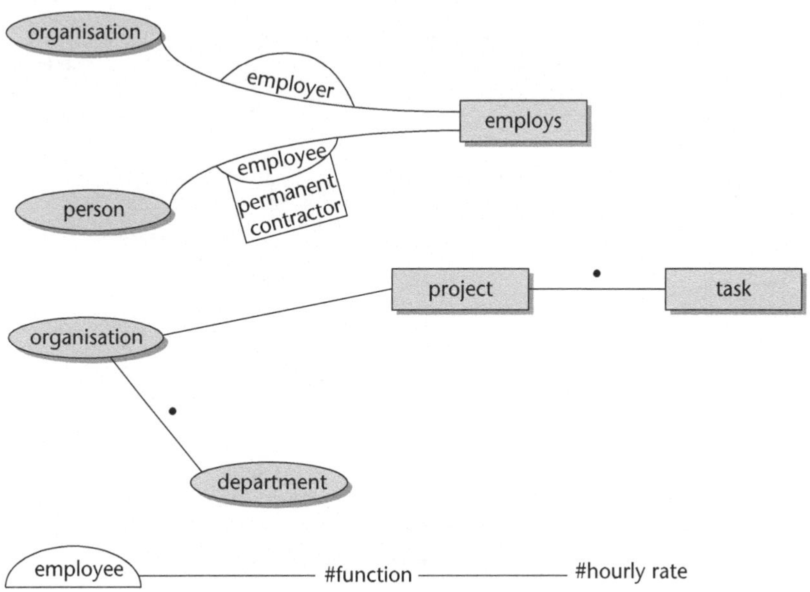

FIGURE 6.6 Candidate grouping (II)

The other piece of chart that has an *organisation*, a *department*, a *project* and so on contains most of information produced in the candidate grouping. For example, the department is a part of the organisation. But in the early analysis, although it was identified that the project is an affordance, it was not clear in terms of its antecedent (supposedly due to a not very careful analysis). Therefore, the question here is, should the project be connected to the organisation or the department? If we read the problem statement again, it can be seen that the project should not belong to any department. Hence, the project is a dependant of the organisation. It has also been found out that there should be two *budgets*, one for each project and one for each department, as denoted in Figure 6.6.

An *employee*, as seen in Figure 6.6, has a determiner, *function*, which itself has a determiner, *hourly rate*. Determiners are attributes that enable us to describe an agent or affordance. For example, an employee can be described by his or her *function*, which can be further described using an *hourly rate* of how much the employee earns per hour. More similar pieces of the chart can be produced for discussion and verification with the user before a complete ontology chart is produced.

Ontology charting

After the candidate affordances have been analysed and grouped into scattered pieces of ontological structures, the fragments will be assembled into an integrated ontology chart. The ontological dependency between the fragments is the key to their connections, and this is constantly checked and maintained. It is unavoidable that some mistakes may have been made in the previous phase, and these will be corrected at this step. Figure 6.7 is the ontology chart for the project management in our example.

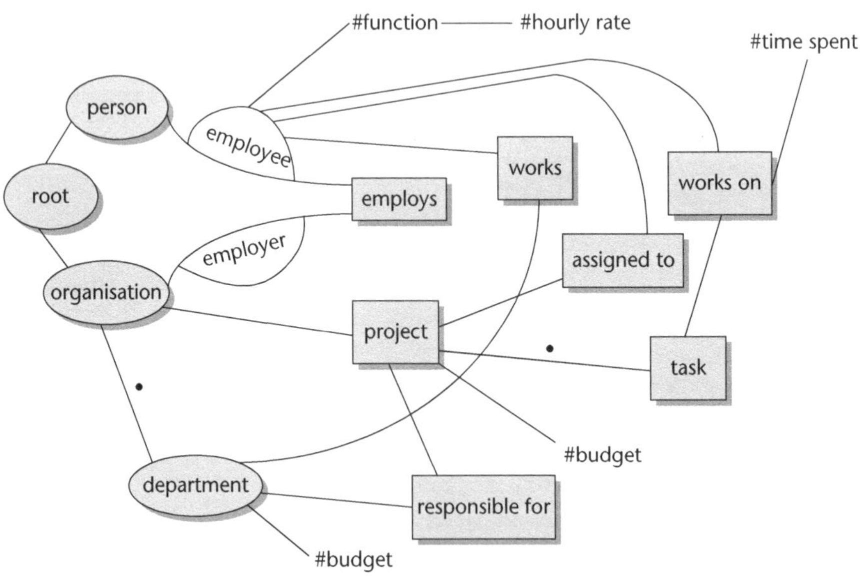

FIGURE 6.7 An ontology chart for project management

The model exposes a few basic assumptions underpinned by the ontological principles. There is a *root* agent in the chart that functions as the ultimate antecedent for the whole problem domain under the study. This root agent is the social community in which all its members share some fundamental concepts and cultures. Without these fundamentals, there would not be agreed meanings of organisation and person. Different social communities may have completely different definitions of an organisation. Differences may even exist in determining the boundaries of a person for the start and finish, which may have to be the cause of debates on moral issues relating to abortion and euthanasia.

In this example, a project is ontologically dependent on an organisation, but not a department. This suggests that a project exists independently of a department. The relationship between a department and a project arises from the department's participation. An employee working in a department may or may not be assigned to a project. An employee who is assigned to a project may work on a certain task, but the actual effort put into the task is measured by the determined *time spent*.

This ontology chart must be read many times by the analysts with reference to the problem statement and other business knowledge that has been gained through various channels. After the draft of an ontology chart has been produced, checks and verifications with input from the users are strongly suggested so that they can give their maximum support and assurance.

Norm analysis

The analysis then proceeds to the phase of *norm analysis* in which norms will be identified and specified as the conditions and constraints for realising the affordances. The norms specified here are kinds other than the ontological dependency imposed on the antecedent and dependant. In the case of the project management, everyone working on a task must be in the first place be assigned to the project. This can be specified in a pseudo-language:

assigned_to(employee, project) <u>while</u> task(project) → works_on(employee, task)

A norm has a validity period of time marked by a start and a finish. Norms are, for example, institutional rules such as the age limit for employees, the maximum number of projects an employee is allowed to participate in, and the total time spent on a project by an employee. Therefore, the validity time during which the norm can be applied must be identified. All the norms are linked to the relevant affordances as constraints. For example, the age limit for employees is linked with the affordance *employs*, and the maximum number of projects an employee can participate in is linked to the affordance *assigned to*. Note that norms should usually be linked to affordances, the patterns of possible actions, rather than to agents, because an agent may have a number of patterns of possible actions, each following a set of norms specifically to that affordance.

A detailed discussion of the method of norm analysis is found in the next chapter.

Commentary on semantic analysis

In an actual practice of semantic analysis, the order of the phases is not strictly followed. For example, some new affordance may be identified even during the phase of ontology charting, and it may then be added to the model. In addition, iterations of the analysis phases may be necessary in order to reach an adequate analysis. Moreover, interactions between the analysts and the problem-owners are essential during the analysis. In this way, opinions and judgements can be inspired by the preliminary results, and comprehensive requirements can be elicited and incorporated into the model well before any system is developed.

It is worth noting a number of special features of semantic analysis. The first is the role of the ontological relationship in modelling. The method always requires the process to begin with a semantic analysis to identify the agents who create the social world around them. An agent has some abilities to accomplish something. These abilities are also identified and put into the analysis model to construct the picture of the world.

In doing this, a rigorous analytical principle must be observed – the existence constraint, or in other words the ontological constraint. The ontological constraint says that a pattern of behaviour can be described only if the agent, who acts, is described in the model. So the agent is a kind of ontological antecedent to their own actions (the latter being the dependants of the agent). The ontological constraint must be fully observed. That means that the existence of the dependants must occur within (or during) the existence of the antecedent. If there are more affordances available when a certain behaviour is realised, they should also confirm the ontological constraint. That is, any added affordance should not exceed the existence of its antecedent affordances already described in the model.

Besides the ontological constraints as a principle for analysis, there is another important principle: it is not allowable for an analyst to invent artificial terms or introduce new concepts when modelling the agent's actions. The purpose of this is to force the analyst to speak the same language as the problem-owners. Any ambiguity in the terms or concepts used in describing the problem should be resolved by putting them into a context of actions that are already described and understood. When doing this, if the problem-owners are inspired with some new terms, they may be used only after a careful justification by the problem-owners and the analyst together. This is because the world to be modelled is constructed by the community of agents, that is, the problem-owners. The agents know the meanings of words in their own world, and their interpretations are the only ones that are justified.

Another feature is the scope of the analysis. Jayaratna (1986, 1990) observes that some methods of systems analysis have a narrow scope of analysis; some issues of enquiry, such as the problem-owners' notional systems (i.e. basic assumptions about the focal problem and the environment), tend to be ignored. Some predominantly 'standard' systems development approaches take the physical world as an entry. For example, with Jackson's development method, a physical world is given as consisting of objects in motion from state to state; the task of the systems worker is to build a model that is an abstract description of the real world (Jackson 2001).

Semantic analysis, however, covers both the 'wet' and 'dry' aspects of the problem (Goguen's terminology; Goguen 1992). It places the problem-owners at the heart of the total enterprise of analysis. The role of the analyst is only to elicit and specify the business knowledge. The analysis is aimed at producing precise requirements specifications that are intelligible to the users, so the responsibility still remains with the users.

Questions and exercises

1. It is extremely important to understand what syntactic and semantic problems occur in the analysis and design of information systems. Discuss and explain what semantic problems an analyst may encounter in information systems analysis and design, especially in the scenario of a large systems development in which a number of stakeholders are involved.
2. Review and understand the notion of the affordance of a technical system and an organisation. Discuss the differences and similarities of the affordances of a technical system and an organisation.
3. In the context of information systems development, discuss how semantic analysis can be utilised in domain modelling and requirements representation.
4. The method of semantic analysis captures the behaviour of agents and behaviour in a problem domain. It focuses on the meaning of the end users' words. Compare and contrast the key notions of semantic analysis (e.g. agents, affordances, ontological constraints and norms) with those of other methods (e.g. the class diagram in unified modelling language), to illustrate the differences and identify the benefits.

7

MODELLING ORGANISATIONAL DYNAMICS

Communications, pragmatics and norms

Modelling an organisation with semantic analysis portrays the ontological relationships between agents and their patterns of behaviour within the organisation. However, the static ontological model is inadequate in providing a comprehensive view of an organisation. Communications based on these ontological relationships represent the dynamic aspect of the organisation. A sign has a meaning, and it can be used with intention during communication. Pragmatics, as a branch in semiotics, is concerned with the relationships between the intentional use of signs and the resulting behaviour of the responsible agents in a social context. Communication takes place successfully when a meaningful sign is used with an appropriate intention between the two parties involved (i.e. the speaker and the listener).

This chapter addresses the effects of using signs in organisations. Before exploring the semiotic approach, various approaches and techniques for the analysis of the pragmatic aspect of signs are introduced, such as speech act theory, functional grammar and deontic logic. The semiotic approach distinguishes a number of elements in an act of communication: propositions, propositional (or illocutionary) attitudes and perlocutionary effects. An act of communication will further result in a variety of commitments and responsibilities. The method of norm analysis introduced in this chapter provides a formalism for identifying and specifying these important notions when analysing and modelling the social and organisational aspects of communication.

Human communication

A social community is a purposeful system in which human beings act and interact with each other to achieve goals that may relate to the community or to individuals. 'Doing things with words' in a concerted way becomes a necessity for fulfilling the ever-complicating objectives of social beings in ever more complex organisations.

Communication is the indispensable means by which agents in society coordinate their actions to achieve their goals.

A language–action view of information systems leads people to design information systems as part of the relevant human communication system; an analysis of communication is therefore the essential entry for the analysis and design of information systems. This school of thoughts sees the uses of language as actions. A radical recognition about language and existence – 'nothing exists except through language', as stated by Winograd and Flores (1987) – typically represents this point of view. In addition to this view of *language as actions*, another complementary view should be advocated, that is, the notion of *actions as language*. The actions should be regarded as a kind of language because they manifest ideas, thoughts and propositions. Non-linguistic means, such as facial expressions, gestures and other ostensive actions, can also perform the communication of messages and intentions.

This integrated language–action view has been adopted here in this book. According to this view, speech acts have the capacity not only to represent the relevant social world, including its actions, but also to constitute part of its (social) actions. Accordingly, information communicated through language has its complement in the social world of situations, norms, institutions and cultural patterns – and vice versa.

Theories and formal methods are available for studying language and the use of language in human communication. Speech act theory and functional grammar provide facilities to analyse the taxonomy and functionality of communication acts that will be discussed in this chapter. In order to analyse the social effects of communication acts, deontic logic will be examined and can be used to link the linguistic and the social acts. As computer-based systems are introduced into business practices, how to utilise modern technology to enhance human performance in terms of interaction and communication becomes an important question. In order to answer this question, the modelling of human communication is addressed in this chapter by analysing the communication acts employed and propositional attitudes expressed. This analysis serves as a theoretical basis for the development of a technical information system.

Approaches to human communication

Speech act theory

Speech act theory originated in Austin's 1955 William James Lectures at Harvard (Austin 1980) and has been further developed by Searle (1969). It studies the roles of language use in communication and focuses on the performative aspects of language. Searle proposes a classification of four sorts of speech acts: utterance acts, illocutionary acts, propositional acts and perlocutionary acts:

- An *utterance act* is simply the act of uttering an expression.
- An *illocutionary act* is a basic, meaningful unit of human communication that consists of propositional contents and carries intentions to be perceived by a hearer.

- A *propositional act* is a subsidiary act within an illocutionary act. It expresses a propositional content that is realised by uttering the expression.
- The effects produced on the hearer by an illocutionary act are called perlocutionary effects, and the acts of producing them are called *perlocutionary acts*. Perlocutionary acts, unlike illocutionary acts, are not essentially linguistic, because it is possible to achieve perlocutionary effects without performing any utterance at all.

For the purpose of studying the effect of a language in communication, the most relevant acts are illocutionary acts and perlocutionary acts. In the course of a conversation, a complete unit is always an illocutionary act that is produced by the speaker with certain meanings and intentions incorporated in the utterance. The hearer receives this communication unit and perceives the meaning from his own perspective, which may result in a different one from the speaker's. In any case, there is always some effect on the hearer (unless the hearer chooses to ignore it). The effects work on the mental world of the hearer; for example, he may change his feelings or mental state. In such a case, the perlocutionary acts are not overt linguistic and not observable. The hearers may also make explicit reactions to the perlocutionary act; for example, they might accept an invitation and change their agenda. In such a case, this becomes observable.

Figure 7.1 illustrates two agents involved in a process of communication to show that the roles of speaker and hearer will change in turn. The speaker addresses the hearer with an illocutionary act that produces an effect on the hearer, although one should be aware that the effect on the hearer may or may not be desirable from the speaker's perspective. However, in a broad sense, the speaker himself is a hearer while performing the utterance; therefore, there is also a perlocutionary effect on the speaker. The consequent behaviour may become observable, reflecting the illocutionary effect. In an example of issuing someone an invitation, the perlocutionary

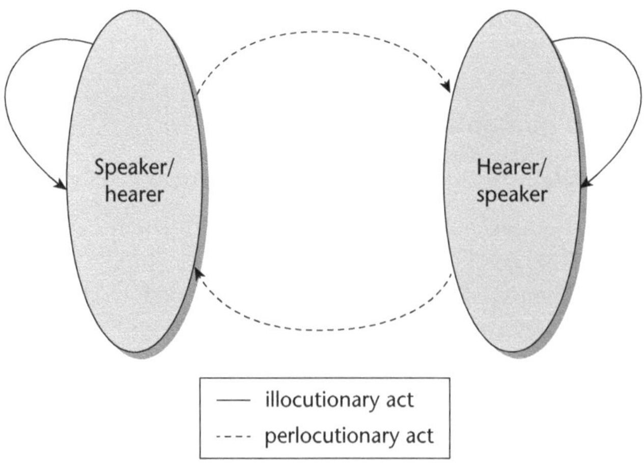

FIGURE 7.1 Speaker and hearer

act that the speaker should perform is that they must make themself physically available and mentally ready for whatever they are inviting the speaker to.

The structure of an illocutionary act consists of the propositional content, illocutionary force and contextual information. The propositional content is contained in the proposition of a message. For example, the two sentences 'You will jump off the car' and 'Jump off the car!' have the same propositional content – *you will jump off the car* – although the former may be seen as a predication and the latter as a command.

The contextual information is concerned with the context within which the speech act is uttered. A context, suggested by Auramäki *et al.* (1988), is delineated by the terms of speaker, hearer, time, place and possible world. The first four terms simply define a situation in which a speaker utters something to a hearer at a certain time and in a certain place. The possible world refers to the 'residual features' of the context that are relevant to the performance of a speech act. The possible world is 'something more than the "actual world"', and it enables us to talk about 'what could be' (e.g. the future). Terms that indicate the jurisdiction (i.e. authority of the speaker over the hearer), the presuppositions of the agents involved in the performance of the speech act and similar aspects are typical constituents of the specification of the 'possible world'.

An illocutionary force is a necessary component of every successful speech act. Searle and Vanderveken (1985) identified seven illocutionary forces:

1. the illocutionary point;
2. the degree of strength of the illocutionary point;
3. the mode of achievement;
4. the propositional content conditions;
5. the preparatory conditions;
6. the sincerity conditions;
7. the degree of strength of the sincerity conditions.

The most important component of the illocutionary force is the *illocutionary point*, while the rest serve as the further specification and consequence of the illocutionary point. The illocutionary point identifies the point or purpose that is internal to its being an act of that type. It determines the direction of fit between the propositional content and the commitments created. The direction of fit determines the direction of matching between the propositional content and the world. There are five types of illocutionary points (Searle and Vanderveken 1985):

- *Assertive*: This is to state how the world is (e.g. to claim, to inform, to predict).
- *Commissive*: This point makes the speaker committed to doing something (e.g. to promise, to offer, to accept, to refuse).
- *Directive*: This concerns making the hearer do things (e.g. to request, to order, to permit).

- *Declarative*: This is used when the speaker wishes to change the world through the utterance (e.g. to declare, to appoint, to approve).
- *Expressive*: This point is employed by the speaker in expressing feelings and attitudes (e.g. to apologise, to thank, to congratulate).

The *degree of strength of the illocutionary point* refers to the degree of an intention associated with an illocutionary act. For example, commanding has a greater degree of strength than asking. Similar contrasts can be made between ordering and requesting, endorsing and agreeing, and instructing and suggesting. Different illocutionary acts may achieve the same illocutionary effect with different degrees of strength.

The *propositional content conditions* determine whether a speech act is non-self-contradictory and feasible. For example, the sentence 'I order you to have finished your homework last week' is self-contradictory; 'Cut a square round shape' is unfeasible; that one promises to have done something in the past is both self-contradictory and unfeasible.

The *preparatory conditions* specify the states of affairs the speaker must presuppose to exist in the world if an intended illocutionary act is to be performed. For example, to let the hearer do something, the speaker must assume that the hearer is capable of doing it. This kind of preparatory condition is normally an ontological constraint by which one can distinguish the speech act, which may be possibly successful and non-defective, from those which are impossible.

A speech act may be performed successfully but defectively so. For example, one may apologise to a hearer for something that one considers disgraceful but the hearer thinks otherwise. Similarly, a speaker can successfully issue a command, but if the performance of its content is not within the appropriate jurisdiction (e.g. the speaker has no necessary authority), the speech act is defective. Therefore, if one can consider that the success of a speech act is largely dependent on the speaker, the effect of it relies fully on the hearer. In other words, the effect of the speech act is realised through self-adjustment by the hearer, or through the perlocutionary act.

Functional approach

The functional view of natural language (typified by Dik 1978, 1989) regards a language as an instrument that human beings use intentionally to achieve certain goals and purposes. To achieve these goals and purposes, human beings perform linguistic actions following complex, socially established patterns. A *speaker* uses linguistic expressions to communicate messages to an *addressee* so as to construct or modify the state of affairs in a certain way.

According to functional grammar theory (Dik 1989), any natural language text can be divided into clauses and extra-clausal constituents. The clauses follow certain underlying structures and can be mapped onto the actual form of the corresponding linguistic expressions by a system of expression rules. The expression rules determine the form of each part of the expression, their orders and the intonation.

The underlying clause structure is a complex abstract structure that can be analysed at several levels:

CLAUSE	→ speech act
PROPOSITION	→ possible fact
PREDICATION	→ state of affairs
PREDICATE	→ property/relation
TERM	→ entity

The constructions at the lower level are the building blocks of the higher level. A *term* is an expression denoting some entity in some (mental) world. *Predicates* designate types of entities and patterns of actions. A *predication* consists of a few predicates to specify relations between entities and/or actions. A *proposition* is composed of one or more predications; it connotes a possible state of affairs. A *clause* (or *message*) is constituted of a proposition associated with a certain propositional attitude; it normally includes the entries of speaker, addressee, speech time, content and perhaps more (Weigand 1990).

Predicates are organised in *predicate-frames*, the structures that specify the fundamental semantic and syntactic properties, such as (a) the syntactic category of the predicate (verbal, nominal or adjectival), (b) the number of arguments, and (c) the semantic functions of the arguments (agent, goal, recipient, etc.). For example, a predicate-frame of 'give' can be specified as follows:[1]

$$\text{give}_V\ (x_1)_{Ag}\ (x_2)_{Go}\ (x_3)_{Re}$$

which states that the category of 'give' is 'v'; it has three arguments that play the roles of agent, goal and recipient.

Predicate-frames can be extended by *satellites* (non-arguments) that pertain to additional features such as the location, the speaker's attitude or the character of the speech act. *Terms* are the noun-phrases to replace the arguments in the predicate-frames and satellites.

There are two types of terms to be distinguished: (a) basic terms, which are expressions given as such in the lexicon (e.g. pronouns, proper nouns or question words), and (b) derived terms (a derived term being a basic term with an optional set of restrictors). *Nuclear predications* consist of predicates and terms. A nuclear predication as a whole designates a set of *states of affairs*, which is used in the broad sense of a 'conception of something that can be the case in some world'.

Core predications are obtained by adding *predicate operators and satellites*. The predicate operators relate *aspectuality* information (e.g. perfective/imperfective, quantificational and phrasal descriptions) to the predications; the predicate satellites are terms that specify manner, speed, instrument and the like to the predications. *Extended predications* are further constructed with *predication operators and satellites*. The most important types of predication operators are tense, external phrasal aspect, quantificational aspect, objective mood and polarity (positive/negative) operators. The satellites are, for example, terms with the functions of time and place.

An example of extended predication can be given by:

Past $read_{V}$ $(\text{John})_{Ag}$ $(\text{the book})_{Go}$ $(\text{quickly})_{Manner}$ $(\text{yesterday})_{Time}$

which reads as 'John read the book quickly yesterday'. Notice that the sequence of the words is supposed not to be significant either in the sentence or in the predicate-frame, although in an actual use of language the word sequence may have some pragmatic effects.

Propositions can be built from extended predications by incorporating *proposition operators and satellites*. Proposition operators are employed mainly to distinguish two modalities: subjective and evidential; proposition satellites indicate the attitudes of the speaker.

The result of these extensions is called *extended proposition*, for example:

Subjective Mood [John writes the book] $(\text{in my opinion})_{Attitude}$

which represents 'In my opinion, he should write the book.' *Clauses* (equally, messages or speech acts) can be composed on the basis of the extended propositions by associating *illocutionary operators and satellites*. Typical examples of the operators are declarative, imperative and interrogative; the satellites are terms describing the action of speaking, namely the illocutionary act itself. This can be shown in an example of a speech act:

Decl [he is stupid] $(\text{frankly})_{Illocution}$

which reads 'Frankly, he is stupid.'

The levels of term, predicate and predication are concerned with representation that is at semantic level, while the proposition and clausal levels deal with interpersonal relationships. In another words, these are typical issues at the pragmatic level in semiotics.

Deontic modality in communication

A communication act may convey the speaker's intention, which is correlated with the illocution of the act. The ultimate purpose of performing a communication act, in business cases, is to establish or alter the social relationships between the agents. This capacity to produce a social effect is called the deontic aspect of the communication act, which can also be examined by means of deontic logic.

The word 'deontic' is derived from a Greek word which can be translated as 'as it should be', or 'duty'. Deontic logic is a branch of symbolic logic or modal logic that deals with a set of notions related to responsibility. It provides a systematic approach to investigating normative concepts, systems of norms and normative reasoning

(Follesdal and Hilpinen 1971). Its subject matter is a variety of normative concepts such as obligations (prescription), prohibition (interdiction), permission and commitment. The first concept of these – obligation – is often expressed by such words as 'shall', 'ought' and 'must'. The second concept – prohibition – is expressed by 'shall not', 'ought not' and 'must not'. The third one – permission – is associated with 'may'. The final notion – commitment – is related to an idea of *conditional obligation*, expressible by 'if . . . , then it shall (ought, must) be the case that . . .'.

Responsibility and deontic logic

The notion of responsibility is crucial in designing information systems, because the goal of an information system is usually to support the relevant members of an organisation (or agents) to fulfil their responsibility. Understand, analysing and representing the responsibility of the agents is essential before an information system can be designed to support the functions of the agents. An examination of the most fundamental legal conceptions based on principles of deontic logic can help us gain such an understanding.

The legal philosopher Wesley N. Hohfeld recognised eight fundamental legal conceptions in two sets (quoted in Allen and Saxon 1986). In each set, the paired concepts are 'opposites' in columns and 'correlatives' in rows:

Right Set:	Right	Duty
	No right	Privilege
Power Set:	Power	Liability
	Disability	Immunity

All eight concepts are related to the terms 'must', 'should', 'must not' and more. Each term may involve more than one of these legal concepts. For example, 'a credit card holder *must* pay any outstanding amount of credit within 25 days of posting without incurring interest'. This implies that a card holder has the *right* to pay, and not to pay till the due day, but a liability of paying interest will occur from the due date if the amount is not paid (Liu and Dix 1997). As pointed out by Allen and Saxon (1993), these terms may also result in multiple interpretations, and it is appropriate to expect a machine such as an information technology (IT) system only to assist the human in interpretation.

An IT system should be seen as an assistant to humans, who can delegate some of their responsibilities. Only when human users have the right and power to do so can they transfer responsibilities to a machine. It should be noted here that what is transferred are duties or job functions rather than liability. In the same manner, the government of a country can delegate responsibilities and functions to an embassy in a foreign country but cannot relinquish the liability for what the ambassador has done. Of course, this does not stop users from attempting to use software to abrogate responsibility by 'sorry I can't help, the computer says so'!

Deontic logic has traditionally been used to analyse the structure of normative law and normative reasoning in law. In the early days, legal analysis and legal automation were typical areas of the application of deontic logic. Only recently, along with those areas of application, has deontic logic been applied to computer applications such as the specification of normative security policies, the specification of fault-tolerant systems, the automation of contracting and the specification of normative integrity constraints for databases.

A norm in a symbolic logic can have the following shape:

protasis → apodosis

which can be elaborated, particularly by incorporating deontic notions, as:

<condition> → <**D**> <agent> <action>

The deontic operator, **D**, can be one of the following: obligated, permitted or prohibited. A norm expressed in this structure has an intended reading 'if . . ., then it is obliged/permitted/prohibited for some agent to take some action'. This offers us a unified method for norm representation that can then be translated into programming and embedded into a computer system.

Pragmatic aspects of human communication

Communication is usually a means rather than an end. Communication is conducted to create, modify and discharge social commitments. An agent can be in any state as far as a social commitment is concerned, for example obliged, permitted or prohibited to fulfil it. These kinds of states are associated with the deontic concepts, and thus they are called the *deontic states*.

The minimal unit of human communication is the performance of certain kinds of communication acts – language acts. Three components are relevant in a communication act: performer, addressee and message. The message is equivalent to a clause, or a speech act. The message can be further divided into two parts: the function and the content.

The *content* of a communication act manifests the meaning of the message as it is expressed in the proposition. The meaning (or semantics) of a proposition is fully dependent on the environment in which the proposition is uttered. The interpretation is realised by relating the proposition to the referent, which is a universal social construct or a pattern of human behaviour; this is done by both agents: the speaker and the hearer. A proposition's semantics can sometimes be obtained by referring to another proposition in case of indirect speech.

The *function* of a communication act specifies the illocution, which reflects the intention of the speaker. The illocutions can be grouped into three dimensions. In one dimension, there are distinctions between descriptive and prescriptive inventions, whereas in another, there are denotative and affective modes. Moreover, the

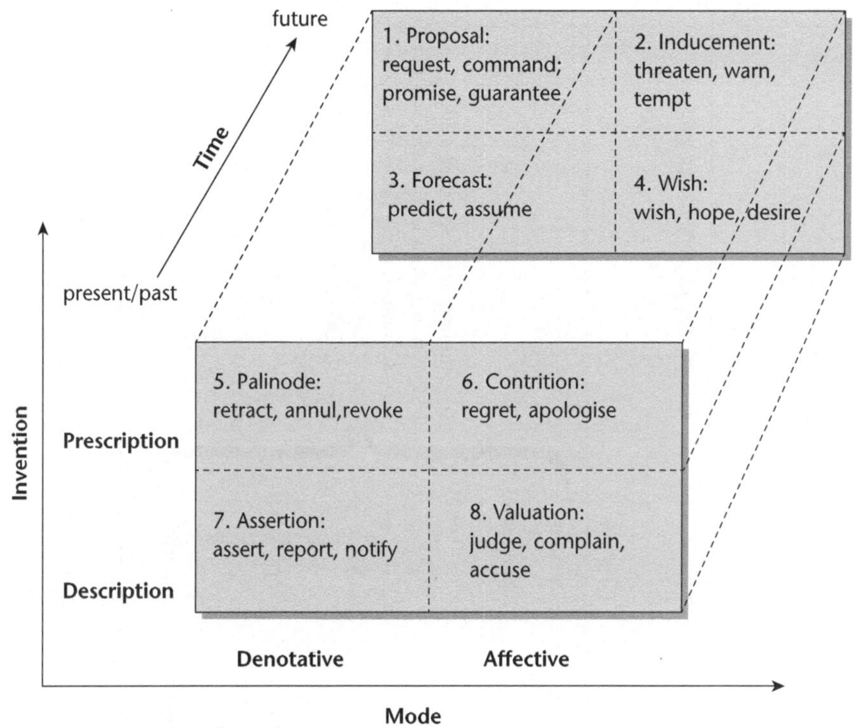

FIGURE 7.2 A classification framework of illocutions (based on Stamper 1973)

illocutions can be associated with different times, namely, now, the future or the past, as they are organised in Figure 7.2. Each cell of the classification framework has been assigned a title and a few representative verbs of those types of illocutions are placed in each cell.

The functions of communication are realised through use of signs. If the illocution in a communication act is related to expressing personal mental states or modes (also modalities or moods, e.g. feeling or judgement), it is called *affective*; otherwise, if it is more about referencing to the external world, it is called *denotative*. If the illocution in a communication act has an inventive or instructive effect, it is called *prescriptive*; otherwise, if it is related more to reflecting and expressing, it is called *descriptive*. The classification on the time axis is based on the social effects produced by the communication act: whether the effect is on the future or the present/past.

The ultimate consequence of the communication act lies in the social context that the speaker and the hearer both inhabit. At the social level of the semiotic framework, issues such as beliefs, expectations, commitments and contracts are typical examples of social consequences. Table 7.1 shows a quick analysis of the types of illocutionary acts and consequences in relation to the propositional attitudes of the relevant parties before and after the communication act has been performed. The labels in the first column indicate the types of illocutions; for example PDf

TABLE 7.1 Perlocutionary acts and propositional attitudes

Illocution Type	*Speaker (S)'s Propositional attitudes*		*Illocutionary acts (=operations)*	*Addressee (A)'s Propositional attitudes*		*Listener (L)'s propositional attitudes*
	Before	*After*		*Before*	*After*	
(1) PDf	wish	expectation	Proposals (to others)	liberty	obligation	Illocutionary acts also influence propositional attitudes of listeners other than addressees, e.g. a listener may have expectations in the cases of *proposals* and *forecasts;* beliefs in the case of *palinodes* and *assertions*
	liberty	obligation	proposals (to self)	wish	expectation	
(2) PAf	wish	expectation	inducements	—	expectation	
(3) DDf	expectation	expectation	forecasts	—	expectation	
(4) DAf	wish	wish	wishes	—	belief that S wishes x	
(5) PDp	belief in x then belief in ~x	belief in ~x	palinodes	—	belief in ~x	
(6) PAp	wish ~x	approval of ~x	contrition	wish ~x	approval of ~x	
(7) DDp	belief	belief	assertions	belief	(stronger) belief	
(8) DAp	judgement	judgement	valuations	judgement	judgement to S's	

means *prescriptive, denotative, future*; DDp means *descriptive, denotative, present/past* – as illustrated in Figure 7.2. The symbols 'x' and '~x' shown in the table represent a proposition or an event and their negations. The illocutionary acts can be viewed as linguistic operators that have certain social and pragmatic functions.

The above analysis, with much simplification in terms of communications, is based on a supposition that the communication is performed in an honest, sincere and reliable manner. In such cases, the speaker's intention will be expressed in the speech act by the illocutions. As a result, there will be a perlocutionary effect on the addressee. The analysis shown in Table 7.1 distinguishes the addressee from the hearer. The former is considered to be the target of the speech act, while the latter is someone 'overhearing' the conversation; very often both are relevant in communication analysis.

The social consequence is the further expansion of the effect produced by the utterance of the act. The social consequence is an interpersonally, jointly established relationship between the speaker and the hearer. The consequences of illocutions in general relate to both the speaker and the hearer, although in some cases one may be more strongly affected than the other. For example, in case of the speaker making a proposal, this can be directed to someone else or to the speaker himself. In the former case, it may be a request or a command, and the primary effect of the speech act will be on the addressee, which totally differs from the latter case. The social consequence, produced by the social and cultural norms, will serve as a kind of 'terms of reference' of socially contracted behaviour for both the speaker and the hearer.

Some more explanations related to Table 7.1 can be offered:

- There are always consequences for both parties of the communication act. The speaker and addressee each and both have propositional attitudes before and after an illocutionary act. The attitudes before are conditions, whereas the ones after are consequences. The ones shown in the table are views from the speaker's perspective.
- Directives (not listed in the table as a basic category) are complex acts that are composed of *proposals* and *inducements*. When a speaker with proper authority makes a proposal, some inducement is implied; therefore, the proposal he makes is in the nature of a directive. Without authority, one can also produce a directive by associating the proposal with an inducement (e.g. a threat or reward). It should be noted that the assumed conditions of honest, sincere and non-defective communications are essential. This implies that the communication will always be carried out normally, not taking into account the abnormal disruption.
- Some illocutions have stronger illocutionary forces than others, which is not taken into account in the classification. For example, the illocutions 'command', 'insist', 'request', 'ask' and 'beg' all create obligations on the addressee, but 'command' and 'insist' have stronger illocutionary forces than the others, of which the first is even associated with authority. 'Beg' has the weakest illocutionary force, but it still creates an obligation for the addressee because of the ideal conditions assumed in the communications.

Propositional attitudes can be roughly indicated by two scales: the *denotative* and the *affective* (Figure 7.3). A propositional attitude can normally be expressed as a position on one of the two scales. Denotative attitudes are related to someone's acceptance of a proposition or event in terms of belief. One can hold a strong or weak belief, a disbelief or a neutral position. A supposition is related to a neutral position of belief, and the neutral belief may be the condition before and the consequence after the hypothesis has been made; very positive or negative beliefs are, for example, related to assertions. The affective scale facilitates in indicating value judgements such as like and dislike, and aspiring feelings such as desire and fear. Desire, wish, hope and fear are examples of such feelings. Deontic consequences are produced on the basis of mixtures of these two kinds of propositional attitudes.

The norm analysis method

The concept of norms

The idea of a norm corresponds at the social level to the idea of an affordance at the individual level. Wright (1963) explains the concept norm in this way:

> 'Norm' has several partial synonyms which are good English. 'Pattern', 'standard', 'type' are such words. So are 'regulation', 'rule', and 'law'.

Norms are developed through the practical experience of agents in a society, and in turn have functions of directing, coordinating and controlling actions within the society. Complex agents can be formed in different contexts for certain purposes, for example cultural clubs, political parties, corporate bodies, governments, nations and multinational alliances. The functions of norms, such as the laws and regulations of organised complex agents, are to determine patterns of behaviour and whether they are legal or acceptable within the social context. Norms also have directive and prescriptive functions, which are sometimes termed *normatives*. When a particular agent is to act, the norms provide guidance for action. However, in each particular case, the agents will evaluate the situation they are in and find norms that they think are relevant to their case. The process of this evaluation

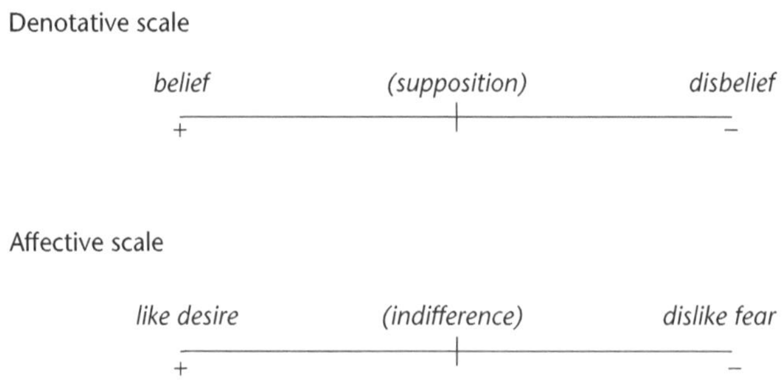

FIGURE 7.3 Propositional attitude scales

and selection of norms may be subjective. In other words, norms do not have a predetermined relationship to particular actions because the norms can be manipulated, applied and disregarded due to subjectivity.

Holy and Stuchlik (1983) explain the non-deterministic relationship between norms and particular actions as follows:

- A norm has to do with a type of situation and not with one particular situation.
- Any action is understandable to at least someone other than the actor, which means that it is performed according to some plan, rule or norm. An action may be considered as deviant or norm-breaking only in relation to some particular norm or cluster of norms; however, it can at the same time be performed according to some other norms.
- An actor may invoke different norms for deciding on his actions. Whether the action is norm-confirming or norm-breaking, one has to speak about the viewpoint of particular norms.

Norms are developed as collective affordances of the complex agent at the social level. The society allows itself or its members to conduct actions on an agreed moral or legal basis. Norms serve as a standard for the members to coordinate their actions, and this makes it possible to expect, predict and collaborate with others in performing coordinated actions. When modelling the agent and the actions, which may reveal the repertoire of available behaviour of the agent, the norms will supply rationale for the actions.

There are six components of norms (Wright 1963):

1. the *character*: the effect of the norm, typically, 'ought to' for a mandatory norm, 'may' for a permissive norm, and 'must not' for a prohibitive norm;
2. the *content*: the action or activity prescribed in the norm;
3. the *condition*: the circumstance or the state of affairs in which the norm should be applied;
4. the *authority*: the agent who gives or issues the norm;
5. the *subject(s)*: the agent(s) who can apply the norm;
6. the *occasion*: location (space) or span (time) in which the norm is given.

The character, the content and the condition are seen as the kernel of the norm. Behind all these components, there are 'promulgation' and 'sanction' as means of enforcement in the application of norms. Brkic (1970) describes such means as 'systems of social control' at multiple levels. Societies employ various systems, such as normative, religio-ideological, educational-cultural-scientific, socio-political and economic ones as the primary control. Other systems of organised forces in the form of the police can be used as an institutionalised form of coercion, whereas military aggression and blackmail are non-institutionalised forms of coercion. Other lower level instruments of control permitted by the higher level systems are, for example, a company's economic means, a business organisation's policies and an employee's codes of conduct.

All these norms and means of control form a kind of vital force that, formally or informally, explicitly or implicitly, governs all the members of the social, cultural community or business institution. Within the scope of this kind of vital force, people use signs and language to establish commitments, discharge responsibilities and fulfil social obligations.

Norms in business organisations

Norms exist in a community and will govern the members of the community in their behaviour, thinking, making of judgements and perception of the world. The shared norms are what define a culture or sub-culture. A sub-culture may be a team who know how to work effectively together, and their norms include a solution to their organisational problems. Norms can be represented in all kinds of signs, whether in documents, oral communication or behaviour, in order to preserve, to spread and to follow. However, one cannot always put one's hands conveniently on a norm, as one might grasp a document that carries information through an organisation. A norm is more like a forcefield that makes the members of the community tend to behave or think in a certain way.

Norms are developed through the practical experiences of people in a culture, and they in turn have functions of directing, coordinating and controlling actions within that culture. A research group or a working team may have a sub-culture and therefore may have local norms. Those norms will provide guidance for members to determine whether certain patterns of behaviour are legal or acceptable within the given context. An individual member of the community will, having learned the norms, be able to use the knowledge to guide his or her actions, although he or she may decide to undertake either a norm-conforming or a norm-breaking action. When the norms of an organisation have been learned, it will be possible for one person to expect and predict behaviour of other members, and further to collaborate with others in performing coordinated actions. Once the norms have been understood, captured and represented in, for example, the form of deontic logic, they can serve as a basis for programming the software applications to perform the tasks on behalf of the human agents.

One way to categorise the norms is by how they control human behaviour. Five types of norms can be identified in this way, each of which governs a certain aspect of human behaviour:

- *Perceptual* norms deal with how people receive signals from the environment via their senses through media such as light, sound and taste.
- *Cognitive* norms enable people to incorporate the beliefs and knowledge of a culture, to interpret what is perceived, and to gain an understanding based on existing knowledge.
- *Evaluative* norms help to explain why people have certain beliefs, values and objectives.
- *Behavioural* norms govern people's behaviour within regular patterns.

- *Denotative* norms direct the choices of signs for signifying; such choices are culture dependent, for example the choice of a colour to signify happiness or sadness.

Another way of classifying norms is based on the effects of the execution of norms. Four types of norms are found in this classification:

- *Standing orders:* The execution of a standing order may result in a change in the physical world. Standing orders are commands to perform actions, and are usually expressed as one 'may', 'may not', 'must' and 'must not' do something. Typically, in a business environment, a department manager can give an standing order to the people in the department.
- *Status norms*: The execution of a status norm often creates or alters a social structure and legal relations. The norm designates a person as having liability, immunity, right or no right in relation to certain events or actions. Job descriptions and company regulations are examples of these norms.
- *Powers of intervention*: Execution here invokes or inhibits the use of existing standing orders and status norms. For example, a judge may have the power to decide which law to apply to a case.
- *Legislative powers*: These change the other norms. The execution of this type of norm may lead to an alteration in the legislative structure. The agent applying the norm must have the right to modify or create a norm. The board of governors in a business usually has the powers to alter the company laws and set up new rules.

Norms can also be classified based on the types of objects that the norms are applied to. In this approach, three classes of norms are found:

- *Substantive norms*: These norms are concerned with core business functions and operations that contribute directly to the organisational objectives.
- *Communication norms:* These norms specify patterns, structures and procedures of communication within an organisation. The role of the norms is to ensure that everyone knows what information should be kept and provided, and when and what actions should be taken. Without these norms, the whole organisation cannot act in a coordinated manner to achieve its objectives.
- *Control norms:* These norms introduce sanctions and rewards. They act as a mechanism to reinforce that everyone does what he or she is supposed to do, as prescribed by the other two types of norms.

These classifications are not exclusive of one another. For example, a standing order can be any of the three types: substantive – if it is concerned with business operations; communication – if it specifies the processes for how the task should be performed; or control – if it provides information about the consequence when one fails to complete the task.

Norm analysis

Norm analysis is useful for studying an organisation from the perspective of agents' behaviour that is governed by norms. From this perspective, specifying an organisation can be done by specifying norms. Norms can be expressed in a natural language or a formal, machine-executable language. They will be incorporated into the database as integrity and consistency constraints, or programmed as software applications.

A norm analysis is usually carried out based on the result of a semantic analysis. After a semantic analysis, the semantic model delineates the area of concern of an organisation. The patterns of behaviour specified in the semantic model are part of the fundamental norms that retain the ontologically determined relationships between agents and actions without imposing any further constraints. A pattern of behaviour is available as long as the antecedent behaviour is there as described in the ontology model. However, in a semantic model, a realisation (i.e. by obtaining an instance) of the antecedent may not necessarily lead to a realisation of the dependent; there are norms to allow the agent to judge the situation and to decide if a particular instance will be produced. The results of a norm analysis can be written using a specific format such as NORMA or other specification language, and further converted into a programming language.

A complete norm analysis can usually be performed in four steps, as outlined below.

Responsibility analysis

This analysis enables responsible agents to be identified and assigned to each action. The analysis focuses on the types of agents and types of actions. In other words, it will answer the question of which agent is responsible for what type of action.

As an instance of behaviour, its lifecycle goes from being realised, through being sustained, to its termination. The first and last states are marked as the 'start' and 'finish', and in between these is the existence of the behaviour. Of interest here are the agents who bring about changes in behaviour, namely, the agents authorising the start and finish of the process. This analysis aims to define these two kinds of agents who influence the start and the end. They are called the start authority and the finish authority of the affordance.

In an organisation, responsibilities may be determined by the organisation's constitution or by common agreements. In the case of organising an international academic conference, as illustrated in Figure 7.4, several committees and other sections may be involved in the organisation process.

Producing a call for papers, to decide whether a topic should be included in the conference, is the responsibility of the programme committee, as is deciding whether a paper should be accepted for presentation at the conference. But issuing an invitation letter to a participant should be the remit of the organising committee. More responsibilities are defined by the organisational rules of the International Federation for Information Processing as follows in NORMA:

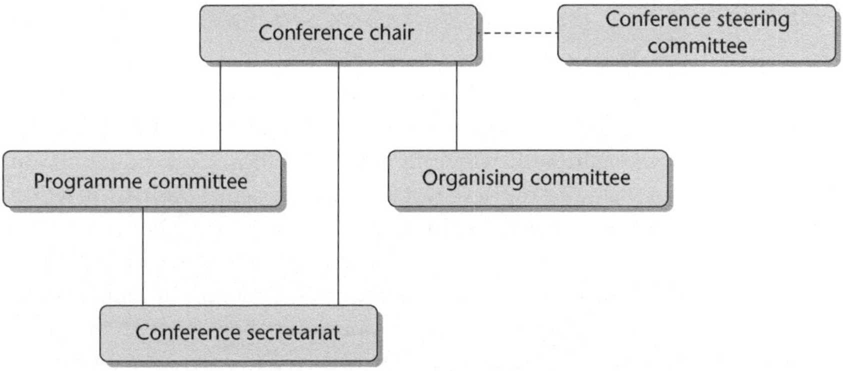

FIGURE 7.4 The organisation of an international academic conference

Scope of conference	+@, –@: Conference steering committee
Conference budget	+@, –@: Conference chair
Call for papers	+@, –@: Programme committee
Issuing invite	+@, –@: Organising committee

Proto-norm analysis

Consider the basic structure of a norm:

<condition> → <D> <agent> <action>

A norm in this form specifies the circumstances in which the action *may*, *must* or *must not* (as indicated by the deontic operator) be performed by the agent. The proto-norm analysis helps one to identify relevant types of information for making decisions concerning a certain type of behaviour. After the relevant types of information have been identified, they can be used as a checklist by the responsible agent to take the necessary factors into account when a decision is to be made. The objective of this analysis is to facilitate the human decisions without overlooking any necessary factors or types of information.

In the comparative review of information systems design methodologies (CRIS) case, for example, the organising committee responsible for assigning priorities to those eligible to attend a working conference must know the following types of information:

- the name of the person to be possibly invited;
- whether or not this person is a member of a working group or a technical committee;
- whether the invitee is an author or a referee.

Trigger analysis

This step of the analysis involves considering the actions to be taken in relation to the absolute and relative time. The absolute time means the calendar time, while the relative time makes use of references to other events. In proto-norm analysis, there is no mention of when the types of information should be supplied, the decisions made or the actions taken. But in actual business practices, all activities are organised in relation to time.

The results of a trigger analysis are specifications of the schedule of the actions. All the actions can be organised in dynamic sequences. By setting up and managing triggers for the actions, the automated system can prompt human agents to respond to the situation in time. The triggers can first be stated in a natural language and later translated into a computable form. The keys to the triggers are the absolute time and relative time linked to the action types contained in the semantic model.

In our example of the conference organisation, the determination of the applicants' priority must be carried out in a certain time before the invitations for the conference are due to be sent. Moreover, the invitations for the conference must be sent to the participants in time.

Detailed norm specification

In this step of the analysis, the contents of the norms will be fully specified in two versions: a natural language and a formal language. The purposes of this are: (a) to capture the norms as references for human decisions, and (b) to perform actions in the automated system by executing the norms in the formal language. For example, in the CRIS case, the rules of assigning priories to applicants that are written in English can be recorded and then translated into a pseudo-language for automatic execution.

In business, most rules and regulations fall into the category of behavioural norms. These norms prescribe what people *must*, *may* and *must not* do, which are equivalent to the three deontic operators 'is obliged', 'is permitted' and 'is prohibited'. The following format is suitable for the specification of behavioural norms:

> **whenever**
>
> **if**
>
> **then**
>
> **is** <deontic operator>
>
> **to**

Adopting this form, a credit card company may state the norms governing interest charges as follows:

> **whenever** an amount of outstanding credit
>
> **if** more than 25 days after posting

then the card holder

is obliged

to pay the interest.

whenever an agreement for credit card is signed

if within 14 days after commencing

then the card holder

is permitted

to cancel the agreement.

The first norm says that after 25 days of posting the bill, if there is still an amount outstanding, the card holder will have to pay the interest on this. The second norm states that the card holder retains the right to cancel the agreement within 14 days of its commencing.

The next norm says that unless there is a special arrangement made, for example with the account manager, the card holder is not allowed to spend more than the credit limit:

whenever purchasing

if no special arrangement is made

then the card holder

is forbidden

to exceed the credit limit.

Card holders are expected to behave according to the norms stated in the agreements. As understood by both the customers and the credit card company, the company may impose sanctions if a customer fails to observe these norms. With this form of specification of norms, a computer program can be written to execute the norms. As long as the norms are specified, computing technologies such as active databases, object technology and artificial intelligence will have different approaches towards software realisation.

Norms in computer systems

A constraint in an information system is, according to Jardine (1984), a 'prescription or prohibition of the behaviour of the Universe of Discourse or parts thereof'. Norms, controlling the behaviour of the agents at the social level, will have to be reflected as constraints in the conceptual models and incorporated into the technical information systems. The norms function as *integrity constraints* that safeguard the systems to behave properly.

One approach is to classify the constraints into three groups (Weigand 1993).

- *Analytical constraints* define the meaning of the objects and operations in a system. For example, a student can attend a class, and a teacher can teach.
- *Empirical constraints* set the rules for the generalisation of the domain. For example, an age acceptable to a system cannot be negative.
- *Deontic constraints* specify the rules that the objects and operations must comply with; for example that a student can take a maximum of five subjects in a semester. The special feature of deontic constraints is that they can be violated. A violation should not lead to an inconsistency in the information system. Instead, the system should incorporate a mechanism to derive corresponding rules of action for sanction and correction.

Norms can be treated as these constraints. In a computer system, these norms are programmed and incorporated into the computer's operations. These constraints safeguard the system to behave 'reasonably' and 'correctly'. The constraints can also function as triggers for the computer system to perform certain actions, such as changing the value of a record or producing a message.

Questions and exercises

1. How can we decide the extent to which human responsibilities should be delegated to an IT system? What are the roles of human users when IT systems do most of the work?
2. Carry out the following role-play in pairs:
    - Replicate the human–machine interactions when withdrawing cash from an ATM in terms of speech acts (indicating the type of speech act).
    - Record the speech acts and use them to specify the functions of the ATM.
    - With reference to the ATM example, discuss how speech acts have been used in information systems design.
3. Suggest how the aspects of semiotics may be integrated into systems analysis and design, and how they may improve the quality of deliverables in the development of information systems.
4. Referring to the norm theory, discuss how we understand that 'norms are to an organisation like software is to a computer system'.

Note

1 This and the next three examples are based on Groot (1992) and Dik (1989), of which the former is also the source of the syntax used in these examples.

8

ORGANISATIONS AS INFORMATION SYSTEMS

Organisational semiotics considers an organisation as an information system in which information is created, processed and used. The organisation as an integral system includes not only technical functions, but also human functions for information-processing and utilisation. As the semiotic framework shows, the issues at the social level are concerned with beliefs, expectations, commitments, contracts, law and culture, as well as business functions. If a technical information system is to serve the organisation well, it is crucial to understand the organisational functions at the social level. Information systems analysis and design must start with understanding and modelling the organisation. Many information systems methods provide techniques to deal with business analysis and modelling. These methods and techniques may be characterised by their different perspectives in modelling:

- the data-oriented perspective;
- the process-oriented perspective;
- the behaviour-oriented perspective.

The semiotic approach takes a step further. It stresses the distinctions as well the interdependent links between the organisation, the business process and the information technology (IT) system. The conceptual models of an organisational onion and an organisational morphology to be presented in this chapter will offer a useful method to understand the whole organisation and will help the modelling of the organisation. Moreover, an architectural grid for information systems design reveals how IT systems work as a part of the organisation.

Organisations as information systems

An organisation is a social system in which people behave in an organised manner by conforming to a certain system of norms. These norms are regularities of perception, behaviour, beliefs and values, which are exhibited as customs, habits, patterns of behaviour and other cultural artefacts. Teams and organisations exist by virtue of their social norms and cultures. An organisation can be characterised as a structure of social norms, which allows a group of people to act together in a coordinated way for certain purposes. The common purposes may be more than just to maintain the existence of the organisation, and may often be to ensure that the organisation behaves cohesively and effectively in achieving its goals.

An organisation can be seen as an information system in which agents employ signs to perform purposeful actions. The organisation must have fundamental values, basic beliefs and intended goals on which the organisational culture is based. These values, goals, missions and intentions will have to be to some extent spelt out so that the members of the organisation can understand them, and so that coordinated actions can be expected when necessary. This unclearly specified part, although it may be understood by most of the members of the organisation, is called informal (because of the lack of formality) and can be seen as the outer circle of the 'organisational onion' (cf. Figure 8.1), as Stamper (1992) has called it.

The explication of the informal part will increase the formality, hence the 'formal' part of the organisational onion. In the formal part, the organisational structure, responsibility, processes and functions are made explicit. Such high regularity that can be described in rules, a staff handbook or company policies can be specified, and these constitute the bureaucracy of the organisation (Mintzberg 1973, 1988; Simon 1960). Within the formalised aspect of the job, part of it may be highly mechanistic

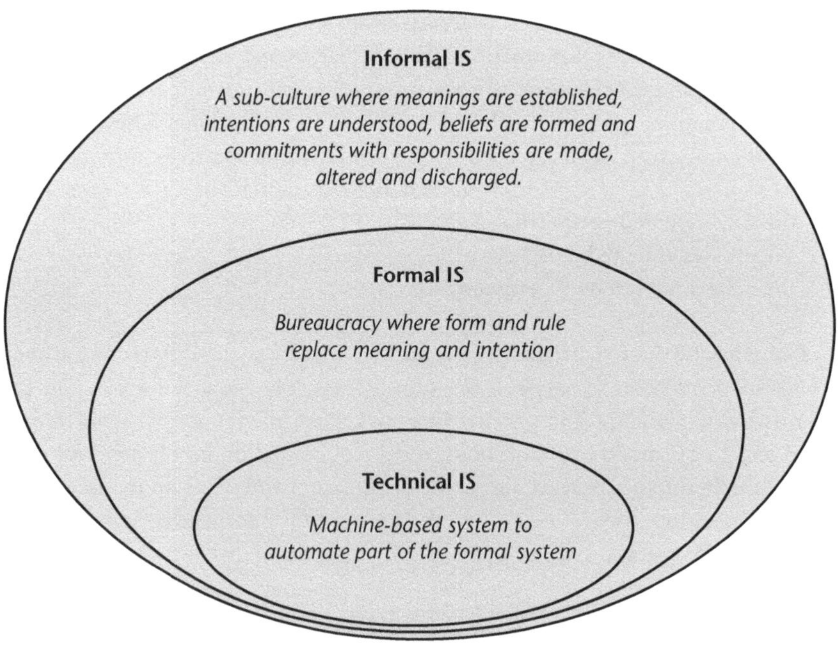

FIGURE 8.1 The organisational onion. (IS, information system)

and repetitive, and this can be automated by computer systems. Therefore, the computer or technical system is part of the formal part of the organisation, which is in turn part of the total organisation.

The informal information system

The whole organisation is first of all regarded as informal information system in which the oral culture plays an important role. The organisational culture, customs and values are reflected in the beliefs, habits and patterns of behaviour of each individual member. A healthy organisation will possess a cohesive culture and personal beliefs, whereas in an unhealthy organisation there may be considerable conflicts between the organisational and personal levels. This layer is a sub-culture where meanings are agreed, intentions are understood, and beliefs are formed. Commitments and responsibilities are made, altered and discharged in this context through negotiation, discussions and, sometimes, physical actions.

The formal information system

Inside the context of the informal information system lies the layer of the formal information system, in which the literature culture plays a dominant role. Rules and bureaucratic procedures are created to explicate and replace meanings and intentions. The rules and bureaucracy specify how the work should be carried out and how the tasks should be performed. They are useful when the tasks are mechanistic and repetitive. The rules and procedures can help to achieve high efficiency.

Those involved in the work do not necessarily understand the meaning of the words and numbers they handle, or the purposes for which they are used. People function as 'machines' that transmit and process sign-tokens, and this de-skilling is the essential step towards automation. However, such a detachment of signs from their meanings in bureaucracy could be dangerous. If the members of the organisation do not understand the meanings of the signs they process, there will be no sound basis for them to check that what they are doing is what they are supposed to do. An organisation may be detached from its members, or it can run efficiently but not effectively as far as achieving its objectives is concerned (Huang 1998).

The technical information system

The technical system, mostly a computer system or an IT system, is placed inside the formal systems layer. The technical system can be programmed according to rules. It can automate some of the functions and procedures needed. The computer system can be developed to read signs, shuffle and rearrange them, store and retrieve them, and finally present them. Many routine and repetitive tasks can be delegated to the technical system to achieve efficiency. However, there are certain prerequisites that have to be met before a technical system can be introduced into an organisation in order to automate some part of the work:

- *Well-defined work processes*: The work process and procedures should be clearly defined. There should be a clear bureaucracy in place into which the technical system can fit.
- *Clearly defined human responsibility*: People using the technical system should know their responsibility clearly. Interfaces between the human system and technical system should be clear in terms of what a user is supposed to do and what a machine is expected to provide. The purpose of using an IT system is to support the work process, but not to hinder the job or to provide excuses for not doing it properly.
- *Explicitly specified rules for operations:* Before introducing an IT system, there should be clear specifications of rules for business operations. These rules can then be translated into the IT system or knowledge-based system for automation purposes.

In summary, an IT system presupposes a formal system, just like a formal system relies on an informal system.

An organisational morphology

In systems analysis and design, a first step is to understand the organisation for which the system is being developed. This includes the structure and functions of the organisation. A traditional method for organisational analysis is to draw an organisational diagram in a hierarchical structure. The diagram (such as an 'org chart') normally represents the officers in different positions and reporting relationships. This kind of analysis is helpful in understanding the structure, but not in understanding what an organisation does.

One approach to understanding an organisation is to focus on the organisational functions (behaviour) rather than just the structure. This approach studies the morphology of the tasks and functions of an organisation. Three areas of organisational

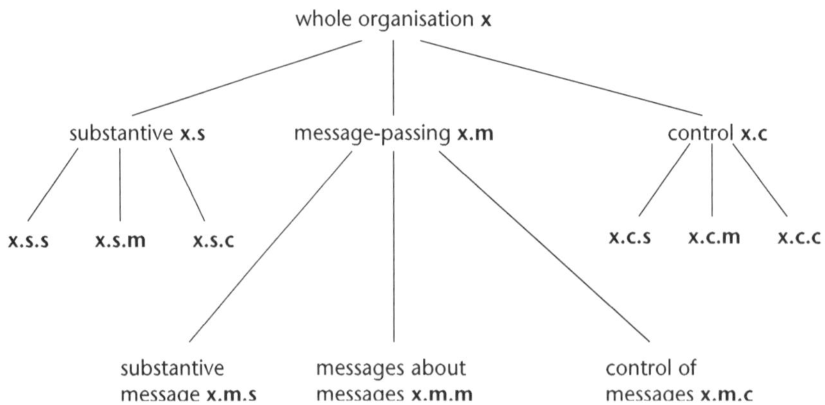

FIGURE 8.2 Organisational morphology (see text for definitions)

functions can be identified, and hence three types of activities and three types of norms can be studied as in the organisational morphology (Stamper *et al.* 1994): *substantive*, *communication* and *control* (Figure 8.2).

The substantive area

The activities in this area contribute directly to the organisational objectives and are productivity related. They are to realise the essential changes in the physical or social world. For example, in an educational institute, the substantive activities would be teaching and research. In an insurance company, they would be sales of policies, the receipt and processing of claims, and payments to customers. In a manufacturing firm, the activities in this area would be material and part procurement, engineering, production, sales and marketing, and post-service services.

The communication area

The activities in this area concern communication. The tasks performed in this category inform the relevant people about relevant facts and work procedures, when and what actions are to be taken, and by whom. Within a company, such communications are required to coordinate the temporal and spatial use of resources for substantive activities. Typical examples of such activities in this area are communications by planning and scheduling, sending memoranda, announcing meetings and events, and sending telephone and email messages.

The control area

The control activities aim to reinforce the whole business system, particularly the substantive and communication areas, so that it will run properly. Tasks in this area include the monitoring and evaluation of substantive and communication actions, followed by appropriate rewards and punishments imposed on the responsible actors. Within an organisation, the power of reinforcement may be informal or it may be explicitly stipulated in rules and regulations. Between organisations, it may be generated by inter-firm agreements or contacts governed by law.

However, the power of enforcement both within and between organisations ultimately rests upon socially established norms within the business sector and on the wider cultural conventions. The formal control norms supplement the informal norms in cases where they are deemed insufficient to ensure that every relevant agent fulfils his or her duties properly. Typical examples of control activities in a company are attendance registers and annual performance reviews. Performance-related reward and promotion opportunities are a consequence of these review exercises and can therefore be regarded as part of the monitoring and control measures.

The substantive, communication and control areas constitute the whole business organisation as described in the organisational morphology. Figure 8.2

shows that an organisation consists of three sub-areas: the *substantive area x.s,* the *communication or message-passing area x.m* and the *control area x.c.* Each of these can be further divided in the same way in more detail, giving, for example, *substantive message-passing x.m.s, messages about messages x.m.m* and *control of messages x.m.c.* Sub-division can continue until the level of detail is appropriate for the purposes of analysis.

All three areas are necessary in an organisation. The communication functions are required to inform people and coordinate actions. The control functions will ensure that other areas function properly. However, based on this organisational morphology, one can see that a 'lean and healthy' organisation should consume minimal resources in communication or message-passing (x.m) and control (x.c) activities. It should direct most of its resources towards substantive (x.s) activities. An 'unhealthy' or badly designed organisation may have to consume a great deal of its energy in building elaborate communication sub-systems and will have to rely largely on the formal control sub-systems to ensure that the substantive part of the work is conducted properly. These two types of sub-systems comprise large parts of typical bureaucratic infrastructures. The more elaborate these two sub-systems are, the heavier the bureaucratic burden is on the organisation.

Modelling organisational architecture

In order to successfully design information systems in an organisation, it is important first to draw an overall picture of what the whole organisation looks like. An organisational architecture, in some cases called enterprise architecture, is a blueprint that defines the structure and operation of an organisation. The intent of enterprise architecture is to determine how an organisation can most effectively achieve its current and future objectives.

Enterprise architecture is important in implementing organisational strategy. Using a holistic approach at all times, it provides a well-defined practice for conducting enterprise analysis, design, planning and implementation for the successful development and execution of strategy.

Organisational architecture

Organisational architecture can be seen in different ways: architecture as a discipline, architecture as an artefact, and architecture as a process.

Organisational architecture as a discipline

Organisation architecture can be seen a discipline for proactively and holistically leading an enterprise's responses to disruptive forces by identifying and analysing the execution of the change towards the desired business vision and outcomes (Box 8.1). Organisational architecture delivers value by presenting business and IT leaders with signature-ready recommendations for adjusting policies and projects to achieve target business outcomes that will capitalise on relevant business disruptions. Organisational architecture as a discipline can be used to steer decision-making towards the evolution of the future-state architecture.

Box 8.1 What is architecture? A metaphor of construction architecture

People who remodel a home are aware that the architect produces detailed drawings that specify information on plumbing, electrical and building construction for the entire structure. The architect responsible for the design produces (or oversees others who produce) blueprints for each phase of the project – from structural changes to the size and layout of the rooms. Moreover, to successfully complete the project, the architect operates within a framework of building codes. City or county inspections ensure that the work complies with building codes.

Enterprise architecture works in a similar manner (Thomas and Cullen, 2001). Enterprise architecture regards the enterprise as a large and complex system or system of systems. Organisational architecture includes more than just an abstract description of the system's structure and behaviour. It includes also principles, policies and standards (akin to building codes) that ensure that systems are soundly constructed. Governance of the enterprise architecture and of its implementation requires organisation and processes (akin to city and county inspectors and the processes for checking building improvement projects). Organisational architecture provides a mechanism to identify and represent, in a unified view, the business processes, data, technologies and customer interfaces that take the operating model from vision to reality.

Organisational architecture as an artefact

Organisational architecture can also be seen as a design artefact that shows the coherence between products, processes, the organisation, the information supply and the infrastructure. The artefact aligns business and technological strategies and communicates the core business processes of the enterprise, together with the building blocks of the application and infrastructure. The artefacts typically include requirements, principles and models that describe the optimal future state, an analysis of the gaps between the future state and the current state, and road maps that support the evolution of the enterprise to the future state by closing these gaps.

Organisational architecture as a process

Organisational architecture is also the process of translating the business vision and strategy into an effective change in the enterprise by creating, communicating and improving the key requirements, principles and models that describe the enterprise's future state and enable its evolution (Lapkin *et al.* 2008). The scope of the enterprise architecture includes the people, processes, information and technology of the enterprise, and their relationships to one another and to the external environment. Enterprise architects compose holistic solutions that address the business challenges of the enterprise and support the governance needed to implement them.

It is important to view enterprise architecture as a process to make the architecture artefacts well connected to the strategic imperatives of the enterprise and leveraged across the organisation. The process should emphasise that organisational architecture is a translation process in which the environmental trends affecting the enterprise and its business strategies are articulated and examined so that the optimal future-state vision can be derived.

Modelling organisational architecture

Architecture models are formal descriptions of an information system, organised in such a way that supports the organisational structure, functions and strategies for changes. These models define the components or building blocks that make up the overall organisation. The models provide a plan from which functions and activities can be performed, and sub-systems developed, that will work together as the overall organisation. It thus enables an organisation to manage its whole social system in a way that meets its business needs.

In organisational semiotics, an organisation can be analysed from an organisational morphological perspective by examining the interactions between the informal, formal and technical sub-systems. An organisation can also be analysed using the organisational onion to group the activities into substantive, communication and control categories in each of the sub-systems. The interactions offer a foundation for an integrated architectural view that is called the organisational architecture grid.

This grid describes and visualises the different architectural layers, the categories of activities and their relationships and dependencies. Although the organisational architecture grid is developed based on organisational semiotics, it coincides to an extent with the enterprise architecture of ArchiMate (Lankhorst 2004), a widely recognised architectural framework in industry. Figure 8.3 explains the derivation of the organisational architecture grid from the two important conceptual models within organisational semiotics:

- Horizontally, the organisational architecture grid can draw an input from the organisational onion and reflect a compositional view of an information system (i.e. the organisation). The grid is composed of four layers. The organisational context is mapped from the informal sub-systems of the organisational onion. The business layer is mapped from formal sub-system. The application layer (consisting of business functions and IT functions) and the technology layer are derived from both the formal and IT sub-systems.

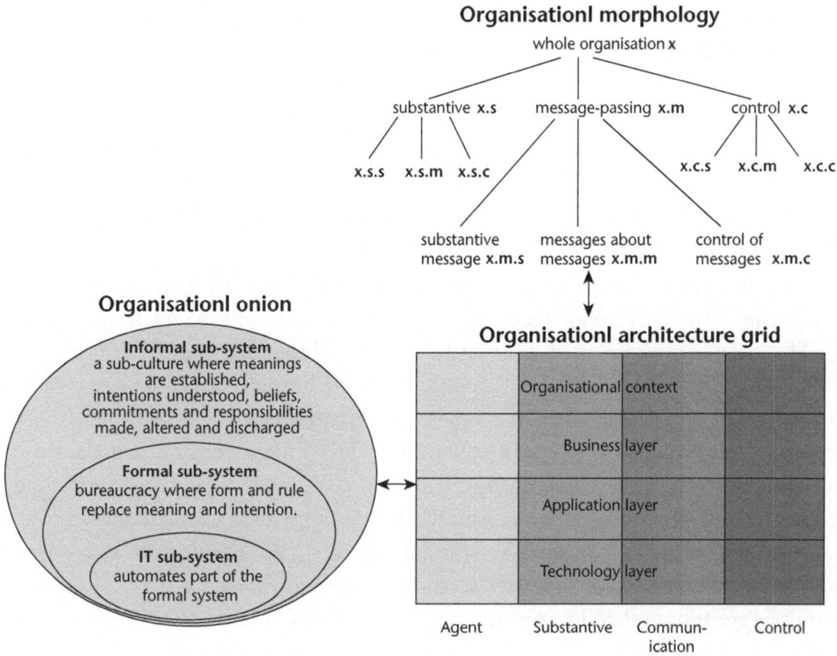

FIGURE 8.3 Deriving an architectural grid for information systems design

- Vertically, the organisational architecture grid can be based on the organisational morphology and reflect the categorisation of activities or functions in an information system (i.e. an organisation). The activities (or functions) can be substantive, communication and control. Equally importantly, each type of activity will be dependent on agents, and this leads to the need for the first left-hand column of the 'Agent'.

The organisational architecture grid at the bottom right of Figure 8.3 converts the theoretical underpinnings (e.g. the organisational morphology and the organisational onion) into a more practically usable technique, and guides the design of the information system (i.e. the organisation), as follows.

The *organisational context* represents the social, cultural, value and other aspects that may not be explicitly defined in the organisation. This layer covers the informal sub-system of the organisation. It constitutes the motivation and justification for the organisational architecture.

The *business layer* describes the shape of the current organisational structure, business processes, formally defined roles, responsibilities and activities. This layer is derived from the formal sub-system of the organisational onion, where rules and bureaucratic procedures specify how products and services are provided. Business processes performed by business actors are important factors in this layer.

The *application layer* supports the business layer with applications and services that are provided by members of the organisation as well as being realised by software applications. This layer is derived partly from the formal sub-system and partly from the technical sub-system in the organisational onion, where routine and repetitive functions are automated and performed by IT applications.

The *technology layer* constitutes part of the technical system in the organisational onion. This layer offers the lower level infrastructural services (e.g. the data-processing, storage and communication services) that are needed to run applications. The architecture in this layer is usually realised by computer and communication hardware and systems software.

From an activity perspective, the organisational architecture grid consists of four main types of activity areas: agent, substantive, communication and control.

The *agent* is relevant in all four layers of the architecture grid. In the organisational context, the agent can be stakeholders; at the business layer, the agent can be actors; at the application layer, the agent can be employees in certain roles or software applications; and finally at the technology level, the agent can be the software components or hardware that performs the actions. The capabilities of such agents in the various layers are affordances, in the terminology of organisational semiotics.

From the activity perspective, the substantive, communication and control activities can be assigned to agents, to show who performs the activity. *Substantive* activities are those related to productivity and directly contribute to organisational objectives. *Communication* activities are referred to as activities that use or exchange information to support the substantive activities. The *control* area in the architecture grid includes reinforcement activities, for example monitoring and evaluating substantive and communicative activities and ensuring that they are performed effectively. The control activities aim to motivate or induce the agents to operate in a proper way. Control is important in organisational architecture but has been neglected in most methods of enterprise architecture.

The sixteen cells in the organisational grid (Figure 8.3) represent all the major factors relevant in designing and running an organisation. Taking the organisational context layer as an example, stakeholders can be agents representing groups or organisations that influence the plans and aims of an organisation. Substantive and communicative activities include meetings, negotiation (communicative) as well as drafting and signing the strategies, plans or agreements within and between organisations. Furthermore, control activities include the identification of key factors and the assessment of substantive and communicative activities performed by the agents. An understanding of strengths, weakness, opportunities and threats in relation to these key factors will help in the formation of plans and aims to address these issues appropriately. Furthermore, the assessment based on these key factors will govern and motivate stakeholders to achieve a better performance.

Figure 8.5 shows an example of modelling architecture in the business layer using the ArchiMate modelling language (Box 8.2). In the example, Client and ArchiSurance are the business actors, the active entities (the subjects) that perform behaviours such as business processes or functions. Business actors may be individuals (e.g. customers or employees), but may also be groups of people and resources that have a permanent (or at least long-term) status within the organisations. A business role is assigned to each actor: Client has the role of Insurant, and in this role makes use of two services offered by the insurance company; ArchiSurance plays the role of Insurer, and in this role it is responsible for the damage-claiming process, which is expressed by the assignment relation between the business process and the role. Note that the use of roles decouples (physical) actors from business activity and provides more flexibility in the allocation of activities to actors.

Box 8.2 Case study: ArchiMate as a language for organizational architecture

The ArchiMate project (http://www.archimate.nl/en/about_archimate/archimate_project.html) aims to provide enterprise architects with concepts and techniques for modelling, visualising and analysing integrated architectures. The ArchiMate project resulted in the ArchiMate enterprise modelling language, which can be used to represent enterprise architecture and assist in information systems design, including technical as well as organisational design.

In ArchiMate, architectural descriptions are made for different 'layers' of the organisation. The lower layers provide functionality to support the higher layers. These include the business layer, the application layer and the technology layer, as illustrated in Figure 8.4.

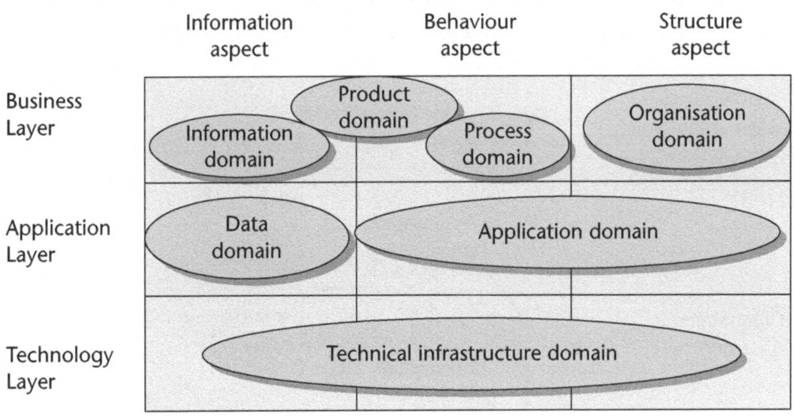

FIGURE 8.4 The ArchiMate organisation architectural framework (Jonekers *et al.* 2004)

- The *business layer* offers products and services to external customers, which are realised in the organisation by business processes performed by business actors.
- The *application layer* supports the business layer with application services that are realised by (software) applications.

(Continued)

(Continued)

- The *technology layer* offers the infrastructural services (e.g. processing, storage and communication services) that are needed to run applications, realised by computer and communication hardware and system software.

Cross-cutting these layers are three aspects: information, behaviour and structure. Structure comprises the static aspects, while behaviour is the dynamic aspect of the organisation. Behavioural concepts are assigned to structural concepts to show who or what displays the behaviour. In the example, role, interface and collaboration are assigned to business process, organisational service and business interaction, respectively.

In addition to active structural elements (the business actors, application components and devices that display actual behaviour, i.e. the 'subjects' of activity), ArchiMate also recognises passive structural elements, that is, the objects on which behaviour is performed. In the domain of information-intensive organisations, which is the main focus of the ArchiMate language, these are usually *information objects* in the business layer and data objects in the application layer, but they may also be used to represent physical objects. The aspects and layers form a framework of nine 'cells', as illustrated in Figure 5.4 (Jonkers *et al.* 2004).

It is important to realise that the classification of concepts based on conceptual domains, or based on aspects and layers, is only a global one. It is impossible,

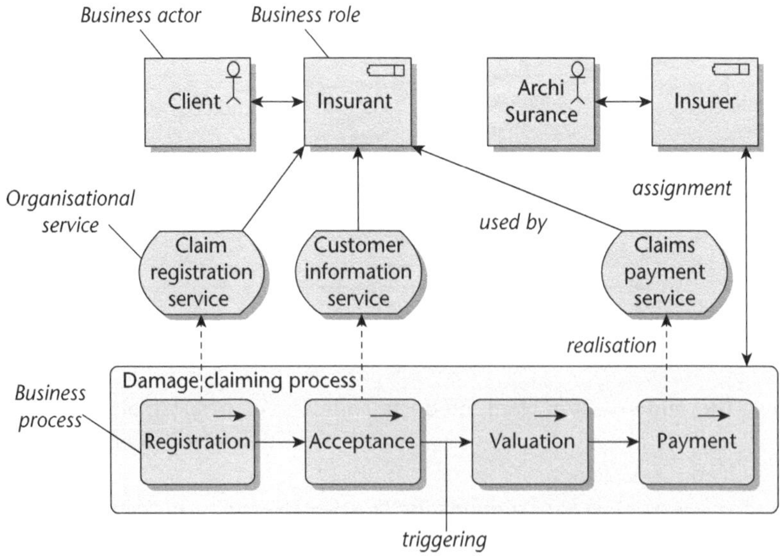

FIGURE 8.5 An example of modelling of the insurance business layer (Lankhorst 2004)

and indeed undesirable, to define a strict boundary between the aspects and layers because the concepts that link the different aspects and layers play one of the most important roles in a coherent architectural description. For example, services and roles serve as intermediary concepts between 'purely behavioural' concepts and 'purely structural' concepts.

Summary: information systems application and modelling in organisations

To model an information system is to represent, by formal means, an organisation in which people use signs for business purposes. A sound modelling method must cover the issues that occur in the semantic, pragmatic and social aspects. Issues at the three semiotic levels are closely related, and Figure 8.6 explains this relationship. The left-hand arrow shows that, in analysis and representation, the focus must be first on the semantic issues. A model containing a clear description of the organisation, which may be in terms of general patterns of actions (i.e. affordances), states and processes, is the first basis for further analysis. Such a model can be taken as a foundation on which the intentions of actions can be discussed.

Furthermore, the rationales, limits and consequences of the actions at the social level can be addressed. But in the case of the practical operations, as the right-hand arrow indicates, the social concern determines the intentions that the speaker needs to express, and they thus decide the words and expressions that will be uttered to represent the meaning. This is the semiotic approach upheld for understanding information systems.

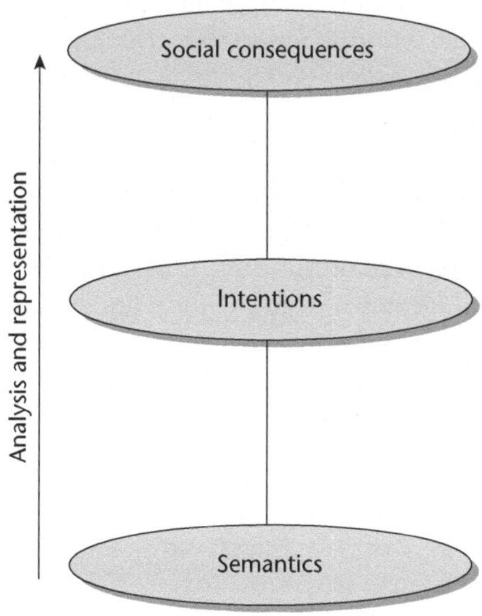

FIGURE 8.6 Application versus analysis and representation in information systems development

Clarifying the semantic problems and representing a social organisation clearly is regarded as the most critical and difficult task. In a practical situation, it is crucial to know how individuals are involved in implementing a plan or conducting an activity by translating the words into actions through which they can understand their tasks and duties. An effective method must provide techniques for eliciting, clarifying and representing users' knowledge and requirements.

For this purpose, the semantic analysis method is advocated for its power in handling semantic problems. Semantic analysis focuses the attention of analysis on the agents and the actions. The semantic principle for solving business problems and interpreting language in the conduct of practical affairs is that meaning must be treated as a relationship between signs and actions. The actions include the physical kinds and the uses of signs (of the semiological kind) to fulfil the purposes of the actions. The semantic model delineates the boundary of concern in the analysis and defines the meanings of the terminology used in the model.

Questions of intentions and social consequences are addressed by means of analysing norms, which govern people's behaviour. The analysis of norms is based on the result of semantic analysis. With the semantically defined words and expressions resulting from the semantic analysis, the intentions and the social consequences can be associated with the actions and the use of signs in communication. The norms acquired, in addition to the semantic model, serve as detailed knowledge of the business organisation. Furthermore, the norms can be used for reasoning and prescriptive analysis of the organisation, for example in planning and behaviour simulation.

Questions and exercises

1. An organisation can be seen as an integral information system. Discuss how to identify and analyse the informal, formal and technical sub-systems in the process of systems planning, analysis and design in order to achieve an alignment between business and technical information system.
2. Discuss how to identify the functional and non-functional requirements in informal, formal and technical sub-systems in the requirements engineering process.
3. Identify substantive, communication and control activities, and discuss the need for these activities in an organisation, using examples in a specific industry (e.g. automotive). Identify how to aim for a 'healthy and lean' organisation by considering these three types of activities in the specific examples and their associated norms.
4. The organisational architecture grid shapes the organisation into sixteen aspects based on the organisational onion and morphology. Discuss each cell of the architecture grid by producing examples in an organisation.

PART II
Applications

9

INFORMATION SYSTEMS PLANNING

Information systems planning is one of the critical processes for an organisation. Planning is the process of deciding on the optimal informatics infrastructure for an organisation, and engaging with the transformation of one informatics infrastructure to another (Beynon-Davies 2009). This chapter discusses how organisational semiotics facilitates systems planning by seeing an organisation as an integral information system and by understanding the organisational morphology. Furthermore, it will discuss how the problem articulation method (PAM) can be used assisting in information systems planning, followed by a case study of an ATM system to illustrate the applicability of PAM in planning complex systems.

About information systems planning

Information systems planning starts with an organisational mission and strategies. It is important to ensure that there is a close match between the strategic direction of an organisation and its information services. Information systems planning can be used to ensure that information systems projects correctly balance business objectives with technical objectives. It is feasible to estimate the effect (and the risk) of proposed information systems projects, in terms of their contribution to business objectives, and to evaluate the effectiveness of current systems. Good planning is a necessary part of the good management of information systems and is likely to improve the ability of an organisation to succeed in complex information systems projects and react to unforeseen circumstances.

Information systems planning falls into the inception phase of the systems development process. As shown in the systems development project lifecycle (Gornik 2004) in Figure 9.1, systems planning focuses on understanding the business context, defining the system's scopes and purposes as well as appreciating the complexity of business domains (e.g. stakeholders, concerns and influences).

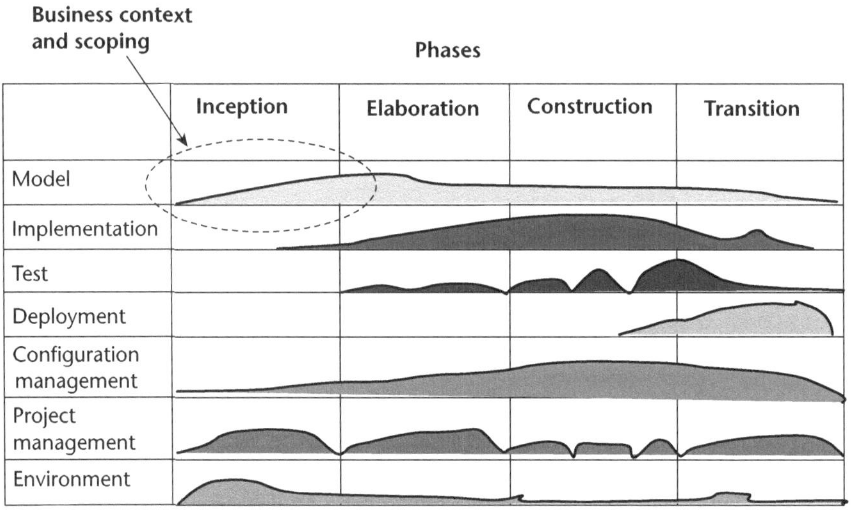

FIGURE 9.1 The project lifecycle of rational unified process information systems (adapted from Gornik 2004)

The driving force for having information systems planning may come from several sources with different aspects. Newly encountered needs, problems and opportunities relating to information systems within the organisation include increased competition in the business environment, the rapid evolution of IT as a result of business pull and technology push, the more sophisticated IT and information systems in use and changes in users' requirements.

These needs for a new and improved information systems system can be initiated by different stakeholders such as management, line managers, users and information systems professionals, all of whom have different perspectives. Typically, high-level managers are concerned with strategic information systems and enterprise-wide applications because they consider the impact of such systems on the entire organisation or on major parts of it. Information systems professionals usually draw attention to new technologies, hardware, software and telecommunications, and suggest ways to use them to improve business processes. Line managers may initiate a consideration of new or improved information systems as a result of talking to colleagues from other organisations or reading an article in a trade journal. Users enquire about how new or improved information systems can solve the problems they encounter in their daily work.

Figure 9.2 shows a typical information systems planning process including four major phases: strategic planning, organisational information requirements analysis, resource allocation and project planning. The purpose of *strategic planning* is to align the information systems plan with the overall business strategies and objectives of the organisation. Methods such as competitive strategies, a customer resource lifecycle and strategy set transformation are often used in this phase.

Organisational information requirements analysis will contribute to the information architecture of the organisation in such a way that various existing information

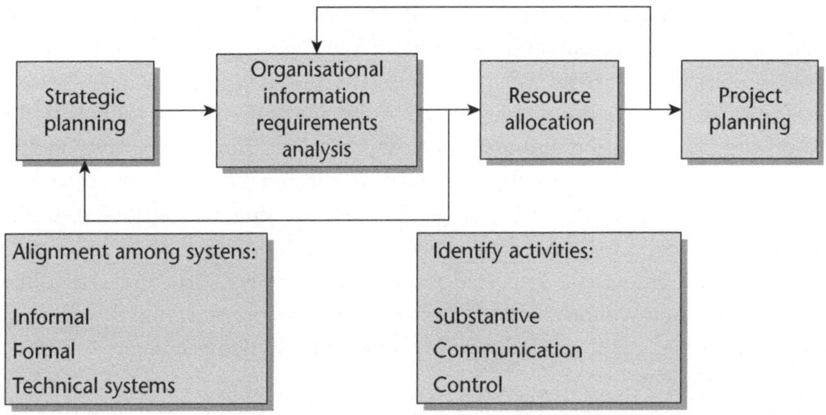

FIGURE 9.2 The information systems planning process

resources (business applications and databases) can be integrated. Business systems planning and critical success are often used to support the analysis.

In the *resource allocation* phase, methods such as return on investment charge-out or in-house/outsourcing are often used in order to allocate information systems development and operation resources among competing applications.

The final *project planning* phase acts to ensure that the information systems projects can be completed on time and within budget. Methods in this phase can involve the critical path method, Gantt charts, milestones and product-based approaches.

The whole process may consist of several cycles among the different phases; for example, the result of the organisational requirements analysis may in turn affect the revision of information systems strategic planning.

Strategic planning: informal, formal and technical systems

Information systems are increasingly embedded into the organisation supporting the core business process, and are sometimes the generator of new revenues. Information systems planning, which formulates strategy for future systems development and maintenance, must be integrated into the overall organisational strategy. Ideally, information systems planning should focus on the alignment between the organisation's strategy and the information systems strategy. Therefore, regarding the organisation as an integral system of both business and technical aspects is one of the prerequisite for effective information systems planning.

From the semiotic perspective, an organisation is essentially an information system, as illustrated in the organisational 'onion' (see Figure 8.1). The process of information systems planning should fully consider the informal, formal and technical systems and their interaction within an organisation. This guides information systems planning in examining all aspects of an organisation. According to the semiotic onion, the three main levels of analysis are needed to analyse the strategy, goal, culture and environment, and to further assess the organisation's current situation and plan the future information systems, as shown in Figure 9.3.

Informal systems planning assesses the environment of the organisation as well as the organisation's mission and goals. The inputs to planning at this level include current and future trends in the immediate environment of the organisation – economic, social, political and ecological trends affecting the organisation. This particularly involves an assessment of its current and potential place in its value network. Furthermore, the expectations, objectives, power structure and culture in the organisation will be analysed. This analysis involves reviewing the organisation's mission and goals, and determining information systems strategies to support corporate strategies.

Formal systems planning requires information concerning the shape of the current organisational structure, business processes, formally defined roles and responsibilities within the organisation, activities and plans for change. The planning activities at this level involve an assessment of the organisation's structure, resource allocation mechanism, management processes and functional capabilities. These contribute to identifying organisational information requirements, including the overall information architecture, and current and potential information needs.

Technical systems planning provides information on trends in IT that are likely to affect the organisation in the short to medium term, and that are likely to stimulate a need for change in its IT infrastructure. Planning at this level involves an assessment

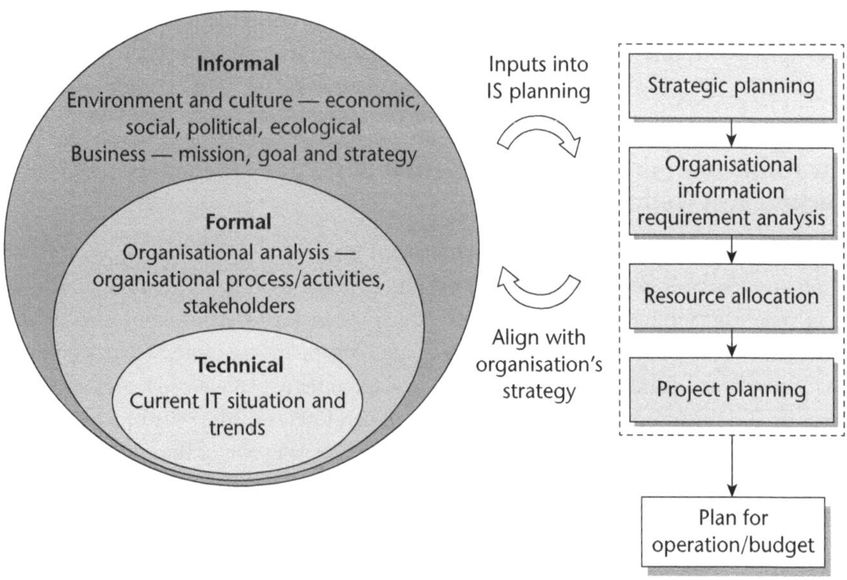

FIGURE 9.3 Planning information systems in informal, formal and technical systems. IS, information systems

of current information systems capabilities, an introduction of new technologies, stages of information systems adoption and a blueprint of IT personnel and skills. This contributes to the specific IT strategy, such as hardware, software and network plans.

In order to achieve an alignment between the organisation and the information systems strategy, the planning outcome of informal, formal and technical systems should dynamically input into the process of formulating the information systems strategy. The notion of alignment suggests that the organisational and information systems strategies are related in a cycle of mutual reinforcement. As shown in Figure 9.3, the information systems strategy will be formulated by examining and transforming all the organisational aspects as the input. In this way, the information systems strategy will align with the organisational strategy, and in turn support the organisation's activities and have an influence on the formulation of the future business strategy.

Relationship between informal, formal and technical systems

The demarcation of each sub-system is not always clear, and the divide between these sub-systems can become blurred. Changing one sub-system will definitely have impact on others. For example, re-engineering business processes will produce a need to redesign the information technology (IT) system, and vice versa. It is important to consider the relationship between sub-systems during information systems planning in order to achieve the alignment. There are three types of relationships between the systems:

- *Interacting with each other*: Interaction means that changes in one system will affect the other, and this is often a two-way interaction. The organisational culture, value, mission and strategy in the informal system are reflected through the rules and bureaucracy in the formal system. The changes of environment and mission will lead to the corresponding adaption of organisational structure – business processes as well as roles and responsibilities. In turn, issues or problems in the formal systems (e.g. the need for an improvement in business processes or for a more effective organisational structure) may also lead to the launch of a new strategy in the informal system. The interaction between the formal and technical systems lies in the alignment of business activities and technical supporting functions. Business processes, roles and responsibilities formally defined in the formal system will determine what functions the technical systems should have in order to support daily operations. In turn, the introduction of new technologies, hardware, software and advanced infrastructures will stimulate new initiatives (e.g. new services and procedures) to improve the business process in the formal system.
- *Conflicting with each other*: Unlike interaction, conflicts between the informal, formal and technical systems refer to some form of friction, disagreement

or discord arising within the organisation when one sub-system is resistant towards the beliefs or actions of another sub-system, or finds them unacceptable. A conflict usually starts from the disruption of interactions, often caused by differences of opinion or disagreements between systems. There is always tension between the formal and informal systems. The divergence between the culture in the informal system and the bureaucracy in the formal system is the main cause of conflict. For example, when an organisation promotes a culture of democracy and equality in the informal system, people may be constrained by rules and authority structure in the formal system. However, the rules and authority structure are necessary to ensure that responsibility is fulfilled and tasks are performed.

The conflict between the formal and technical systems lies between, on the one hand, the possibility for people to make judgements and apply discretion even within the formal system, and on the other hand, the rigid 'pre-programmed' rules incorporated into computer operations to prevent such happenings (Box 9.1). The processes and rules implemented by individuals in the formal system could be realised based on people's judgement when an exceptional situation arises. However, the automated functions and procedures programmed into the technical system cannot adapt to the flexibilities in the formal system, which lead to the conflicts between the two. The conflicting status needs to be resolved in order for the business functions or services to be performed. It is usually resolved by assigning a higher precedence to people in the formal system rather than entirely relying on the capabilities of the technical system.

Box 9.1 Can the deadline be changed? – conflicts between formal and technical systems

One typical example of conflict between formal and technical systems is the submission system for academic papers, for example for a conference. A conference usually sets important dates such as the paper submission deadline and acceptance notice date to control the progress of collecting, selecting and compiling papers. Therefore authors need to submit their papers through the submission system before the deadline. The technical system is programmed to accept papers until the deadline, and any submission after the deadline will not be accepted.

However, there are unexpected situations such as an author's internet failure or a system crash due to too many authors submitting at the same time. Despite such situations, the technical system will automatically close the submission facility after the deadline, which leaves authors no further opportunity to submit. But the conference secretariat, which is considered to be part of the formal system, is able to accept a paper manually or even extend the deadline when necessary. This is a typical conflict between the formal conference management system and the technical submission system. To solve the conflict, the individuals involved in managing the conference will usually have precedence over the technical system.

- *Overlapping with each other*: Overlap between sub-systems means that one sub-system may have some services and functions in common with another system. In some case, even the data content or information may be duplicated in the two sub-systems. The redundancies brought about by the overlap serve several purposes. For example, the overlap in services or functions will increase the reliability. Even when the IT system is down, the formal sub-system can serve as a fall-back solution to ensure continuity of business.

Overlaps between the sub-systems that exist in every organisation have to be allowed. Existing business processes may be changed or adapted by the individuals involved; as a result, new process patterns may emerge and may gradually become standardised. Part of the standardised patterns may then be incorporated into the IT system. During the course, overlaps in functions and services may be encountered.

Some functions and procedures that are automated in a technical system are the same as some repetitive tasks in the formal system, which means that the technical IT system can only be delegated to perform routine and repetitive tasks for the purpose of improving efficiency. These tasks can also be completed by people not using IT, which then ensures the human's control over the organisation.

To achieve the alignment between the organisational strategy and information systems strategy, it is important to consider and manage the relationships between the informal, formal and technical systems during information systems planning. As shown in Figure 9.4, the ideal alignment can be achieved by solving the conflicts, identifying the overlaps, reinforcing the strategies and norms, and finally realising the organic interactions throughout the systems. The planning of the informal, formal and technical systems will contribute to the first phase of strategic planning in order to align the information systems strategy with the organisational strategy.

Organisational information requirements analysis: substantive, communication and control activities

Information requirements must be met at the organisational level for planning information systems, identifying applications and planning the information architecture. The second stage in information systems planning is an analysis of how information is to be managed in the organisation in order to support the organisation's objectives and operations. The analysis describes organisational information needs as well as the structure and content of the overall information architecture. Unlike the detailed information requirements in later systems design phases (e.g. identifying data attributes), broad information requirements will be identified

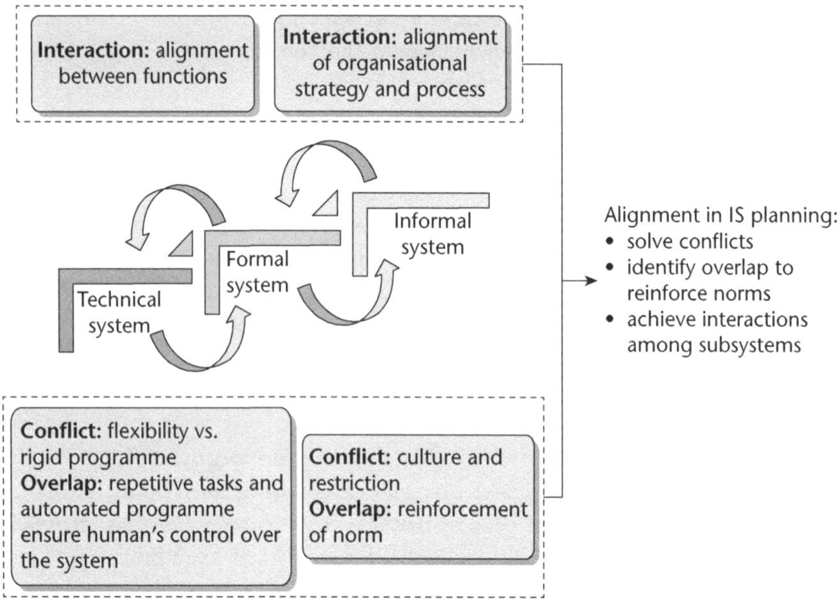

FIGURE 9.4 Alignment of information systems (IS) planning by managing relationships between sub-systems

to establish a strategic information architecture that can be used to determine information systems projects and allocate resources.

It is important to identify organisational behaviours and functions in order to deliver a strategic information architecture that will direct the development of specific applications. The organisational morphology (see Figure 8.2) provides an insight into the areas of tasks and functions in the organisation. Understanding the three types of activities (substantive, communicative and control) will provide an underpinning for the analysis of organisational information requirements in the business domain.

As illustrated in Figure 9.5, the information requirements at the organisational level can be analysed into three types of interrelated activities, which constitute the strategic information architecture. The figure shows that the information architecture for a business domain (e.g. production) consists of three sub-areas: the substantive area x.s, the communication area x.m and the control area x.c. Each of these can be further divided in the same way in more detail until the information architecture is informative enough to direct application planning and resource allocation.

Information requirements for substantive activities

The identification of substantive activities is essential for organisational requirements as they contribute directly to the business domain to be planned. These activities will usually result in economic changes in the business domain under consideration. Therefore, identifying norms governing substantive activities is

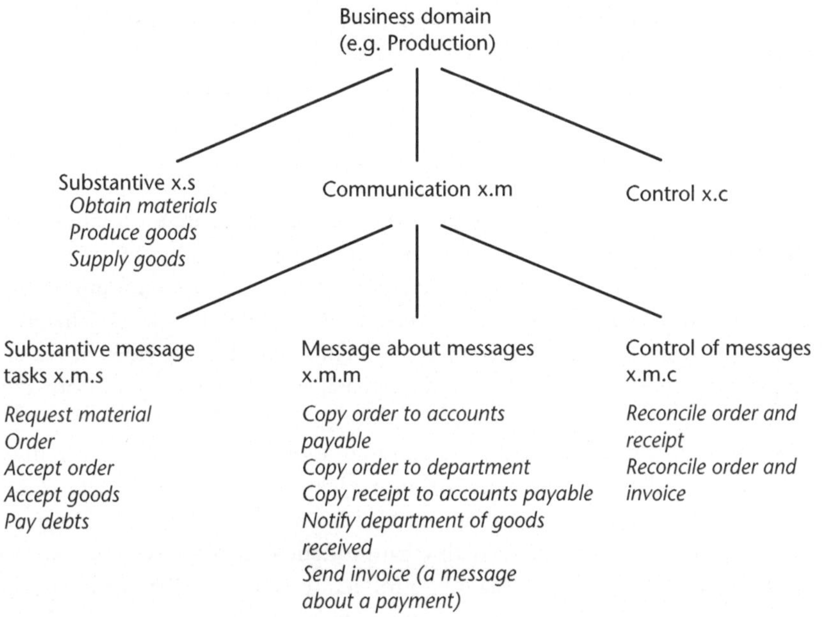

FIGURE 9.5 The morphology of organisational information architecture in systems planning

important in organisational information analysis in order to ensure attainment of the basic goals in the domain to be planned. The main task in analysing substantive information requirements is to find out details of how to perform these substantive activities and make these norms explicit, for example the norms concerned with core business functions and operations.

Let us take the production domain as an example. If systems are going to be planned in this domain, norms governing core production functions and operations, such as 'obtain materials', 'produce goods' and 'supply goods', need to be identified. Furthermore, the information requirements can be divided into details by analysing each substantive activity (x.s) in terms of substantive (x.s.s), communication (x.s.m) and control (x.s.c) activities. For example, 'obtain materials' could be further analysed into its substantive activity (e.g. actually get materials), communication (e.g. schedule and feedback on goods received) and control activity (e.g. quality inspection). This sub-division can continue until sufficient information requirements have been satisfied for the system to be designed. The outcome of the information requirements analysis for substantive activities includes the norms of key processes and norms in the business domain, which underpin the fundamental part of the strategic information architecture.

Information requirements for communication activities

These aim to identify the communicative patterns, structure and procedures within the business domain. The aim of analysing communicative information requirements is to ensure that everyone knows what information should be kept and provided, and what actions should be taken and when. This information is important in the strategic information architecture as the planned business domain cannot act in a coordinated manner to achieve its objectives without communication activities.

Communication activities pass messages from one agent to another for the purpose of supporting successful performance of the substantive activities. Signs are employed and sent between agents with meanings agreed by the both parties involved in the communication to express their intentions. Communication is important in the management of the firm and the conduct of business. Therefore, the analysis of information requirements of communication activities in relation to supporting substantive activities is indispensable for the strategic information architecture.

The information requirements in communication activities involve the information needs both within the organisation and between it and other organisations. For example, in the production domain, there is a need to identify the communicative information requirements with regard to temporal and special information in order to coordinate the substantive production activities. Between organisations, information requirements (e.g. enquiries, orders, invoices and reminders) need to be identified to support communication activities such as establishing legally binding contracts and coordinating the discharge of the contracts by the business partners.

The communicative information requirements can be further detailed in terms of their morphological features. As shown in Figure 9.5, in order to identify detailed communication requirements, the activity (e.g. coordination to obtain materials) can be further analysed through the substantive message x.m.s (e.g. request materials), messages about messages x.m.m (e.g. copy the order to the accounts payable department) and control of messages x.m.c (e.g. reconcile the order and the receipt). The details needed at this level of analysis of the communication information requirements can be determined by whether or not they meet the requirements for the organisational architecture.

Information requirement for control activities

This constitutes the third part of the organisational information architecture. The analysis of the control activities involves identifying the enforcement norms that prescribe appropriate rewards and sanctions. This control part of organisational information in the business domain will ensure that every agent acts properly in performing the substantive tasks, which are necessary to maintain the social and organisational orders. The incentives are provided as part of the control activities to stimulate a positive achievement of the goals in the business domain. The control information requirements can be analysed based on stipulated rules and regulations within the organisation or on inter-firm agreements, treaties or contracts between organisations.

Take the production domain as an example (Figure 9.5). Here, the requirements of control of information could be performance measurements and a checklist and policy for staff evaluation, which would act as a mechanism to reinforce that everyone did what they were supposed to do as prescribed by the organisation's substantive and communicative information requirements.

The substantive, communicative and control information requirements together constitute the organisational information architecture with the purpose of prioritising information categories and allocating resources. It is important to notice that a *healthy* organisation should consume a small amount of resources in communication and control activities, and will direct most of its resources towards undertaking substantive activities. However, an *unhealthy* or badly designed organisation may have to consume a great deal of its energy in building elaborate communication sub-systems, and may have to rely largely on the control sub-systems. It is therefore important to achieve proper planning or possible re-engineering during the organisational information requirements analysis in order to achieve greater effectiveness in the business domain to be planned. In other words, the planned organisational information architecture should enable the organisation to operate effectively by ensuring that the substantive activities are best supported by the communication and control activities.

Infrastructural analysis and planning – an ATM case study

PAM, as a semiotic method for infrastructure analysis, has been applied in enterprise infrastructure modelling. The architecture of PAM is shown in Figure 9.6.

Unit system definition (USD) articulates an enterprise in which the requirements and artefacts are analysed and decomposed into unit systems (U). Within the context of these U, stakeholder identification (SI) will identify the relevant stakeholders, followed by integrating the outcomes obtained from USD and SI in the form of a collateral structure (CS) that conceptualises an enterprise infrastructure. Valuation-framing acts as a feedback mechanism to: (a) prioritise the importance of the viewpoints of the stakeholders involved in the Us; and (b) iteratively verify and refine the analysis in the other three stages.

As shown from the architecture, the PAM focuses on the alignment between systems and users' needs, which can be applied in enterprise requirements modelling and producing the requirements specification of the enterprise's system. These requirements specifications can be further used for planning and designing the scoped system. This section describes how the PAM techniques discussed in Chapter 4 can be used in enterprise modelling through a case study of an ATM system (Liu *et al.* 2009).

Unit system definition

An ATM machine should be able to provide consumers with certain banking services, such as enabling them access with authentication, to obtain cash in a different

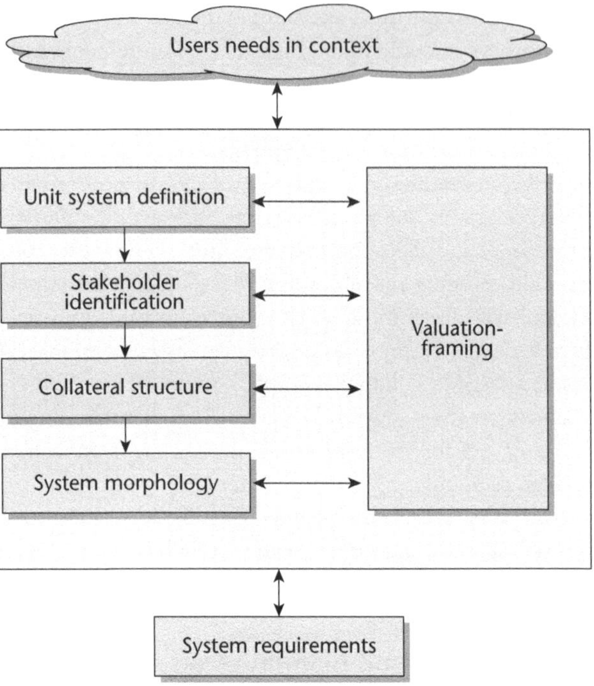

FIGURE 9.6 Architecture of the problem articulation method

currency, to check the status of their account, to print receipts for different service requests and to receive general information about the services available. In order to perform these business functions, the ATM should be supported by an infrastructure with resources, such as refilling the cash when the stack is empty, replenishing supplies (e.g. printer paper), monitoring the safety of the premises, notifying the staff of breakdowns, arranging alternative banking services and maintaining the ATM machinery.

The scenario here describes a problem situation of the ATM in operation, which is in turn defined as the U. Box 9.2 depicts the recourses required by the U that supports consumers, bank clerks and ATM suppliers to fulfil the tasks within the capacity of their responsibilities.

Box 9.2 The unit systems representing the ATM domain requirements

<U – ATM in operation>

U_1 = ATM machine construction
<Ui>

$U_{1.1}$ = recourse planning for parts (hardware/software) supplies
$U_{1.2}$ = assemble the specified ATM machine
$U_{1.3}$ = test the machine for the user's acceptance
</U1>

U_2 = ATM machine launching

<U2>
$U_{2.1}$ = install the supplier's hardware and software on the machine
$U_{2.2}$ = test the entire system for operability
$U_{2.3}$ = training bank clerks on operating the machine
</U2>

U_3 = day-to-day operations

<U3>
$U_{3.1}$ = provision rules, policies and safety of operation
$U_{3.2}$ = replenishment of different back notes
$U_{3.3}$ = replenishment of paper for receipt
</U3>

U_4 = breakdown circumstances

<U4>
$U_{4.1}$ = reporting breakdown by consumers
$U_{4.2}$ = handling breakdowns notified by designated bank clerks
$U_{4.3}$ = arranging alternative banking services by bank clerks
</U4>

U_5 = maintenance of ATM

<U5>
$U_{5.1}$ = setting up service agreement with suppliers
$U_{5.2}$ = regular servicing of machinery
$U_{5.3}$ = reviewing service agreement U5.4 = troubleshooting and repairs
</U5>
</U - ATM in operation>

The infrastructure for the U has been articulated and represented by the sub-unit systems, such as that the ATM machine should be built as the bank specifies, the ATM machine should be installed for enabling the operation, the ATM machine should perform the day-to-day specified operations, the ATM machine should be properly dealt with when it breaks down, and the ATM machine should be serviced as required. Each of the sub-unit systems details the activities contributing to the U. The sub-unit systems can be further decomposed where appropriate until the U has been clearly analysed.

Stakeholder identification

In the example of the ATM service, the stakeholders are identified and their roles and responsibilities are further described for U_1, U_2, and U_3 as follows:

U_1 – ATM machine construction

$U_{1.1} \supset$ {coordinator, facilitator, recourse planning for hardware/software supplies, value}

$U_{1.2} \supset$ {manufacturer, provider, assemble the specified ATM machine, value}

$U_{1.3} \supset$ {manufacturer, provider, test the ATM machine, value}

$U_2 \supset$ ATM machine launching

$U_{2.1} \supset$ {supplier, provider, install hardware/software of ATM machine, value}

$U_{2.2} \supset$ {engineers, facilitator, test the operability of entire system, value}

$U_{2.3} \supset$ {engineers, facilitator, training bank clerks, value}

$U_3 \supset$ day-to-day operations

$U_{3.1} \supset$ {bank officer, governing body, provision rules, policies and safety of operation, value}

$U_{3.2} \supset$ {clerks, facilitator, replenish banknotes, value}

$U_{3.3} \supset$ {supplier, provider, replenish paper for receipts, value}

The value for the each stakeholder at this stage is unknown until a valuation process has been conducted in the stage of valuation-framing, where a set of criteria in a matrix are applied. The value perceived by the stakeholders will be used to support decision-making on a priority of a specific U in the entire system's development.

Collateral structuring

Figure 9.7 illustrates the four cycles for the problem situation of the ATM machine in operation, that is, the U. The *construction cycle* is the state in which the U is being constructed by assembling the components provided by the *resource system*. The resources include the screen, keyboard and so on. This cycle will create a working system for the ATM machine that is available for configuration and installation. In the construction cycle, there will be instances where a fault triggers the dismantling of components for maintenance. The dismantled resources may later be reassembled as the available system and relaunched for operation.

The *launching cycle* will change the state of U_1 from construction to set-up, and will require the commissioning of equipment in the available system. This cycle will necessitate unpacking, configuration, installation and testing the hardware and software. After this stage, U_2 will enter the *operating cycle*, where it functions to provide the ATM's services. The routine operation of the operating system takes

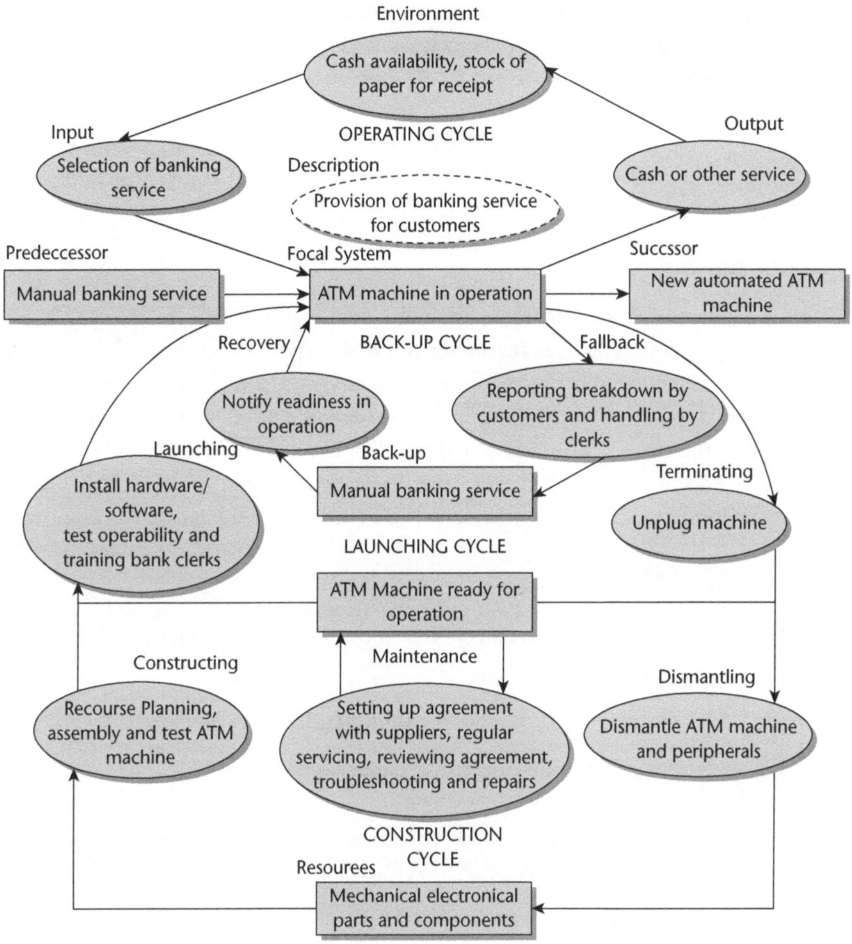

FIGURE 9.7 Collateral analysis for the ATM system

an input (i.e. the banking service request) and generates an output (i.e. cash or another banking service). The environment has a profound influence on the input system. It serves to capture the internal and external factors exerted on the U, for example the requirements from the customers for service. These requirements will inadvertently determine the number of banknotes needed.

In the operating cycle, the system may require periodical maintenance. Consequently, U_1 will be terminated and decommissioned by entering the launching cycle and constructing cycle where appropriate. The termination of use of the ATM machine will require the system to be uninstalled and subsequently dismantled for servicing.

The back-up cycle handles the state of the Us when the system fails. In the event of a system breakdown, a fall-back service will alert the duty member who is responsible for liaising with the engineers to arrange the repair, and for redirecting users from the ATM service provision to the traditional manual banking service in the branch with free tokens. Once the ATM machine has been serviced, a notification will be sent that the system is back in operation. The recovery service will switch the procedures according to the operating cycle.

The analysis in the collateral structuring provides a coherent view of the lifecycle of such problem situations, and helps in producing the complete requirements specifications that will then be used for the systems planning and technical design.

Valuation-framing

To assist decision-making relating to the functional requirements for the ATM system, each user's concerns over the presence of the system were assessed. Table 9.1 shows the assessment results obtained using Equations (2) and (3) (Chapter 5) for the focal system U_3: the ATM machine in day-to-day operation. The interests of key users such as the bank officer, clerk and supplier have been valued on the basis of their gains and losses because they are the direct beneficiaries of the ATM system. The results computed for S can be assigned to equation (1) (Chapter 5) as follows:

U_3 – day-to-day operations

$U_{3.1} \supset$ {bank officer, governing body, provision rules, policies and safety of operation, 18}

$U_{3.2} \supset$ {clerk, facilitator, replenish banknotes, 26}

$U_{3.3} \supset$ {supplier, provider, replenish paper for receipts, 13}

Here, *S* refers to the calculated value as perceived by the stakeholders for a priority of a specific U in the development of the entire system.

TABLE 9.1 Valuation of the impact of the ATM on the stakeholders

U_3	*Bank officer*	*Clerk*	*Supplier*	$A_i = \sum_{j=1}^{n} V_{ij}$
Subsistence	2	3	0	5
Classification	3	3	0	6
Territoriality	3	3	3	9
Temporality	3	3	3	9
Learning	2	1	2	5
Recreation	1	3	2	6
Protection	3	3	3	9
Exploitation	–2	3	–1	0
Association	0	1	0	1
Interaction	3	3	1	7
$S_j = \sum_{j=1}^{10} V_{ij}$	18	26	13	

For example, the clerk, with his role of facilitator, scored S = 26. This result implies that the clerk would gain highest benefits from the ATM system to support his day-to-day job. The valuation results of a corresponding focal system can guide the decisions on prioritising functions and further system upgrading.

Questions and exercises

1. Why is information systems planning necessary?
2. We understand that no one can plan in turbulent times, but planning is nevertheless crucial. How would you reconcile these two viewpoints?
3. If we consider outsourcing as a possible option during systems planning, what are the risks of outsourcing and how should we cope with them? How do we do 'smart sourcing'?
4. If an organisation wishes to outsource its information systems, what factors will it have to consider according to the semiotic onion and systems morphology?
5. Discuss how the semiotic onion, systems morphology and the associated PAM support operational planning, tactical planning and strategic planning in an organisation.
6. How can semiotic methods support activities in the lifecycle of an information systems project, especially in terms of systems planning. Which of the existing frameworks of systems planning seems most useful? Why is this?

10

CO-DESIGN OF BUSINESS AND TECHNICAL SYSTEMS

Information technology (IT) has an important role to play in business organisations. The assumption that the use of IT is necessary in any business is almost taken for granted. It can be witnessed that continual investments in IT have to be made to sustain productivity in industry. However, it has been widely observed that there is often a gap between an operational IT system and the current business requirements of a organisation. An IT system that was at one time highly supportive could, after a period of time, impose constraints on business operations, and could be regarded as a legacy system.

Such a problem can be caused by a number of factors. One is that IT systems and business processes are not treated as one integral unit but are designed separately. The calibration and adjustment of IT and business systems can overcome some of the problems, but more costly exercises such as process re-engineering or redevelopment of the IT system sometimes have to be involved. Many research communities, such as those from computing and management sciences, have made great efforts in searching for a solution through the investigation of flexible architecture for IT systems, evolutionary information systems (IS) and the co-evolution of IT systems and business processes.

The co-design of business and IT systems is a step in this direction. When an IT system is viewed as a part of the business organisation, and both the IT and business systems are designed at the same time, the gap between them can be minimised. In this chapter, we will first discuss the interplay of business and technical systems, and then present the co-design framework covering infrastructural co-design, organisational co-design and operational co-design. We will then discuss the implementation of co-design given in the context of integrated healthcare management.

Co-design to address gaps between business and IT systems

Many IT services businesses have recognised the gap between the desire to address business issues (e.g. to reduce costs, create new business models, implement new business processes and gain competitive advantages) and the limitation in their ability to implement successful solutions using IT. The gaps between business and IT threaten businesses' success because they prevent companies from unleashing the power of technology to enhance their efficiency, gain a competitive advantage and drive their business goals.

The gaps between business and IT arise in various circumstances. A gap can arise when there is a lack of effective communication between business people and technical people. Sometimes the technology works but the organisational factors are not aligned with its implementation. Or the organisational factors may be in place but the technology is not delivering as promised. Sometimes the technology works and the organisational factors are in place but the needs of the business or other external factors have unexpectedly changed.

The complex and changing business requirements always result in a constant gap between IT and business systems, as illustrated in Figure 10.1:

- *Complex business systems versus predefined technical systems:* Current business systems comprise the goals, people, structures, processes, IT, resources and constraints of a business. All of these constitute complex and dynamic business systems. Business systems become more complex when conflicts arise between the different interests and priorities of multiple stakeholders. In parallel, the technical aspects relating to platforms, middleware, networks, applications, legacy systems and functionality do not stay unchanged. It is hard for the programmed IS to cope with these constant complexities.
- *Varied human communication versus structured and formal information-processing in IT systems:* Business communication tends to be varied in terms of the form, channel, context and often the involved natural language, which may be hard to formalise, while IT aims towards formal, structured communication and machine-based languages.
- *Business versus technological perspectives:* IT specialists place an emphasis on technical capabilities, while business managers are more concerned with business service capabilities, even though these are often enabled by the IT infrastructure and systems.
- *Business pull versus technological push:* Organisations become knowledge-centric, decentralised and agile in order to respond to the market and environment, and

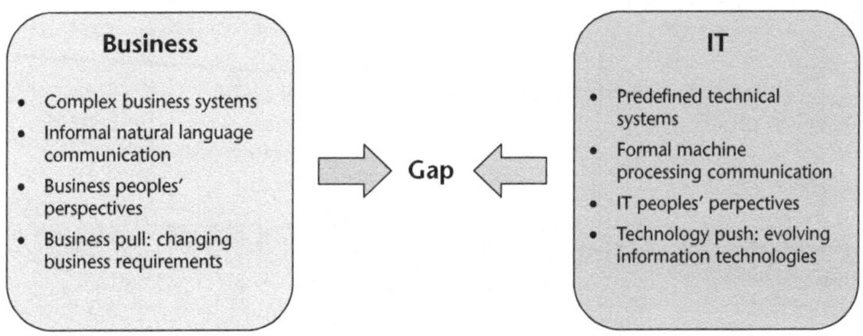

FIGURE 10.1 Driving forces affecting the gaps between business and IT

to maintain business competitiveness. The economic climate and corporate social responsibility also impose requirements on business organisations over time, and these business requirements determine the functionality of the IS. On the other hand, new technical capabilities emerge as technology advances, which opens up additional possibilities for performing business. This sometimes presents to the business organisation as opportunities, but sometimes as pressure for change.

Bridging these gaps is now more critical than ever because of the increased competitiveness in the business environment.

Theoretical foundations for co-design

The essence of co-design is the integration of IS business systems, which allows both systems to evolve naturally. The co-design framework should have the ability to capture and portray both business and technical information in an interrelated fashion. This will then allow enterprises to be more adaptable to the continuous flux by using IS functionalities to meet their business requirements. A co-design is often featured as follows:

- The IS design places a focus on the business systems, the IT system being a by-product. That is, meeting business requirements is the primary concern and IT systems are treated as part of the business.
- The IT system will be designed in such a way that it can evolve when the business system changes.

To achieve these features, the co-design framework should first have a holistic view of an organisation and recognise the interaction between people and technology in the organisation. Furthermore, in a more practical way, the co-design framework should contain a mechanism to decompose complex problems in the enterprise and to provide a shared view of the business and IT landscape so that the business strategy can be translated into an effective change in the enterprise. Therefore, as shown in Figure 10.2, the theoretical underpinning of co-design includes

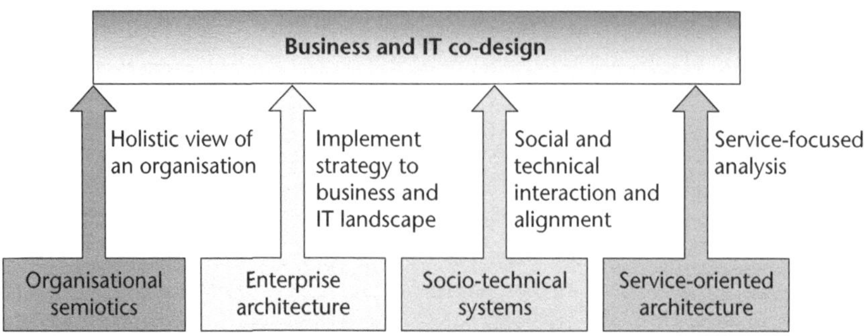

FIGURE 10.2 The theoretical foundations of co-design

organisational semiotics, enterprise architecture (EA), socio-technical systems and service-oriented architecture, each supporting the co-design from a particular angle:

- *Organisational semiotics* leads to a holistic view of an organisation by regarding the organisation as an information system.
- *Enterprise architecture* translates the business vision and strategy into an effective change in the enterprise by creating, communicating and improving the key requirements, principles and models that *describe the enterprise's future state and enable its evolution.*
- *Socio-technical systems* provide insights into the complex work design by recognising the interactions between people and technology in the workplace.
- *Service-oriented architecture* (SOA) results in solutions by focusing on the services that IS provide, and by integrating technical functionality into enterprise systems.

Viewing organisations through a semiotic lens

Organisations as information systems

From the perspective of organisational semiotics, an organisation is regarded as an information system composed of formal, informal and technical systems (as discussed in Chapter 8). The organisation is able to provide services and perform functions that are determined by the organisation's capability (or affordance). Most of these service capabilities and functions are explicitly defined and described. They are regulated or governed by explicit norms (e.g. business rules). These are called formalised activity or formalised behaviour. Within the whole range of formalised organisational behaviours, some services and functions are mechanistic and can be automated by computer-based systems. In such cases, technical solutions or automatic systems can be employed to perform these functions instead of humans.

Organisational semiotics suggests that an IT system is part of a formal area of the organisation that is in turn part of the total organisation. In this way, IT is seen as part of the entire organisation and should be subject to the formal and informal aspects of the business. It is essential that the informal, formal and technical levels should be combined together to provide seamless support to the business.

Organisations as systems of norms

An organisation is governed by norms, which allow every part of the organisation to work together in a coordinated manner for certain purposes. As shown in Figure 10.3, the whole organisation (enterprise) may have a number of functional departments, for example marketing, sales, production, finance, and research and development. These departments support the different processes and functions in an organisation but may overlap. For example, the sales department and the production department share an IS function in terms of assessing the inventory level in order to tell whether the items are in stock before placing an order. Similarly, the production and finance departments will overlap when planning for new production.

Each department has a set of norms to govern its activities and IT systems. For example, each department has standard operating procedures to control its activities and ensure consistency. Each department has IT systems to support the business functions. There may be departmental IS such as the payroll system in the human resources department and the purchasing system for managing raw materials in the production department. The whole organisation is placed within the context with which the organisation is required to interact.

Norms act as a forcefield governing every part of the organisation as well as the IT systems:

- Norms enable members to communicate and coordinate by specifying the patterns, structures and procedures of communication within an organisation. For example, there are patterns such as using email for information exchange but telephone calls for urgent issues; in addition, group teleconferences may be adopted to reduce the number of regular face-to-face meetings.
- Norms govern members' behaviour. For example, the processes, procedures and rules are specified to direct members in conducting activities such as processing orders and purchasing materials.
- Norms sustain the organisation by providing regulations, standards and conventions by which members can act accordingly. The obedience of the members is reinforced through exercising appropriate rewards and sanctions.

Service-oriented approach

In order to strategically align the IT with the business, the service-oriented approach has been adopted to redesign business operations into business services that will improve the business's agility (Clarke and Nilsson 2008; Larson 2008). The SOA provides solutions to managing large problems by decomposing the

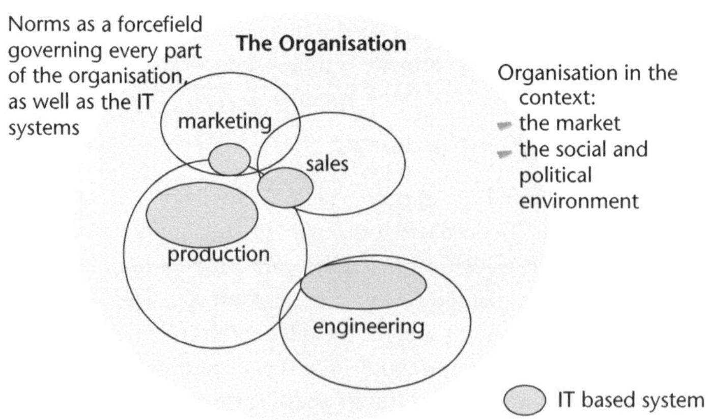

FIGURE 10.3 Norms governing organisations

problems into pieces. The solutions to the sub-systems can in turn be combined to form a solution to the complex problem.

A *service* can be seen as a discretely defined set of contiguous and autonomous business or technical functionalities. It consists of information and processes. In an organisation, services act as a solution logic implemented in a service-oriented manner, or as a set of business or technical solutions.

Service orientation is a paradigm for organising and utilising distributed capabilities that may be under the control of different ownership domains. It provides a uniform means to offer, discover and use capabilities to produce the desired effects consistent with measurable preconditions and expectations.

Service orientation leads to a design for linking business and computational resources (principally organisations, applications and data) on demand to achieve the desired results, especially in supporting the integration and consolidation of activities within complex enterprise systems. The conceptualisation of service orientation in a business enables the focus on core business competences to generate added values for customers. The business competences are classified into *core business competences* (which create value to meet the business goal) and *supporting business competences* (which facilitate the primary business activities).

An organisation adopting an SOA should usually be more dynamic in coping with changes under pressure from the business environment. SOA enables the enterprise to be redesigned or improved more easily by identifying underperforming components and removing them without affecting the other parts of the business. Similarly, ineffective IT components can be rationalised without affecting the business operations.

The SOA Reference Architecture technical standard

The Open Group (2009) has announced the most important standard for SOA – the SOA reference architecture (SOA RA). The SOA RA standard provides organisations with a foundation for the architecture and implementation of SOA solutions. Organisations using the standardised SOA RA as a starting point will have a common understanding of SOA and a way to communicate clearly and concisely across lines of business, business roles, vendors and partners.

The logical solution view of the SOA RA (Figure 10.4) depicts an SOA as a set of logical layers. Note that one layer does not depend solely on the layer below it and is thus named a partially layered architecture: a consumer can access the business process layer or the services layer directly, but not beyond the constraints of an SOA architectural style.

Note that there are, in Figure 10.4, five horizontal layers that are more functional in nature and relate to the functionality of the SOA solution. The supporting layers are supportive of cross-cutting concerns that span the functional layers but are clustered around independent notions themselves as cross-cutting concerns of the SOA architectural style. The lower layers (services layer, service component layers and operational systems layer) are concerns for the provider, and the upper ones (services layer, business processes layer and consumer interface layer) are concerns for the consumer.

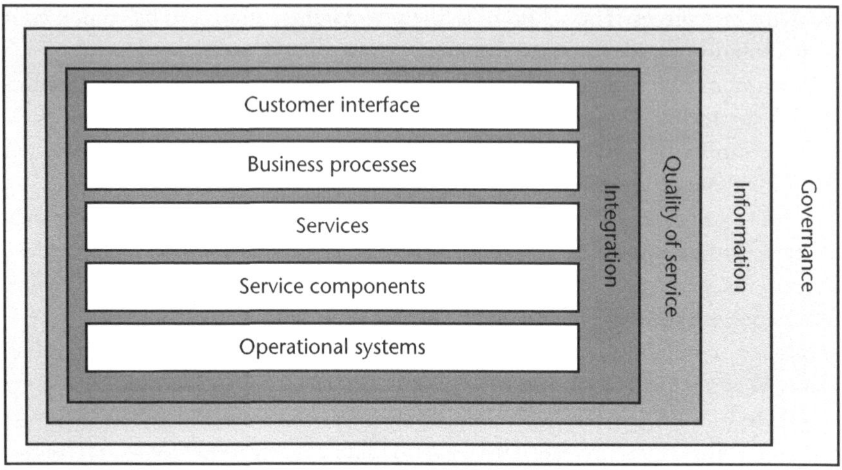

FIGURE 10.4 The logical solution view of the service-oriented architecture reference architecture (adapted from Open Group 2009)

The main point of the provider–consumer separation is that there is value in decoupling one from the other along the lines of the business relationship. Organisations that may have different lines of business use this architectural style (where one is the consumer and the other is the provider), customising it for their own needs and integrating and interacting between themselves; in such a case, there is still real value in maintaining a decoupled consumer–provider relationship. Each layer and the relationships between the layers will now be described.

Socio-technical systems approach

The socio-technical systems approach in organisational development recognises the importance of the interaction between people and technology in the workplace. The term also refers to the interaction between society's complex infrastructures and human behaviour. In this sense, society itself, and most of its sub-structures, is a complex socio-technical system. Socio-technical theory is about the joint optimisation (Cooper and Foster 1971) of the interaction between the social and technical factors that create the conditions for organisational performance and the optimisation of each aspect alone (social or technical; Box 10.1).

Box 10.1 Mini case study: Why social-technical? Social and ethical issues around technical system

Let's take as an example a relatively simple technology: a set of 10 microcomputers connected by a network. The social and ethical issues associated with these networked computers will change dramatically depending upon the socio-technical system in which they are embedded. For instance, are the networked computers:

- part of the intake unit of an emergency room
- a small, public lab at a university
- the computing lab of an elementary school
- a risk analysis office in an insurance firm
- a military supplier testing manufactured parts

The networked computers in each of these different circumstances are part of different socio-technical systems. The "ethical issues in computing" arise because of the nature of specific socio-technical systems, not because of the computers in isolation. Many of these ethical issues are intimately related, however, to the technology: issues of reliability of the system in the emergency room, data privacy in the insurance company, free speech and misuse in the public university lab. These are not just social systems, they are socio-technical systems, and the ethical issues associated with them are based in the particular combination of technology and social system. It is the technology, embedded in the social system that shapes the ethical issues.

(Source: http://www.computingcases.org/general_tools/sia/socio_tech_system.html)

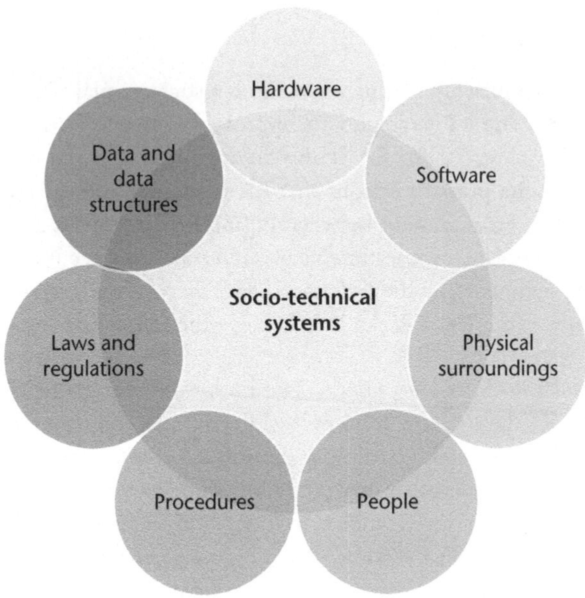

FIGURE 10.5 What constitutes socio-technical systems

As shown in Figure 10.5, a socio-technical system typically consists of technical components such as the infrastructure, network, database and IT systems, as well as socio-organisational components such as the organisation, process and people representing different stakeholders:

- *Hardware*: Mainframes, workstations, peripherals and connecting networks.
- *Software*: Operating systems, utilities, application programs and specialised code. Software often incorporates social rules and organisational procedures as part of its design.
- *Physical surroundings*: Buildings also influence and embody social rules, and their design can affect the ways in which a technology is used. Moving a technology that assumes one physical environment into a different environment may cause problems of mismatch.
- *People*: Individuals, groups, roles (support, training, management, line personnel, engineer, etc.) and agencies.
- *Procedures*: Both official and actual; management models, reporting relationships, documentation requirements, data flow, rules and norms.
- *Laws and regulations*: These might be laws regarding the protection of privacy, or regulations on the testing of microchips in military use. These societal laws and regulations might be in conflict with the organisation's internal procedures and rules.
- *Data and data structures*: What data are collected, how they are archived, to whom they are made available, and the formats in which they are stored are all decisions that go into the design of a socio-technical system.

Enterprise architecture

EA can be seen as a process. In this view, EA is a strategic planning approach that integrates business and IT strategies to improve business effectiveness and performance (Lapkin *et al.* 2008). EA is also an artefact that is the outcome of EA planning. One of the primary reasons that EA is adopted in organisations worldwide is to promote an alignment between business requirements and IT solutions because, for many organisations, strategic planning and the execution of the resulting projects are hampered by the lack of a shared view of the current business and the IT landscape – the EA. EA can help achieve the following:

- *Management's needs for a big picture:* The business's management needs a view that combines the strategy, business architecture, IS and technology domains. This is crucial for quickly analysing the impact of any proposed changes and prioritising the projects that drive the most value to the business.
- *Aligning IT investments with business goals*: Creating a platform for collaboration between business and IT stakeholders is essential. Effective EA supports strategy, analysis and planning by providing stakeholders with a blueprint of the current state of the business and IT landscape as well as the desired future state.

- *Managing complexity to achieve transformation*: Today's applications, systems and platforms have complex interdependencies that make it challenging to enhance the IT capability. An EA strategy is essential to achieving successful, lasting transformations – such as major SOA initiatives and packaged application implementation – and managing the inherent risks of a technology-enabled business transformation.

An EA framework provides a collection of best practices, standards, tools, processes and templates to assist in the creation of the EA and architectures of various scopes. Widely adopted EA frameworks, such as TOGAF (Open Group 2011) and the Zachman framework (Zachman 2008), currently exist to define EA. Taking the Zachman framework as an example, this is an EA framework that provides a formal and highly structured way of viewing and defining an enterprise.

As shown in Figure 10.6, the headings (horizontal and vertical) in the framework are not just about the business or technical systems. They are about the entire enterprise of which the IT system is a part, that is, systems within systems. Therefore, the EA is considered important to support the alignment between business and IT, and to manage change in organisations.

The business–IT co-design framework

The business–IT co-design framework provides a set of architectures, methodologies, processes and techniques to assist in designing business and IT systems at the same time. As shown in Figure 10.7, the framework has three components: infrastructural, organisational and operational co-design.

	Why	How	What	Who	Where	When
Contextual	Goal List	Process List	Material List	Organisational Unit and Role List	Geographical Locations List	Event List
Conceptual	Goal Relationship	Process Model	Entity Relationship Model	Organisational Unit and Role Relationship Model	Locations Model	Event Model
Logical	Rules Diagram	Process Diagram	Data Model Diagram	Role Relationship Diagram	Locations Diagram	Event Diagram
Physical	Rules Specification	Process Function Specification	Data Entity Specification	Role Specification	Locations Specification	Event Specification
Detailed	Rules Details	Process Details	Date Details	Role Details	Location Details	Event Details

FIGURE 10.6 Zachman's enterprise framework (Zachman 2008)

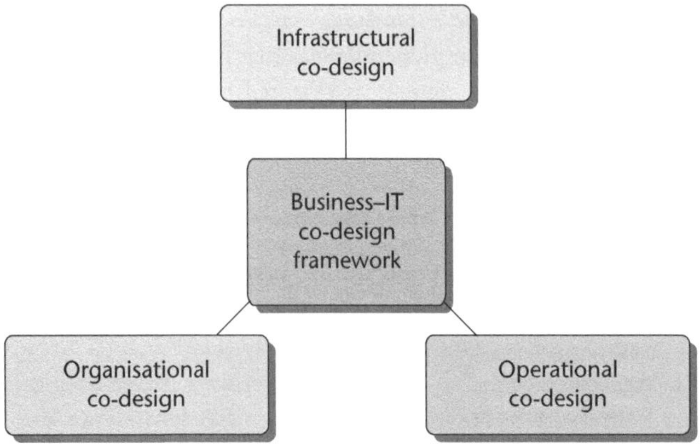

FIGURE 10.7 A business and IT co-design framework

The infrastructural, organisational and operational co-design each focus on different aspects of the business and IT systems (Table 10.1):

- *Infrastructural co-design* investigates the organisation's mission, vision, market context and stakeholders. The main task of this aspect is to examine the infrastructure of the organisation as a whole and align the organisational strategy with the IT strategy. The EA can be used to deliver IT strategies and IS systems.
- *Organisational co-design* focuses on the organisational aspect that involves the organisational structure, organisational behaviour, business rules and responsibilities. The main task is to construct the business components, structure, capability and services that IT systems support. The organisational structure and capabilities can be modelled as an organisational affordance through ontological modelling.
- *Operational co-design* emphasises the dynamic aspects of the organisation, for example the operation of services, processes and operational rules. The main

TABLE 10.1 Infrastructural, organisational and operational co-design

	Infrastructural co-design	*Organisational co-design*	*Operational co-design*
Factors to be considered	Organisational mission and vision, market environment and stakeholders	Organisational structure, business rules, roles and responsibilities	Services, processes, business rules
Methods/ techniques used	Enterprise architecture, strategic alignment, problem articulation method (PAM)	Semantic Analysis Method (SAM), Organisational Morphology, Norm Analysis Method	Process modelling, norm specification, UML
Deliverables	Strategies and objectives	Services, components, structure, capability	Processes and functions

task is to embed the dynamic aspects of business systems into the processes and functions of the IT systems.

Infrastructural co-design

Infrastructure co-design aims to produce a blueprint of the business and IT landscape. An effective utilisation of IT resources in an enterprise is normally dependent on and driven by business strategies. The infrastructural co-design leads to an alignment of the business and its IT systems at two levels, as shown in Figure 10.8.

- *Alignment at the strategic level*: This aims to achieve an integration between the IT and business strategies, which determines the capability of the IT at the strategic level. Business and IT systems are examined at this level to address issues such as scope, competencies and governance. Business scope, competencies and competitive advantages, as well as business governance, are considered from the business perspective. Similarly, the scope of the technology, IT systems competencies, IT governance and their relationships are considered from the IT perspective.
- *Alignment at the operational level*: This aims to achieve the functional integration between the IT infrastructure and applications on the one hand, and the organisational infrastructure and business processes on the other hand. At this level, the business and IT systems are examined from an internal perspective including infrastructures, processes and skills. The administrative infrastructure, organisational processes and skills are considered from the business perspective, whereas the IT architectures, IT processes and skills are considered from the IT perspective.

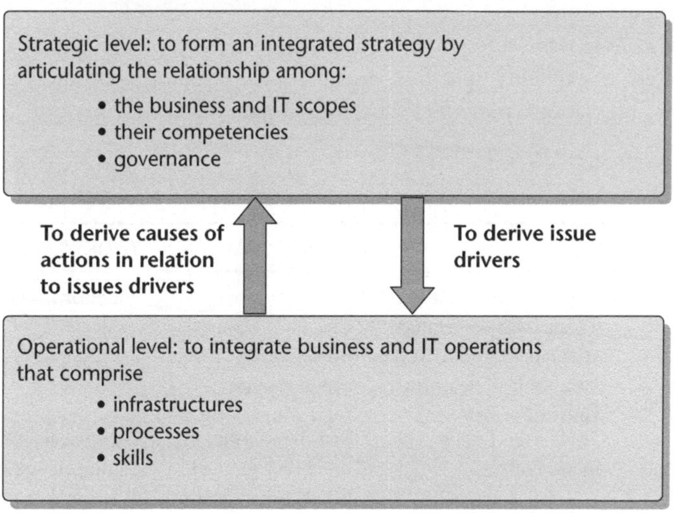

FIGURE 10.8 Two levels of business and IT alignments: strategic and operational

Each of the two levels of alignment seeks IT to fit with the business internally and externally, which allows the enterprise to maximise the business value of its investment in IT. The infrastructural co-design at the strategic level forms an integrated strategy by articulating the relationship between the business and IT scopes, their competencies and governance, while the design at the operational level integrates the business and IT operations.

Organisational co-design: organisational and operational requirements

Co-design at the organisational level analyses the business and IT systems from multiple dimensions consisting of the informal, formal and technical perspectives (Liu *et al.* 2001). Accordingly, the organisation can be designed from an EA perspective consisting of informal, formal and IT systems. Each system can be analysed in terms of organisational requirements and systems requirements, as shown in Table 10.2.

Informal systems requirements are rooted in business practices that include stakeholders, cultures, beliefs and behaviours. The organisational requirements are reflected in the organisational culture, vision, mission and strategies. The operational requirements are described in guidelines and policy documents. Many stakeholders will play roles such as those of an actor, client, provider, facilitator, governing body and/or bystander. However, in this informal part of the organisation, not all processes and procedures are clearly specified. Consensuses are reached mainly through discussions and negotiation; decisions are mainly made based on human interpretation and a justification of the issues in relation to considerations such as organisational values, visions and objectives. In other words, no formally specified rules and procedures can be adopted as the key foundation for making decisions.

Formal systems requirements make up the bureaucracy of the organisation and are reflected as explicitly specified organisational structures, business processes, workflows, regulations and rules. The formal part of the organisation can often

TABLE 10.2 Applying the organisational onion in organisational co-design

	Informal systems	*Formal systems*	*Technical systems*
Organisational requirements	Organisational culture, vision, mission, strategies, articulation of norms (i.e. communication norms, control norms)	Organisational structure, business processes, procedures, regulations	Functions, capability of services
Operational requirements	Guidelines, policy documents	Staff handbook, operating manual, process specification, workflow design	Functional requirements, non-functional requirements, systems design

be specified in a staff handbook, operating manual, process specification or workflow design. Such formalism ensures that the business performs its functions in an orderly and reliable manner. Both the informal and the formal perspective can often only be executed with appropriate support from the technical perspective.

Technical systems requirements represent the capabilities and functions of the IT systems that are required to support business processes and improve business performance. The services and functions of business systems that are supported by IT systems need to be specified as one of the enterprise requirements. The functional and non-functional requirements of a system, as well as its design, need to be specified to guide the IT systems design.

These requirements exist as the three important dimensions of the enterprise. Organisational co-design integrates the informal, formal and technical systems requirements for the business and IT systems, respectively. Design at this stage will provide guidance to specify the way in which the business operates and the IT resources are exploited, as well as the quality of the end products or services.

Operational co-design

The aim of operational co-design is to cover the business and IT systems with regard to business operations and IT functions. Figure 10.9 shows the process of operational co-design, given that the strategic business context has been identified and understood, in which key factors such as the business strategy, location and norms are identified. These will provide the input for the process of operational co-design.

The infrastructural and organisational co-design provides inputs to construct the *strategic business context*, the fundamental concepts for representing an enterprise being defined as follows:

- *Location* defines a business environment (e.g. economic region, culture implication and investment priority) in which the *organisation* is situated. The location may affect resources procured to conduct its business operations.
- *Norms* defines the formal, informal and technical aspects of the organisation and influences organisational behaviour in the form of culture, process and communications. Norms are executed to direct, coordinate and control the business operations in which stakeholders, processes, constraints and resources (including computing resources) are required (Clarke 2001; Liu *et al.* 2003).
- *Strategy* ensures that business operations will be carried out to meet customers' needs as well as the business's expectations in terms of strategic sustainability. Strategy is formulated to ensure that business operations are carried out to achieve a strategic goal and satisfy the end customers' expectations in the market environment.

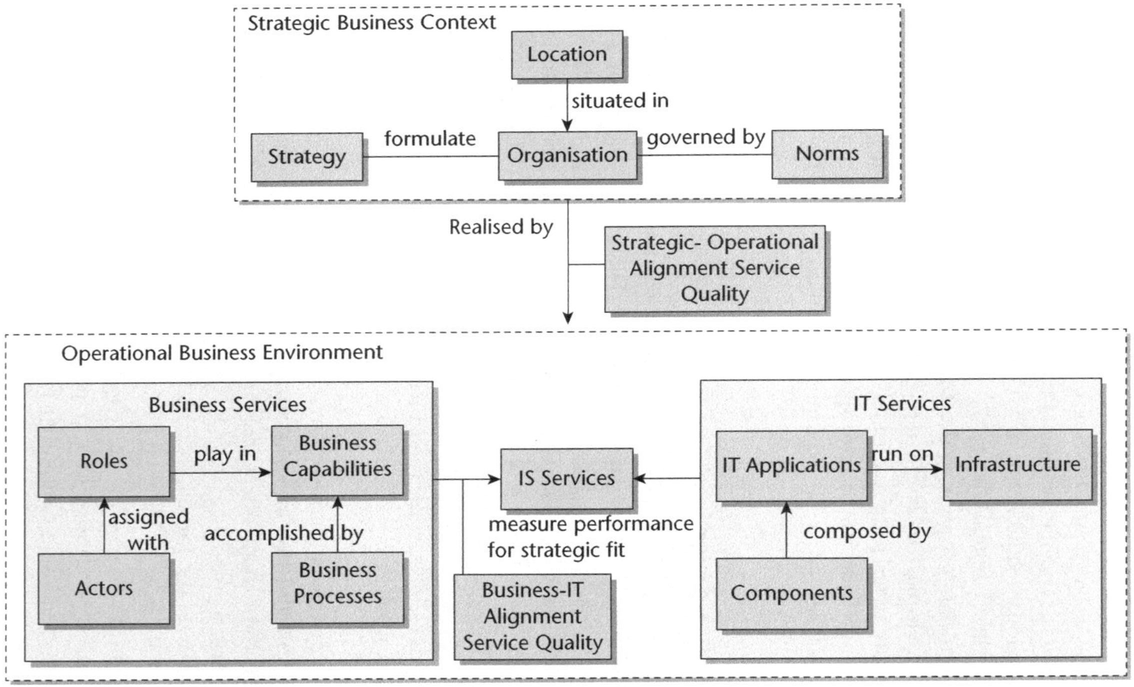

FIGURE 10.9 Operational co-design

Organisation sets out an *operational business environment* based on the strategic business environment. In the business environment, service is a key concept to achieve business and IT alignment in operational co-design as large problems will be broken down into small pieces for specific alignment. The performance of this environment is measured and controlled by the service quality of the strategic–operational alignment, and affects the quality of customer service.

Operational co-design between business services and IT services is conducted in an operational business environment, continuously driven by the requirements of the strategic business environment. Therefore, business services, IT services and IS services are the three key elements in operational business environment:

- *Business services* defines a scope of *business capabilities* that describes how the *organisation* is able to implement the *strategy* to deliver value to its customers. *Business capabilities* are accomplished through *business processes* that formulate a flow of events for how the business service is carried out. Within defined *business capabilities*, the right stakeholders as *actors*, with their *roles* and resources, are engaged in the *business processes* to achieve the strategic goal and objectives. Each stakeholder may participate in the business operation with their own social and cultural background, and their behaviour will be governed by the organisational norms. The *business services* are supported by computing resources (i.e. *IT services*).
- *IT services* comprises IT applications with their corresponding technical *components* and *IT infrastructure*. The IT infrastructure refers to hardware, data storage, networking and security. IT services are driven by business services to achieve specific efficiency and effectiveness.
- *IS services* connect business and IT services together. IS services must *match* the technical logic with the business purposes to optimise these metrics as *IS services* represent the interface between the *IT services* and *business services*. One business service often relates to one or more than one IT service and vice versa. An optimal IS service should assure *business–IT alignment service quality* that should in turn maintain a high *customer service quality*.

Case study: organisational co-design for care pathway management

Complexities in care pathway management

Clinical pathways – also known as integrated care pathways, coordinated care pathways, care maps or anticipated recovery pathways – are task-oriented care plans that detail essential steps in the care of patients with a specific clinical problem and describe a patient's expected clinical course (Coffey *et al.* 1992; Kitchiner and Bundred 1996; Box 10.2).

Box 10.2 Complexity of care pathway: the 'knowing-doing gap'

The complexity of the treatment process is manifested in many ways, including various types of activities, different levels of knowledge and processes, as well as coordination among stakeholders. The core part of the treatment process comprises clinical pathways where various clinical activities are defined in certain sequences. These activities include clinical evaluation, inspection, medication, laboratory tests, surgery and so on, which are formalised in the form of medical documents. These pathways should be patient-specific and dynamic in response to the patient's evolving status. The pathway knowledge is the 'knowing' aspect of the treatment process, but currently this is static in paper-based documents.

On the other hand, each activity in the pathway is also supported by several sub-activities. For example, the laboratory test in the clinical pathway will be supported by several sub-activities such as test requests, reporting, evaluation of the results, recording the results and so on, which are daily routines relying on organisational knowledge and are mostly automated by the current hospital information systems. These are the 'doing' aspect of the treatment process, involving coordination among stakeholders and systems, but they are mostly separate from medical knowledge and the patient's status. Therefore, the treatment processes are composed of the interactions and coordination between various activities at different levels of activity and multiple types of knowledge.

This is what leads to the complexity of clinical pathway management. One major problem resulting from this complexity is the separation of the formal clinical pathway knowledge and the activities supported by the technical information systems in the treatment processes – the 'knowing–doing gap' or 'clinical pathway–guideline implement gap' (e.g. Muscholl 2005). Therefore, an approach that involves designing the business process knowledge and the computer system together is important in order to fill the gap in clinical pathway implementation.

Although the applications of clinical pathways improve the quality of care, the complexity of clinical processes leads to shortcomings in practical treatment. For example, some of the drawbacks are the lack of knowledge-sharing and the inadequacy of computer support for pathway information. Another weakness of clinical pathways is the lack of accuracy of information in the treatment process (Li *et al.* 2013). We will describe here a co-design approach that captures the knowledge in the clinical pathway and designs the pathway management system in parallel to integrate the pathway knowledge seamlessly into the treatment process.

Co-design methodology in care pathways

The co-design methodology is adapted to design the knowledge in the clinical pathway and the integrated management system in parallel, as illustrated in Figure 10.10.

As shown in Figure 10.10, the co-design methodology is composed of three phases: (1) organisational co-design for the problem-scoping at the informal level; (2) organisational and operational co-design of the business and technical systems; and (3) evaluation for refinement. These three phases constitute the design processes where the gaps between business and technology will be minimised, and the integrated system combining pathway knowledge and existing IS will be designed.

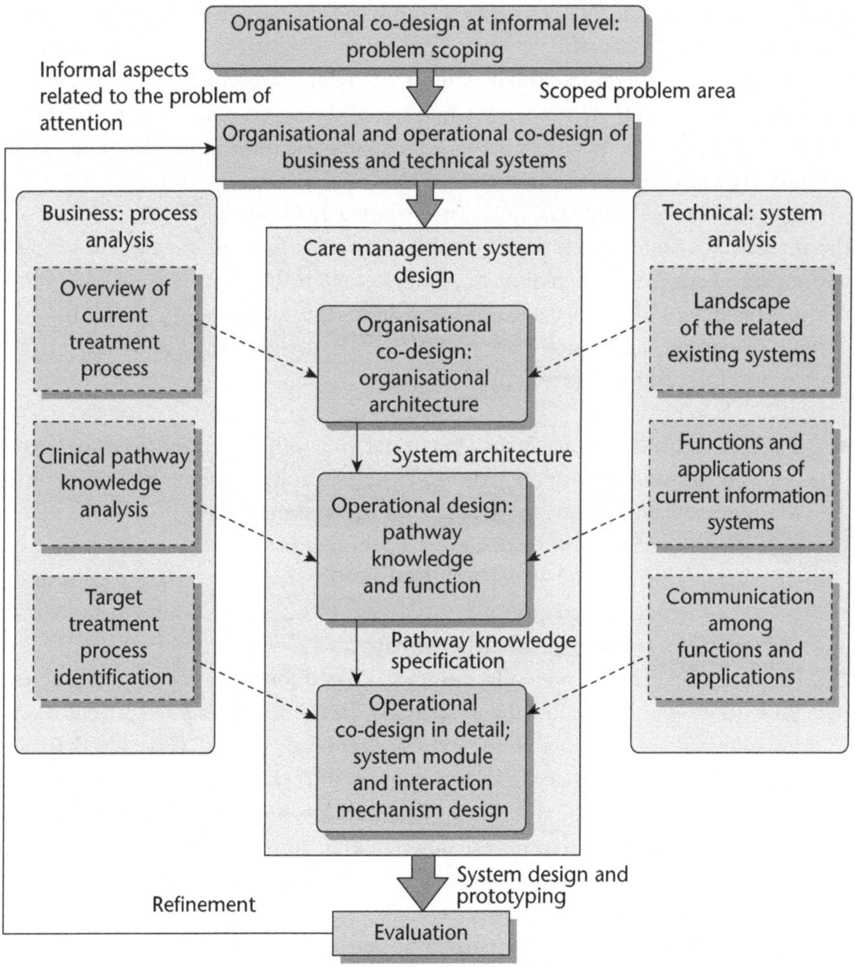

FIGURE 10.10 Co-design of business and technical systems in clinical pathway management (adapted from Li *et al.* 2013)

Organisational co-design for problem-scoping focuses on an understanding of the informal level of the organisation and an identification of the business requirements and the problems that need to be solved. This phase defines the problem space in which organisational practice, stakeholders, culture, patterns of behaviour, strategy and opportunity reside. Together, these define the business needs or problems. In this phase, business problems are analysed and scoped within the context of organisational strategies and practice, culture, stakeholders and patterns of behaviour. The outcome of this phase leads to a prioritised scope of the business issues to be addressed in the co-design. This guides the following co-design process for integrated clinical pathway management.

Furthermore, different informal factors such as the leadership, workforce, language, community engagement, quality improvement and patient safety will influence the provision of care through the business strategy, culture, stakeholders' beliefs and patterns of behaviour. The cultures of patient safety and quality improvement have been identified as the most related informal factors in clinical pathway management. At the same time, methods to promote the patient safety culture to improve the quality of medical provision also need to be identified as the informal part of the integrated system.

Organisational and operational co-design of business and technology systems focuses on the integrated system design tightly coupled with the formal pathway knowledge and technical systems, which aims to seamlessly align the treatment processes and the systems design. The co-design phase includes three stages – organisational co-design, operational co-design and operational co-design with the details of the systems modules and interaction mechanisms:

- *The organisational co-design* takes a structural view of the current treatment process and the landscape of the existing IS in the problem scope. By considering the overview from both the formal and the technical aspects, the integrated systems architecture will be designed combining both aspects as the output of this stage. This is a high-level architecture that leads to an overall picture of how the integrated system supports different levels of the treatment process.
- *The operational co-design* specifies the formal pathway in the form that can be fully supported by the IT services. In this stage, related formal pathways and business knowledge will be identified and analysed. In the meantime, the inventory of functions and applications of the existing technical systems, as well as the corresponding IT services and activities supported by the applications, will also be identified. As a result of considering the two aspects concurrently, the pathway knowledge from related sources in different modalities, for example tacit knowledge, explicit knowledge, experience, recorded discussion and observations, protocols, educational resources and procedures, will be extracted, modelled and specified in forms such as the workflow, activities, norms, rules and constraints that the integrated system and IT services can be aligned to.
- *The operational co-design with the details of systems modules and interaction mechanisms* will lead to a further design of the systems modules and their interactions.

> In this stage, the target treatment processes supported by the integrated system and the ways of communicating between the existing technical systems will be identified and analysed. Furthermore, based on the pathway knowledge specified in the previous stage and the combined view of the formal process and technical communication, the modules and their interaction mechanisms for coordinating different stakeholders and systems applications will be designed. In particular, the interoperability and communication standards within the integrated system and current applications will be considered.

The *evaluation phase* will focus on evaluating the efficacy of the integrated system. The evaluation and the measurement will be conducted using different dimensions of the application domain, leading to a further refinement of the co-design process. The case study method is used to evaluate the integrated clinical pathway management system with regard to the dimensions of technical and medical quality. The technical dimension of the approach will be demonstrated by a trial implementation of the system in the clinical pathway. The impact on medical quality, as well as the cost and efficiency of the treatment process, will also be evaluated through the case study. Co-design methodology is an iterative process; therefore, the evaluation result will be used to refine the integrated system from problem-scoping to system modules design.

The outcome of organisational and operational co-design for care pathway management

Organisational co-design

The outcome of organisational co-design for care pathway management is shown in Figure 10.11. The systems architecture for the integrated clinical pathway management is proposed based on organisational semiotics and organisation co-design architecture that regards IS as a part of the organisation. In this architecture, the informal level where the practical treatment process happens, the specified formal pathway knowledge and the technical healthcare IT systems are integrated in order to provide seamless support for the knowledge pathway at every step of treatment process, as well as to coordinate the multidisciplinary team in the care process.

Informal culture of patient safety where practical treatment processes happen

In order to improve medical quality throughout the integrated system, the informal level where practical treatment processes happen will be consolidated by promoting the patient safety culture. Therefore, the shared beliefs and values for treating patients safely and successfully will be established at this level. This further enables a cohesive culture of high medical quality and impacts on health professionals' behaviour throughout the treatment processes.

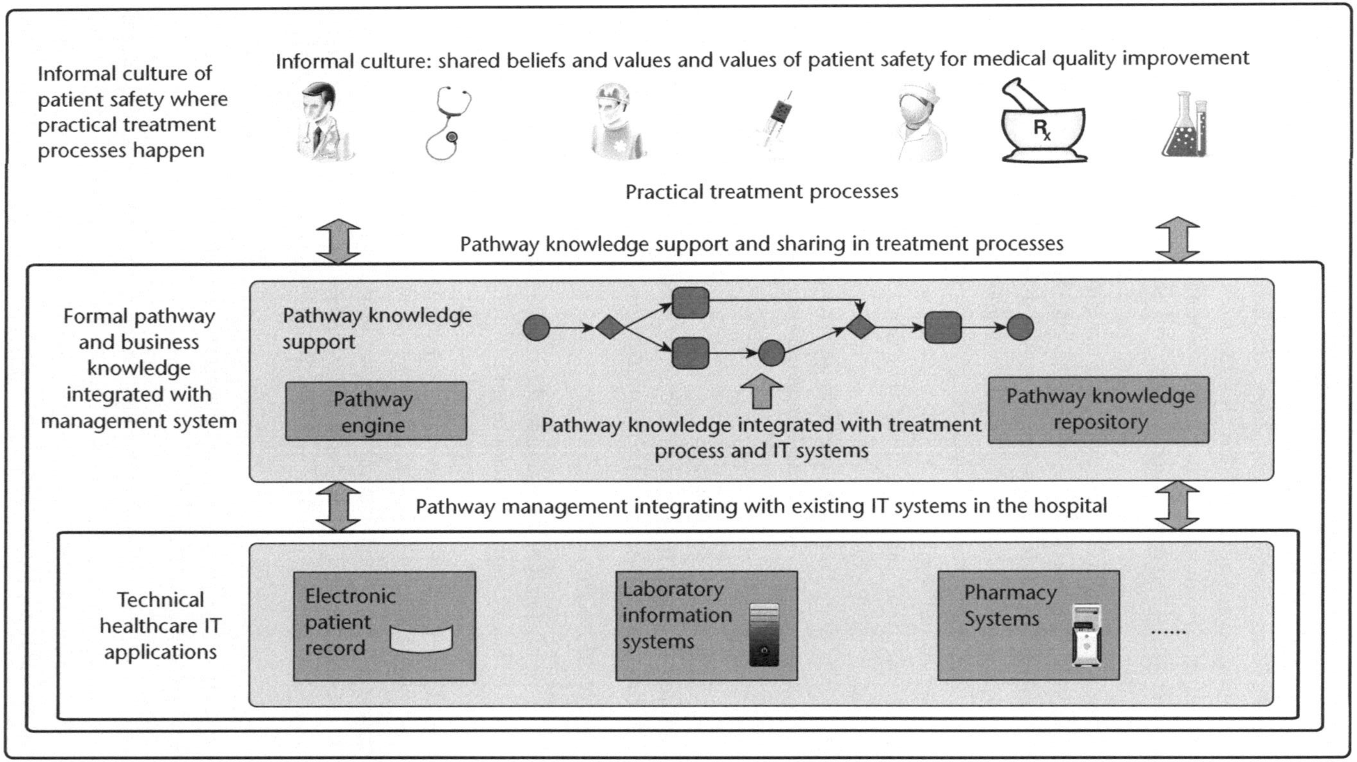

FIGURE 10.11 Organisational co-design for care pathway management. RIS, radiology information systems

New strategies to improve medical quality and updated guidelines for implementing the clinical pathway can be seen as the informal actions applied to improve medical quality. The changing strategy and guidelines could help to promote a culture of reducing medical errors. For example, staff in all departments of the hospital could be encouraged to improve their prescribing and recording accuracy by being more specific and detailed.

Formal pathway and business knowledge integrated with the management system

The formal level in the middle with the specified pathway and business knowledge plays a central role, both supporting the informal treatment process and connecting with the current IS. At this level, pathway knowledge is specified in the business knowledge repository, and the pathway engine supports the treatment process based on predefined knowledge and patient information. Together, these provide healthcare staff with pathway information at the informal treatment process level and support the execution of each step, as well as cooperation within the treatment team.

Technical healthcare IT applications

The formal pathway and business knowledge is also integrated with the existing healthcare IT systems in the technical level. The pathway engine communicates with various IS according to different activities during execution of the pathway. In addition, by integrating with current systems, the pathway engine is able to provide appropriate pathway information based on real-time treatment information for healthcare staff at the informal treatment level. Here, we will focus on the co-design of the formal clinical pathway knowledge and the integrated pathway management system.

Operational co-design of clinical pathway and IT system

In the management environment for the operational clinical pathway, co-design is conducted between *clinical pathway services* and *IT services*. As shown in Figure 10.12, the clinical pathway encompasses the business services that describe how healthcare professionals plan treatment for a certain disease. It is extracted from a different source of business knowledge, which is predefined as guidance for healthcare professionals. The clinical pathway services define a scope of business capabilities including medication, clinical evaluation, nutrition, observation, nursing, surgery, consultation, inspection and testing. These capabilities are accomplished through business processes that formulate a flow of clinical events relating to how the clinical pathway service is carried out.

The operational environment of the clinical pathway usually involves the main IT services in a hospital, such as the management of inpatient and outpatient

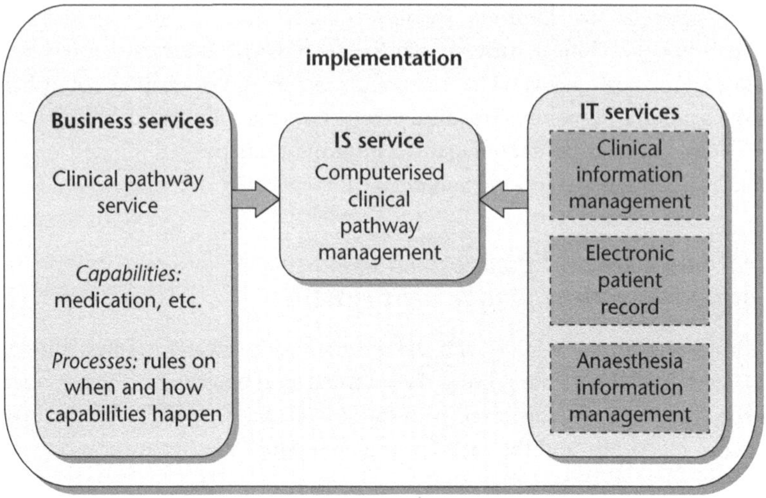

FIGURE 10.12 Operational co-design of clinical pathway services and IT services

information, clinical information management, anesthesia information management and pharmacy information management, management of patient records and so on. The IT services have their own applications (e.g. clinical information services including laboratory tests, radiology information systems, pathology and the management of inspection information) with their servers and data storage, as well as a network of intranet and internet systems. However, these IT services are separate from each other, which means they can only support certain business capabilities of the clinical pathway (e.g. pharmacy information management supports the business capability relating to medication), and they are not able to combine together to achieve a whole clinical pathway.

The *computerised clinical pathway management service* is the IS service that connects the business services and IT services. The IS service on one hand connects with the clinical pathway on the business side, and on the other hand matches the technical logic with IT services. Therefore, the design of the IS service will contribute to the alignment of the pathway knowledge with the hospital IT systems, where the computerised clinical pathway is available to advise personalised treatment guidance based on specific patients. Furthermore, it enables a dynamic collaboration between the IT services to support the seamless integration of pathway knowledge into the system-supported treatment process. This helps to narrow the 'knowing–doing gap' in the implementation of the clinical pathway.

System modules and interaction mechanism through operational co-design

The system modules and their interaction mechanism are designed through the operational co-design process (as shown in Figure 10.13). They are designed to implement the system architecture and to achieve an alignment between the business and IT systems at the operational level. The system modules are divided into

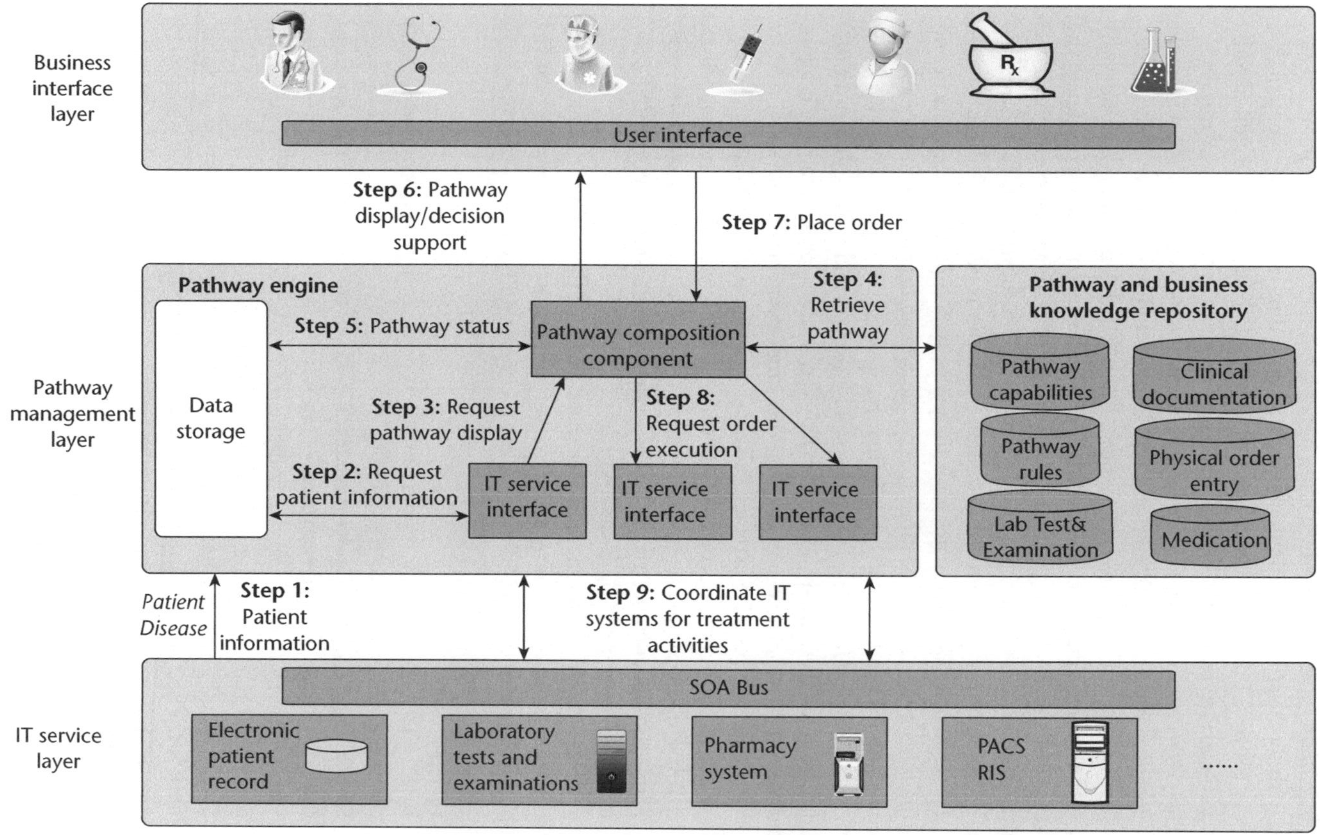

FIGURE 10.13 The result of the operational co-design: system modules for care pathway management

three layers: the interface layer that supports the treatment process, the pathway management layer and the data source layer.

The *business interface layer*, which is the upper layer, is designed to support interactions with the healthcare staff in the business services dimension of the practical care pathway process. This allows healthcare staff to access knowledge in the clinical pathway and guidance related to pathway execution in terms of the practical processes.

The *pathway management layer* is the key component that realises the alignment between the business and IT services. This layer includes the pathway knowledge repository where all the pathway and business knowledge is stored, and the pathway engine that implements the knowledge in order to guide and coordinate the execution of the treatment process. The *pathway composition component* enacts the clinical pathway based on the pathway knowledge in the repository and recommends the appropriate treatment activities according to a patient's health status. The *IT service interface* collaborates with the pathway composition component and information service and applications to execute certain capabilities in the pathway by collecting data and exchanging information.

In the *IT services layer*, the existing hospital IT services and applications constitute the data source layer. Many treatment activities such as prescribing medication, undertaking laboratory tests and carrying out surgical operations are supported by the existing IT systems. The latter are the data source for patient treatment activities and are derived from heterogeneous IS. In order to overcome these heterogeneities, the SOA is adopted in the data source layer, which breaks the functions of the existing IS into components that are viewed as services using a unified protocol security guarantee and loose coupling interface.

Figure 10.14 also shows the *interaction mechanisms* of the pathway management system in guiding the execution of the clinical pathway by integrating the pathway and business knowledge into the treatment process and IT services. This occurs in several steps:

- Step 1: The hospital's IT services (e.g. physician or nurse workstations) send the new patient data into data storage.
- Step 2: The IT service interface retrieves and collects patient information from the data storage as a pathway case.
- Step 3: The IT pathway service component invokes the pathway composition to perform retrieval of the pathway knowledge.
- Step 4: The IT service interface retrieves the corresponding pathway information, including all the clinical facts and rules, from the knowledge repository.
- Step 5: The pathway composition component sends the corresponding pathway information and updates the pathway status in the data storage.
- Step 6: The pathway composition component displays the clinical pathway information to the physician to guide the execution of the treatment process.

These six steps ensure the support of decisions taken in the clinical pathway information based on a patient's situation during the treatment process. Steps 7–9 further integrate the pathway information with existing IT systems to execute treatment activities:

- Step 7: Based on the recommended pathway information, physicians select or enter their medical orders (e.g. test, inspection, etc.) via a user interface.
- Step 8: The pathway composition component invokes the IT service interface to send a message to the IT applications in order to execute the treatment orders.
- Step 9: The IT service interface sends messages to the corresponding information applications to execute these medical orders in the treatment process.

Questions and exercises

1. What business pressures are related to environmental, organisational and technological factors? Use examples to explain your answer.
2. The term 'co-design' is originally rooted in user-centric and participatory design in which design professionals empower, encourage and guide users to develop solutions for themselves. Discuss this difference using co-design of the business and technology framework, and think about how to implement this framework in infoIS.
3. The co-design framework can be used in different areas of IS from systems design to the evaluation of IT strategies. Discuss how the co-design framework guides the activities in information system projects, for example requirements engineering, systems design and evaluation.
4. Discuss the possible challenges encountered when conducting co-design in systems development. Think about possible issues in informal sub-systems (e.g. culture) and what methods are suitable for conducting an infrastructural co-design.
5. What are the roles of the enterprise architect? What are the distinctions between an enterprise architect and a solutions architect?

11

CASE STUDY 1

Systems planning for police organisations

This chapter aims to provide an example of information systems planning. Aligning business and information technology (IT) strategies is often a key part of information systems planning. This example presents a semiotic approach that treats IT systems as an integral part of the business organisation. The applicability of the semiotic framework in e-government, particularly in an evolvable architecture for e-policing, is discussed in this chapter. The implementation of the national Information Systems Strategy for the Police Service and the Crime Justice Information Technology community is evaluated to demonstrate how organisational semiotics is practised in system planning in industry.

Organisational and technological context

e-Government and e-policing

e-Government

Drawing experience from e-commerce and e-business in industry, the advocates of e-government agree that its aims should not be cost-saving, but other more profound benefits. The United Nations Public Administration Network (UNPAN 2012) has suggested that expanding the usage of e-service will help to realise the full benefits of a government service. The perceived benefits of e-government can be summarised as follows (Pacific Council for International Policy 2002; National Office for the Information Economy 2003; Organisation for Economic Co-operation and Development [OECD] 2003; Alshehri and Drew 2011):

- an improvement in services to citizens through a better understanding of users' requirements, thus aiming for seamless online services;

- an improvement in the productivity (and efficiency) of government agencies;
- better transparency and accuracy, the facilitation of information transfer between government and customers, as well as the sharing of information and ideas between all government agencies and departments to build one mega-database;
- a strengthening of the legal system and law enforcement;
- the promotion of priority economic sectors;
- the creation of new business and work opportunities;
- an improvement in the quality of life of disadvantaged communities;
- a strengthening of good governance and a broadening of public participation. This will help in building trust between governments and citizens, an essential factor in good governance, by using internet-based strategies to involve citizens in the policy process, illustrating government transparency and accountability.

This list of perceived values represents the vision of governments and organisations in most countries. However, the success of e-government will reply on multiple factors, for example:

- an appropriate telecommunication infrastructure;
- business process re-engineering;
- an integration of IT and business processes;
- citizen participation;
- the readiness of government staff to adopt IT skills in providing e-government services;
- officials' readiness for change.

Of all these, human and organisational factors are more crucial than technological aspects. In 2012, UNPAN conducted a survey on e-government for the people (UNPAN 2012). This survey was prepared in the context of multiple challenges relating to an open, responsive and collaborative government for the people. The survey says that citizens' usage of e-government services (the demand side) has become a priority issue in e-government studies and policy-making (Box 11.1).

Box 11.1 Mini case study: e-government – the Government to Citizen portfolio in USA services

The e-government initiatives aim to serve citizens, businesses, government employees by delivering high quality services more efficiently at a lower price. Instead of expensive "stove-piped" operations, agencies work together to develop common solutions which achieve mission requirements at reduced cost, thereby making resources available for higher priority needs.

(Continued)

(Continued)

USA Services were merged and consolidated into the General Service Administration GSA's Office of Citizen Services in the winter of 2008–09. Therefore, USA Services is now referred to as the Office of Citizen Services (OCS). The Office of Citizen Services at GSA creates a more citizen engaged government by enabling citizens to have easy access to accurate, consistent, and timely information, regardless of the source. OCS ensures that citizens get information and service via their channel of choice, ranging from Internet, phone, email, or print. These channels include the USA.gov and GobiernoUSA.gov portals, as well as a family of other consumer websites such as kids.gov and pueblo.gsa.gov. Currently, OCS is implementing social media and other Web 2.0 technologies to create a collaborative government with a state-of-the-art environment that will accommodate new ways of interacting with the public.

(Source: Office of Management and Budget (OMB) Whitehouse. Executive Summary for E-Government Benefits Report to Congress 2010, United States)

However, according to the survey, the overall level of usage remains relatively low compared with traditional service delivery methods, even in countries that are making greater efforts to enhance take-up, and notwithstanding continued progress in the provision and sophistication of e-government services. Many potential benefits of e-government are thus concealed and have not been fully realised. This presents a major challenge for policy-makers, who need to rethink how public services can be taken up more by citizens so as to help realise the full potential benefits of these services, and therefore contribute to the sustainable development of government services for the people.

In response to this, recommendations for an e-government implementation strategy have been made, with an emphasis on the following aspects (UNPAN 2012):

- designing and providing citizen-centric services with a user focus;
- narrowing the usage divide across and within countries;
- leveraging social media for a greater take-up of e-services;
- using open data for better public service and greater usage;
- increasing public awareness and promoting e-services.

e-Policing

Police forces around the world face unprecedented challenges: the needs to tackle high volumes of crime, address the increasing challenge posed by transnational criminal networks and deal with the ongoing threat of international and domestic terrorism. At the same time, they must meet citizens' increasing expectations of more visible community-oriented policing and greater public transparency and accountability. Moreover, police forces must meet these challenges while reducing costs and resources, improving efficiency and eliminating waste.

Information management supported by information systems plays a crucial role in all policing activities. Effective information management enables the police to reduce costs by minimising waste and duplication. Effective information management can, for example, remove unnecessary recording for officers, enable police forces to share services and systems, allow for a better use of analytics to support cost-based decision-making and ensure that specialist policing skills are utilised effectively in the community.

Information management also increases the effectiveness and performance of policing services in a number of ways. It enables collaboration and information-sharing between police forces and other agencies, supports the use of analytics to strengthen intelligence-led and preventive policing, and enables officers to access critical information remotely. It also helps to increase public confidence in the police by enabling them to engage with the communities they serve through tools, such as crime maps, that help citizens to understand policing operations and hold the police to account (Accenture 2010, 2013).

e-Policing means that the capabilities of information systems become an essential part of police services and capabilities in supporting policing and administrative processes and enabling the delivery of policing services. e-Policing plays an important role in e-government and prepares the police service for the future by engaging citizens, empowering police officers, optimising ways of working, predicting and improving services through analytics, enhancing collaboration and proactively managing change. Information systems deployed in business processes enable police forces to unlock the value of information and improve their efficiency and effectiveness by:

- reducing the cost in terms of time and other resources involved in business processes;
- providing timely access to the high-quality information held by different organisations;
- enabling police forces to share high-quality information securely and effectively with their partners, hence improving the quality of service;
- feeding business and performance analytics that deliver insight to enable improved decision-making and resource allocation.

As an important part of the e-government initiative in the UK, an e-policing programme was set up at the beginning of the twenty-first century to revolutionise the police service and improve the effectiveness of crime prevention and detection by providing the following (Police Information Technology Organisation [PITO] 2002):

- ready access for the public to police information and services through a variety of easy to use, safe and secure channels, including the use of intermediaries;

- information and services of relevance to citizens, particularly to victims of crime, in a timely and efficient manner;
- support for joined-up working across police forces and with other criminal justice agencies and local authorities;
- a better use of information across all police forces and with other criminal justice agencies to support the implementation of the National Intelligence Model and to make policing more effective in combating criminality;
- the collection, exchange and storage of information in a secure and trusted environment;
- flexibility to accommodate new business requirements and to take advantage of changes in technology.

Implementing and rolling out the e-policing programme demands an extension of the traditional police service using the more efficient, more transparent, more citizen-centred business process and underlying technical infrastructure. This requires changes both in the organisational context and in terms of IT systems re-engineering:

- A change is needed in the culture and business processes that have been in place for crime-reporting, intelligence-gathering, crime analysis, command and control, and many other parts of the business.
- An integrated and modernised police IT system needs to be deployed in the business in parallel to the national systems re-engineering and modernisation programmes being introduced into police IT systems throughout the country.

Organisational background: the Police Information Technology Organisation

Historically, more than fifty police forces in the UK independently developed their own IT systems to support their work. Although this process was guided by principles defined by the UK Home Office, it resulted in separate systems with different structures and functions. These IT systems, usually initially developed in the 1980s, are based on dated technologies – some are still running on the terminal–mainframe platform. The Police National Computer (PNC), launched in 1977, provides police forces with the key information needed for crime investigation, usually via direct access via a computer terminal. An important question is now how to deal with these legacy systems to meet the new business requirements in the police and criminal justice systems.

PITO was established as a non-departmental public body in 1997, with the Home Office as its sponsoring department. In 2007, PITO was subsumed into the National Policing Improvement Agency, whose functions were transferred in 2012 into the National Crime Agency, the UK's national law enforcement agency. PITO served its function at the time, with its defined remit to include England, Wales and Scotland. It provided IT and communications systems and services to the police and other criminal justice organisations within the UK. Recognising that 'information and communication technology (ICT) capabilities play a key role in meeting the Government's objectives and the Home Secretary's priorities for policing' (PITO 2003), PITO was leading the strategic planning and implementation of the organisational and technological infrastructure for e-policing. One of the important items on PITO's agenda was the re-engineering and migration of the legacy police information systems to a web-enabled platform that would support online police information exchange and information-processing, and would enable the revolutionary concept of e-policing.

Problem domain analysis

Challenges for police services

Baseline situation

A well-established and fairly efficient business process existed in the UK police service that was being applied in the fifty-three police services throughout the country. This was supported by an underlying technical infrastructure that had been developed in the 1970s–1990s, including:

- a portfolio of core IT systems used in these police forces;
- a substantial data repository in the PNC;
- a backbone of a secure communication network.

A wide range of IT systems has been developed in the last few decades in the forty-three police forces in England and Wales (not counting Scotland), serving thousands of on-duty police officers throughout the UK as well as the criminal justice system (CJS) community. Many of these systems are currently being upgraded with added functionality, while new systems are continuously being developed and rolled out.

The backbone of the IT systems that support policing nationwide is the PNC, which has been in service for thirty years. Over the years, the system has grown to embrace many technological advances, incorporating advice from the government and policing bodies, as well as from in-house and industry technical experts. It has developed from a record-keeping service into a sophisticated intelligence tool. It holds extensive data on criminals, vehicles and property, which is accessible in a matter of seconds through more than 10,000 terminals in police forces across the country (PITO 2003).

The police IT systems and PNC are connected via Police National Network communications that link all police forces, the Home Office and other criminal justice organisations.

Challenges

Although the police–public interface had been improved by the introduction of the Police Portal and in some areas 'one-stop shops', there was no formally agreed strategy to ensure the development and delivery of a coherent programme. Common facilities across the service would only succeed if supported by the introduction of standard business processes. There was a slow adoption of best practice in individual forces, little central promulgation of best practice and little overall programme management function to drive the business process improvements forwards.

More generally, there was only limited interoperability and integration between systems within forces and a low level of data-sharing both between forces and with other criminal justice agencies. This affected the forces' abilities to make best use of the valuable data held throughout the service. While interfacing and business process improvement may be seen as part of the overall Information Systems Strategy or as contained within other programmes of work, the police–public interface programme set the goals for improving these interfaces to deliver all the benefits of e-policing.

There was also little coordination of approaches to common services such as security and presentation of information. A wide range of interfaces with core systems existed as there were no service-wide standards to follow and a plethora of local applications operating in individual forces. As there was no mandate for forces to adopt common systems and standards, there was an inconsistent approach, and the potential for duplication of effort was enormous. Data quality was also variable between forces. These factors impacted on the service's ability to present a 'joined-up' appearance and could not be regarded as cost-effective or as providing best value.

Many of the initiatives of PITO were in the form of studies or pilot projects. There was a danger that the strong messages to come out of these might not be disseminated to forces or embraced by the wider police service, partly because of the absence of an overall strategy and programme management function. Moreover, with the police service as one of the key members of the CJS, it was within PITO's remit to enable a full integration between the police IT systems and other parts of the CJS, so that a seamless collaboration would be achieved. Figure 11.1 shows the key member organisations within the CJS and how information is shared between them (Parsons-Hann 2003).

Business requirements and architecture for e-policing

Various business targets for e-policing were identified by PITO:

- *Communications*: This target aimed to achieve a clear and secure voice and data communication as these are vital to any successful police operation. This area is important because officers rely on it for their own safety and that of their colleagues.
- *Criminal justice*: All police information systems should be able to share information with other CJS systems, and CJS agencies would be provided with access to police systems. IT would hold the key to joining together criminal justice organisations and improving the way they worked together.

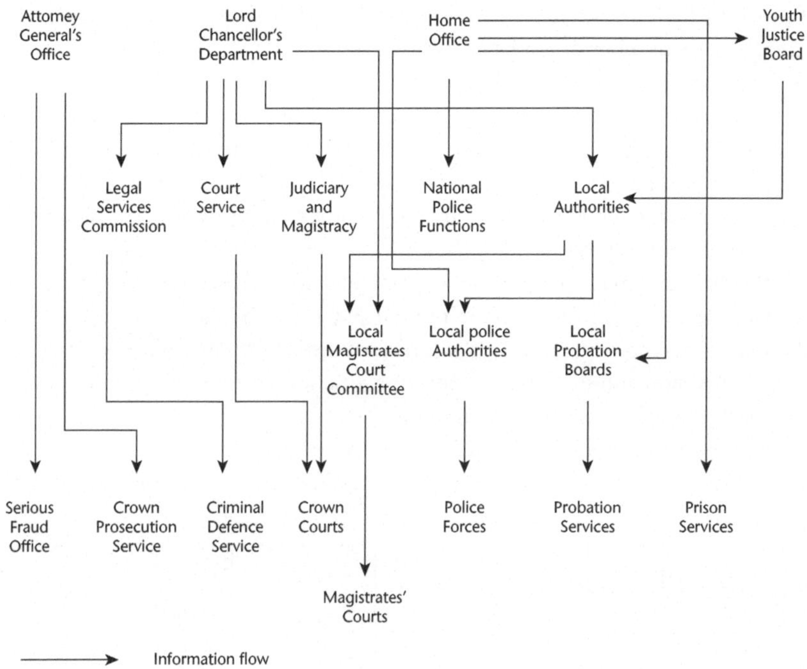

FIGURE 11.1 Information shared between the key members of the criminal justice system

- *Identification*: The ability to identify 'one person from many' is a fundamental concept in policing. Technology should enable the police to do this more quickly and accurately than ever.
- *Intelligence and investigation*: Successful police operations need to be founded on reliable intelligence and sound investigative practice. Collating that intelligence, sharing it with police colleagues and giving them the tools to unlock its potential were key aims in this area.
- *PNC*: The PNC is an unparalleled source of police intelligence available to all forces nationwide. A steady upgrade of the infrastructure and the addition of new databases would be implemented to make sure that the PNC would continue to meet police needs.
- *Police support services*: Improving police efficiency and effectiveness is not all about front-line policing. Forces needed IT applications that would help them to report and analyse their performance and get the most out of the resources they had available.

While the definition of e-policing could at first glance include the whole spectrum of policing, it was appropriate to focus the initial e-policing programme on the police–public interface as that had to be delivered electronically by 2005 to meet the government's targets. This would build on the current police–public interface programme and was consistent with the agreed scope of the Police Service

Information Systems Strategy (code name Valiant), as shown diagrammatically in Figure 11.2. A number of core systems are listed for illustrative purposes only, and not all potential channels for public access are depicted.

For the police–public interface to be effective, there was a requirement for the scope of the e-policing programme to include interconnections between those back-office or legacy systems that were necessary to achieve the vision. The scope would also be extended to include areas of data warehousing so as to make effective use of the information held in the core systems. Apart from the necessary links to back-office systems, all other police core business systems and systems serving staff were considered to be outside the current scope of e-policing. In addition, although e-policing depended on the Criminal Justice Extranet (CJX) for its delivery, the provision and operation of this network was considered to lie outside the scope of the initial e-policing programme.

In the long run, police information systems in the UK would go through the modernisation and transformation process specified by the national Information

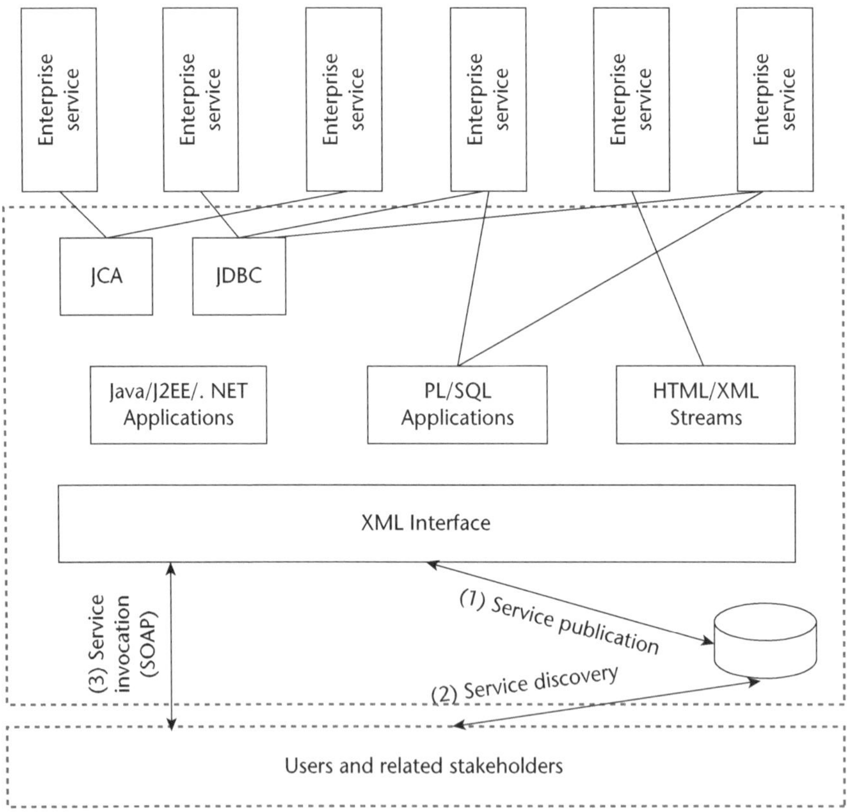

FIGURE 11.2 The Police Services Information Systems Strategy architecture. JCA, Java EE Connector Architecture; JDBC, Java database connectivity; SOAP, Simple Object Access Control

System Strategy. The modernised systems would provide ubiquitous access for police forces and officers. The capability of knowledge-based processing was also required to support effective policing and collaboration between the police and the CJS organisations.

Systems requirements for e-policing

PITO, as a national organisation responsible for IT policies and strategies for the UK police force, had set up many task forces to look into different issues, including the IT infrastructure and functionality of the e-policing systems. As a result of this investigation, it emerged that the environment for future e-policing should include:

- information from all police and criminal justice organisations that was up to date and readily available for use at the point of decision making;
- an enhancement of data- and information-sharing between police forces and national agencies, and between the police and other criminal justice partners;
- the capacity for a coordinated response across police force boundaries using the intelligence generated from multiple information sources;
- a greater capability to tackle serious and major crime;
- more direct, efficient and interactive interfaces between the police and the public;
- common standardised business processes to harness 'best of breed' police systems to support business processes endorsed by the Association of Chief Police Officers (ACPO);
- a business information framework that would point the way to the reuse of such systems (as software components) at a minimum cost within other forces and/or complex processes;
- a common minimum standard for the technical infrastructure, with advancements that were planned and coordinated;
- solutions to address local, regional and national business problems as appropriate.

Many current initiatives were driven by immediate business needs. For example, the online vehicle number plate enquiry system enabled police traffic officers to check vehicle details on the road. On top of all these, a more thorough understanding of police work led to significant changes in the manner and quality of services. Understanding police business processes became the basis for embedding web-enabled technologies into the daily workflow of police forces, which would provide a solid foundation for the e-policing strategies and implementations.

Semiotics diagnosis in strategic planning

In some organisations, such as in a service industry like banking, insurance or consultancy, information-processing may be the core business. In this type of industry, information and services are the products. In other organisations, information-processing and communication exist to support the production of physical goods and other substantive activities. To a large extent, e-government involves a great number of the first type of activities, which produce information. An IT system should be viewed as an integral part of the business organisation, and the design of both the IT and business systems must be conducted simultaneously. The organic integration of IT into the business processes allows both systems to evolve naturally.

An organisation, as an integrated business and IT system, can be seen as an architecture with multiple layers, three of which constitute the technical infrastructure:

- *physical* devices and their interconnections – computer hardware, the network, optical fibres, satellites and so on, which generate and carry a cause-and-effect chain of events quickly and cheaply, across the globe if necessary;
- *signalling* protocols – the validation, authentication and encryption routines that exploit the basic physical phenomena, so that a varied stream of patterns originating in one place can be reproduced, ideally without error, at another place, or corrected in case of error;
- *structures* that enable signals to be combined into messages, analysed into parts (parsed), stored in files, retrieved, used in calculations and recombined into new messages.

The design, implementation and maintenance of these three layers are the tasks of the IT department, whose responsibilities are to make sure that these technical components are functional and adequate to support the business operations.

Three other layers in the system architecture are perhaps more important in conducting business:

- the *meanings* of the numbers, words and expressions that form a message, and the ways in which these meanings are combined to create the meaning of the message as a whole;
- *communicating* the intentions of the message through interaction and negotiation between appropriate actors;
- *social consequences*, in the form of established commitment, obligation and responsibility between the people involved.

All these are close to the core business issues that are related to the business objectives of police operations. Adopting Stamper's semiotic framework (Stamper 1996), the key issues of an IT-embedded system at the six semiotic levels can be summarised as shown in Figure 11.3. On the left of the diagram are suitable names for the levels, the key issues are mentioned in the middle, and on the right are listed the solutions available or approaches to be attempted.

The physical-level solutions are implemented in the form of interconnecting networks of standardised telecommunication devices and computers. It is necessary

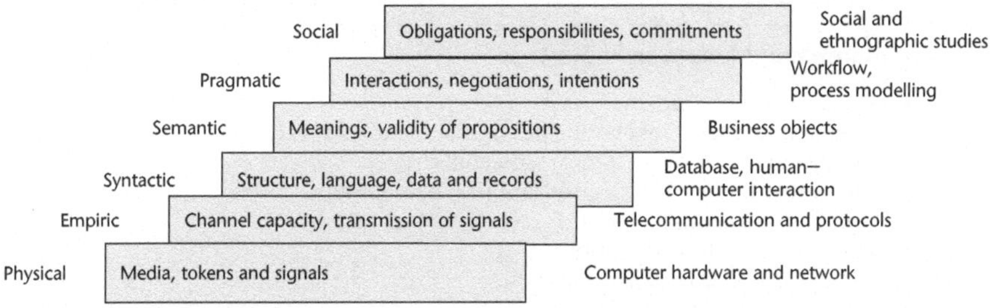

FIGURE 11.3 Key issues of internet-based systems analysed using the semiotic framework

to establish when these are correctly established and when they break down, so the quality of the physical systems can be assured. At the empirical level, various standard communication protocols (such as Transmission Control Protocol/Internet Protocol) can be used to exploit the physical devices. These take care of encoding, switching, error detection and correction, the confirmation of transmission and so on. Like the physical standards, they are established globally.

At syntactic level, it is more difficult to establish global standards. Great efforts have been made in industry to bring in standard forms of communications in computer and information technology, for example Simple Object Access Control and Universal Description, Discovery and Integration in web services. Some standards have been established, but it is difficult to agree on global solutions, and the standards tend to be modified at the local level according to the industry's business norms.

Assessment of the strategic plan: e-policing strategies

In this section, the semiotic framework (Figure 11.3) will be used to evaluate the design and implementation of the IT infrastructure for e-policing.

To meet the requirements for e-policing, PITO developed a strategic framework to address the challenges of organisational and technological issues, and the management of expectations and the implementation of infrastructure. The strategic framework for e-policing illustrated in Figure 11.4 comprises five component strategic areas:

- the Governance and Management Strategy;
- the Applications Strategy;
- the Information and Content Management Strategy.
- the Enabling Services and Infrastructure Strategy;
- the Procurement and Implementation Strategy.

This framework summarises all the important aspects of the current practice of design and implementation of the organisational and technological infrastructure for e-policing. An analysis based on organisational semiotics is provided below to evaluate the e-policing framework by examining its methodological underpinnings.

Governance and Management Strategy

- Organisational structure
- National and local responsibilities of ACPO, ACPOS, PITO and forces for e-policing systems and information content
- Integrated Project Teams and National Focus Groups
- Top-level policies, procedures, measurement and controls
- Long-term strategy development

Applications Strategy

- Applications portfolio/priorities
- Corporate systems and services
- Local initiatives
- e-policing migration strategy
- Interoperability and integration requirements

Information and Content Management Strategy

- Branding and style guides
- Information content creation and management
- Collection and validation of data
- Database management and data warehousing

Enabling Services and Infrastructure Strategy

- Central service provision
- Multichannel supporting infrastructure
- Networking and communications
- Integration with Forces
- Technical standards (inc. web browsers)
- Technology innovation

Procurement and Implementation Strategy

- Procurement and development of e-policing systems
- Catalogue of services – national and local
- Planning, implementation and management of e-policing systems

FIGURE 11.4 The strategic framework of e-policing

Governance and Management Strategy – the social aspect

In the planning and implementation of the IT infrastructure, governmental requirements and the commitment of the police organisations to UK society were seen as the fundamentals. The Governance and Management Strategy covers the following:

- the organisational structure to support e-policing;
- top-level policies, procedures and controls;
- the development of the long-term strategies for e-policing;
- the responsibilities of different government agencies and each individual force in e-policing.

A semiotic analysis

As suggested by the semiotic framework, the design of any information systems infrastructure must start from a definition of responsibilities, obligations and commitments. The strategic framework for e-policing is consistent with this theory by putting the Governance and Management Strategy as the fundamentals. e-Policing requires a full collaboration between the police forces and other criminal justice services. The technologies deployed are only part of the infrastructure, but coordination and collaboration between all the organisations involved is more essential in a functional e-policing infrastructure. Guided by the top-level policies and a definition of responsibilities, collaborative work processes between agencies, institutions and forces is building an organisational foundation, while modern technologies can enhance collaborative e-policing.

Applications Strategy – the pragmatic aspect

To meet the vision for e-policing, the single biggest challenge was to move from a systems developments environment that was police based to a citizen-centric business model. In the traditional model, the central customer office acts on behalf of police forces by establishing the service requirements and priorities for development. The focus of e-policing at the police–public interface necessitates an extension of this role to capture citizens' expectations as well.

In the first instance, developments were to be prioritised based on the recent consultation exercise with all forces and ratified by the Central Customer and the EPMG team. PITO would continue to manage the central programme portfolio including the systems, services, infrastructure and common practices. Some systems and services within the central e-policing programme portfolio would be provided locally by the forces.

The Applications Strategy would be developed to include:

- a strategy for corporate systems and services in e-policing, and local initiatives;
- an e-policing migration strategy;
- a specification of interoperability and integration requirements to meet the long-term e-policing strategy.

A key issue was to determine what should be provided centrally and what could be considered at a local level. The proposed strategy for systems and services to be provided centrally would be based on the premise that these would provide:

- corporate single points of contact for the public to engage electronically with the police service; or
- e-policing systems and services that were generic to the police service as a whole and could be replicated across police force boundaries.

The e-policing business process model is shown in Figure 11.5. Citizens' expectations, as seen in the model, are the fundamentals to determine the criteria for technical and service performance. These criteria are then applied to the measurement of current services, systems, practices and infrastructure.

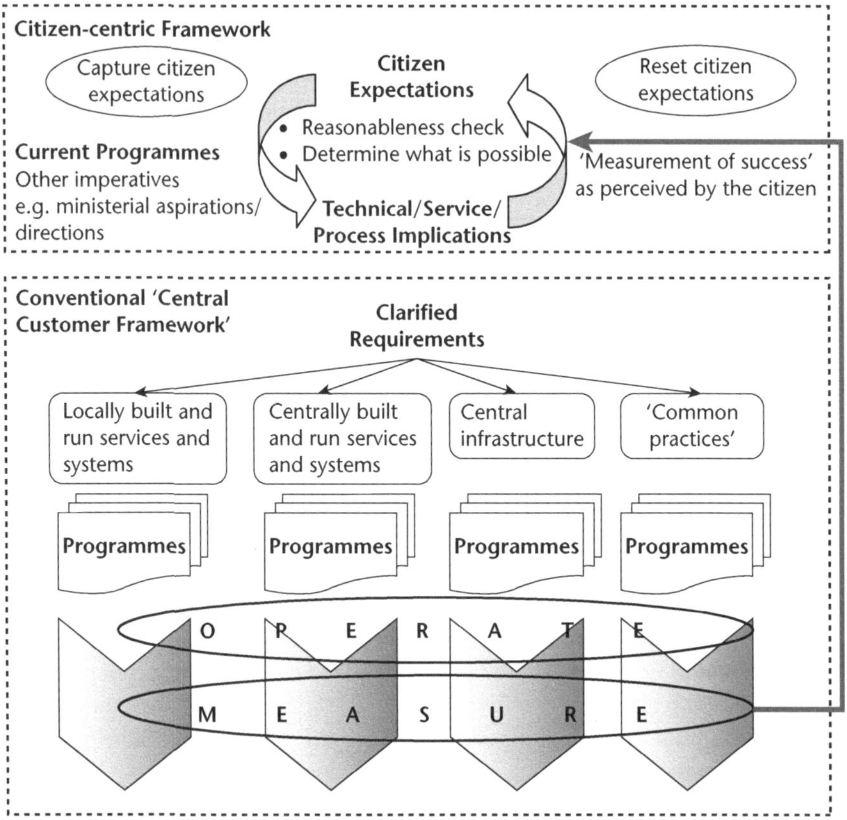

FIGURE 11.5 An e-policing business process model

A semiotic analysis

The Applications Strategy covers the issues identified in the pragmatic aspect. It takes into account the different perspectives of the various stakeholders and aims to achieve effectiveness of the integrated systems. The strategy considers how the systems and services interact with citizens as well as other users (i.e. police officers and CJS staff). Measuring the systems and services leads to an identification of the possible gaps between what is expected and what is available with the current infrastructure, which may lead to an identification of further improvements and solutions to reduce the gaps.

Information and Content Management Strategy – the semantic aspect

An overall strategy for the management of data submitted by citizens and the provision and updating of published information was to be developed. This strategy was to be provided to the forces as a 'toolkit' to ensure that a generic framework was used in information and content management throughout the forces. For the majority of the projects within the police–public interface programme, the information and content management was to be the responsibility of the forces following policies and procedures issued by ACPO and the Association of Chief Police Officers of Scotland (ACPOS) and the EPMG team within PITO. Part of the planning, design and training for each project was to focus on this important area.

The strategy would focus on the branding of police service websites and other electronic display facilities so that the public could gain assurance of the ownership of the information and the security of the communication channels used. Other aspects of content and information management would also be covered in this strategy, including responsibility for the collection and validation of data through e-policing channels, database management and data warehousing as it affects e-policing, and the creation and management of the content published electronically by the police service.

A semiotic analysis

The Information and Content Management Strategy addresses issues at the semantic level. Information content, meaning and validity are the essence for all systems that provide information and services, as described in the semiotic framework. Information should be provided in a timely manner and shared by the relevant stakeholders. The quality of information provision directly affects the quality of police services through e-policing. As shown by experience in many information systems development projects, the semantics of information presents the most challenges as it is difficult to capture in information models and to represent in information systems. Effective methods for dealing with information semantics have to be identified and deployed in the implementation of the e-policing infrastructure.

Enabling Services and Infrastructure Strategy – the syntactic and empiric aspects

In order that the public might be encouraged to use the Police Portal and other channels in providing often sensitive information to the police, and for the police service to make better use of the information in its possession in combating criminality, a suitable resilient multichannel supporting infrastructure was to be provided.

The strategy to be developed for enabling services and infrastructure was a key component in the delivery of trusted, secure and joined-up e-policing services. It was to include strategies for:

- the provision of central services (e.g. web hosting, common directories);
- a communications infrastructure to support multiple channels (e.g. channel strategy);
- integration with local force infrastructures (e.g. browser interface standards).

A backbone communications infrastructure, CJX, was in place linking all forces, and the Police Portal was to be connected to it. This would ensure a secure routing of data traffic and the ability of forces to share information. Forces were to be responsible for compliance with data protection legislation, conformance to system security policies and the observance of the Government Protective Marking Scheme. The accreditation of other criminal justice agencies to use CJX would continue to be the responsibility of ACPO. The requirement for and viability of adopting the replacement government-wide secure communications network being delivered under GSISP, as the principal communication network for the police service or for connecting CJX to it, was to be assessed centrally at the appropriate time.

While the strategy was being developed, additional features were to be provided through the Police Portal, and police forces were to become more dependent on it. As the Police Portal was supporting operational policing, a rigorous testing of new features was necessary prior to their introduction in a live environment, and resiliency was to be introduced to ensure its continuous availability.

PITO was well placed to provide information and guidance to forces wishing to link their systems into the e-policing infrastructure. There was a series of national focus groups already in existence, which were used to review elements of this framework to accommodate e-policing as a priority covering policy and role issues across a range of topics. For example, guidance notes were provided to cover the following:

- security elements to be considered across all channels;
- the technical and architectural standards to be adopted;
- the infrastructure installed to provide the recommended functionality that would be used;
- standards for interfaces to back-office legacy systems (e.g. web browsers);
- performance measures and targets for the fulfilment of citizens' enquiries and the commitments made;
- business process standards (e.g. call centre procedures and practices, data quality, data validation and data-cleansing);
- presentation standards for police websites (e.g. branding, image and style guides);
- the protection of information and codes of practice.

In the longer term, the whole premise, in line with modernising government, would be to provide choices. There was no desire to limit the public's use of any channel to access e-policing services. A national channel strategy would be developed, and it was the intention to provide choices for the public in being able to access police services through a range of channels including:

- the Police Portal;
- internet websites;

- one-stop shops;
- kiosks;
- call centres;
- digital telephony including text messaging;
- intermediaries (e.g. local authority staff);
- face-to-face contact (e.g. at police stations).

It was important to develop and maintain coherence between the channels so that an individual could choose to use different channels (e.g. the internet to report a minor crime, the telephone to report additional information and SMS text messaging to enquire about progress), while the police officer responding was made fully aware of all the information received to date through all channels. This was a central feature of the commercial call centre and client relationship models and has important reference value for integration with the back-office systems.

e-Policing services delivered through the Police Portal were to continue to be provided centrally, but the content for specific features was being requested to be provided and maintained locally. The use of internet websites by police forces was to be encouraged to provide information and discrete services that would be better handled at a local level. Consideration would be given to the provision of a national web-hosting service, and to standardising the appearance and the function of police force websites. It was the intention to recommend a form of branding to enhance the appreciation of the police service as a whole and to provide guidance on the overall appearance and functional content of the websites. Links through to police force websites would be provided on the Police Portal and vice versa.

It may be appropriate for one-stop shops, kiosks and call centres to be operated on a joint agency basis, and the use of intermediaries would be encouraged where it was to the advantage of both parties (e.g. abandoned vehicles or noise nuisance), did not compromise security and was likely to provide a higher level of service to the public (e.g. in rural areas). Police forces would determine locally with their partners the most effective and efficient method of providing these facilities.

The provision of conventional face-to-face contact and telephone services locally would be supplemented by a shared non-emergency telephone number if proven by the concept demonstrator. Calls would be routed to the local force for response. Additionally, the provision of a single number for text messaging was being considered and was at an early stage of investigation. In the long term, to ensure that e-policing was citizen-centric, all channels would be supplemented by strong links with back-office systems. Due to the disparate nature of these legacy systems, local forces had to provide interfaces with systems that have been developed in-house.

The key decisions required were the extent to which e-policing in the long term moves towards a fully functional customer relationship management environment. This would determine the extent of the citizen focus provided, the integration with back-office systems required and the data warehousing facilities needed. Customer relationship management implies potential intelligence-gathering opportunities, and we needed to be aware of the implications of this, particularly with regard to the customer relationship. Assuming that full citizen-centric capability was required, the integration strategy would provide a road map for the two-stage migration from the current CJX-connected forces to:

- limited interoperability with back-office systems in forces as required for the first phase of e-policing;
- a full integration of core systems, data warehousing and e-policing applications as envisaged in the Police Service Information Systems Strategy (Valiant).

It was recognised that for many years forces would be at different stages on their migration towards the fully integrated solution. The integration strategy would be developed as part of the ACPO Information Systems Strategy and the need to cater for the diversity of local infrastructures and systems, together with the expectation that different elements of the police community would migrate at different speeds to the centrally provided infrastructure.

A semiotic analysis

The Enabling Services and Infrastructure Strategy covered the issues relating to the syntactic and empiric aspects. It defined standards for data structure, information exchange, communication between systems, and interfacing between application layers and back-office or legacy systems. Channels for accessing police services and information sources were also defined, for example, the Police Portal, internet websites, call centres and digital message exchanges. The appropriate syntactic and empirical setting provided the necessary basis for the correct representation of semantics.

Procurement and Implementation Strategy – the physical aspect

PITO took responsibility for implementing the centrally provided and managed projects within the overall e-policing programme for the police–public interface. Police forces were expected to provide project management for local implementations and initiatives. During the implementation, business continuity was a priority, and the migration to new systems was to be achieved in a manner commensurate with maintaining operational capability at all times. PITO assisted the forces in training for new systems and aimed to provide support to local initiatives, taking into consideration the fact that forces would be at different stages in their adoption of e-policing techniques.

A semiotic analysis

The Procurement and Implementation Strategy was concerned with the physical aspects of the e-policing infrastructure. PITO had deliberately allowed freedom for the individual forces to choose their own hardware platforms, as long as syntactic and empirical standards that enabled the correct representation and interpretation of information semantics were reinforced. This separation between the physical platforms and the other aspects of the semiotic framework maximised the flexibility for systems changes. As witnessed in many cases, the need for systems changes arose from both the changes in business requirements and the technologies available. The separation between the hardware platforms and the other aspects of the e-policing infrastructure enabled the whole set of integrated systems to evolve with the least number of unnecessary interruptions to the other areas.

Discussions and outlook

PITO, as an organisation responsible for the UK's IT strategies, policies and advice on IT systems implementation at the time, played an important role in the organisational and technological infrastructure for e-policing in the UK. In this project, an input was drawn from the research work of other e-government and e-policing projects such as the US Criminal Justice Integrated Team and Intelligence Service, and the Dutch and Belgian police forces. An emphasis was placed on the co-design of business and IT technology using the semiotic framework in the analysis of e-policing strategy.

A business organisation is composed of people and technology. People are teamed up in a certain structure, have defined responsibilities and are governed by norms (rules and regulations). From the perspective of organisational semiotics, these organisations produce and consume information, and are therefore information systems. The organisational as well as technological components of such information systems have to be co-designed so that the technologies are best fitted into the workflows and business processes. The semiotic framework offers a guideline in analysing and designing information systems by carefully examining the issues at the six semiotic levels.

e-Government involves a large group of stakeholders: government and non-government personnel, service providers and users from all sectors of society. The key 'product' and 'commodity' is information, which will be produced and consumed by the government and citizens (note that both will be providers and consumers as the interactions can be bi-directional). Understanding the nature and characteristics of information is crucial for the design and implementation of e-government systems, and is also necessary for the effective use of information both in the provision of the service and in the response to it. These services are different from those in the traditional form of governance but should supposedly be equivalent socially and legally. Delivering and enjoying the information-based service through e-government will require an integrated social, legal and technical system that encompasses the technical infrastructure, government and citizens. This system should be built on a sound technical and non-technical basis, covering all semiotic aspects.

The advantage of semiotic analysis in information systems planning lies in the completeness of examining all aspects of strategies of information systems in an organisational context. Semiotic analysis regards systems planning as the hand-in-hand planning of both technical systems and business systems. The effectiveness of systems planning relies heavily on the alignment between IT and business. Organisational semiotics provides a holistic view of planning how IT platforms serve technical business operations as well as human information functions supporting the social dimensions of business activities. The semiotic analysis of the e-policing strategy examined the completeness of the strategy by considering the interests of different stakeholders. It shows that the e-policing strategic framework satisfactorily covers a range of issues as illustrated in the semiotic framework.

Questions and exercises

1. Identify examples of information systems in different application domains (naming the systems if preferred), for example:
    - e-government
    - e-learning
    - e-health.
2. Give examples of the tasks performed in information systems design for each layer of the semiotic framework. Identify who is likely to perform those tasks.
3. Discuss the challenges inherent in strategic planning and discuss how semiotic diagnosis can be used in different industries (e.g. manufacturing, banking, logistics or healthcare) in addition to policing.
4. Discuss and identify specific analysis techniques that could support and enrich the semiotic diagnosis at different stages of an information systems project in an organisation.
5. The semiotic framework provides the fundamental concepts of sign for communication at different levels. Interoperability can be seen as the ability of information systems to produce effective communication between different systems or organisations. Discuss how the interoperability of information systems can be assessed and diagnosed using the semiotic framework.

12

CASE STUDY 2

Legacy systems re-engineering for university libraries

Legacy information systems are often part of an organisation's assets. Some of them play an important role in serving the organisation. From time to time, however, there is a need to improve these information systems to produce a better performance or better interoperability with other systems. It is sometimes necessary to re-engineer these systems. Organisational semiotics and methods have been used in such applications. This chapter illustrates an organisational semiotics approach to legacy systems re-engineering in a university library in which the three key Methods for Eliciting, Analysing and Specifying Users' Requirements methods – the problem articulation method (PAM), semantic analysis method and norm analysis method – were applied.

Background

Legacy systems

As business scopes expand and business processes change, many information technology (IT) systems become inadequate in terms of their capacity and functionality. However, these 'legacy systems' may provide critical information and essential support for business operations as many of them have long been integrated into the core business processes and therefore cannot be simply scrapped.

Unlike routine software maintenance, the modernisation of typical legacy systems involves coarser grained, higher level and structural changes that can be realised by a combination of renovation activities from both bottom up and top down. While the former approach reconstructs the system design by analysing the source code, the top-down methods treat the system as a black box and examines 'the inputs and outputs of a legacy system within an operating context' (Seacord *et al.* 2003: 9), which is preferable for achieving a high-level understanding of the systems.

An organisational semiotics approach to systems re-engineering

This case study is based on a research project on Analysing and Modelling the Behaviour of Legacy Systems (AMBOLS) (Liu *et al.* 1999a, 1999b). The project aims to deliver a set of methods for recovering user requirements for a legacy system through an observation of the system and its users' interactions with the system during operation, and by interviewing its stakeholders about what capabilities it provides to them.

The derivation is to be made under the assumption that nothing but the operational system and its users are capable of providing the relevant information. We assume that any documentation, including source codes, is out of date or inaccurate. We also assume that there is no one available who has insight in terms of a technical knowledge of the system. These conditions are common in commerce and government. Our aim in the project is to construct a top-down, black-box, reverse requirements engineering approach.

The AMBOLS approach is useful for enhancing or replacing systems. The recovered legacy system requirements can serve as a reference point for the new systems to ensure that the new technical solutions surpass the old legacy systems. The old requirements can be used as a basis for a validation of the new requirements, and can also enable the developers to learn from the experience and lessons of the old systems.

The AMBOLS approach to requirements recovery

Based on organisational semiotics, an IT system is an integral part of an organisation, and the system's functions are governed by the organisational norms. Requirements recovery for an IT system must start from an analysis of the business domain and operations, as reflected in the AMBOLS approach (Figure 12.1). The whole process of requirements recovery is organised into a series of activities in three stages: *behaviour capture*, *dynamic behaviour modelling* and *requirements derivation*.

AMBOLS uses a number of techniques available from the fields of software engineering, requirements studies and information systems design, with extensions and alterations based on organisational semiotics where appropriate. These techniques are described, and the derivation of requirements is then addressed.

Stage 1: Behaviour capture

This stage of analysis in AMBOLS focuses on the external behaviour of the system and the context in which the system operates, and is achieved mainly by observation and interviews.

Context analysis

The first task in this stage, the context analysis, is to examine the organisational and business environment in which the IT system is operating. The analysis

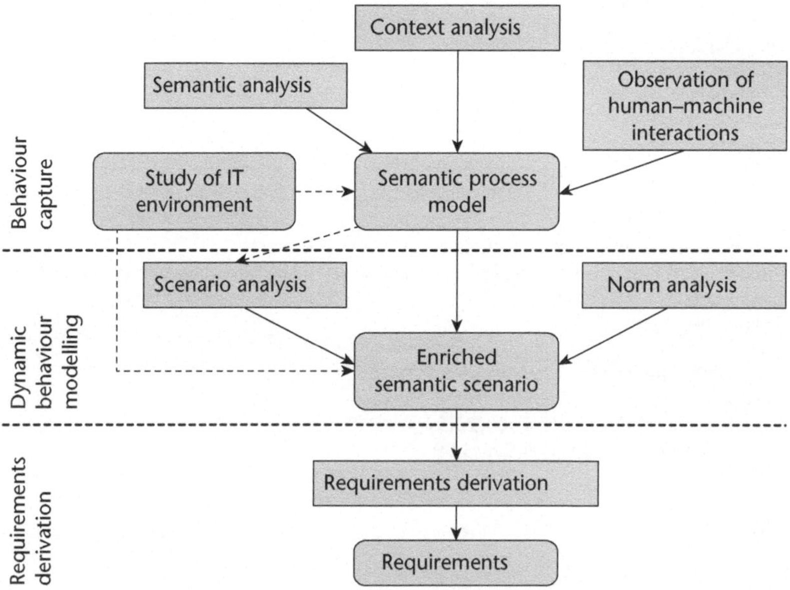

FIGURE 12.1 The AMBOLS approach

covers the domain, organisational structure and business processes. The purpose is to understand the nature of the business and the major business functions, and to identify the stakeholders. A 'soft systems method' (Kolkman 1995) provides a basis for developing a checklist for stakeholders, which includes suppliers, customers, competitors, governing bodies and users of the system. The case method (Booch *et al.* 2007) is used to represent the relationships between stakeholders and major clusters of system functions. This investigation is carried out through interviews and the collection of any relevant literature.

Observation of human–machine interactions

The observation of human–machine interactions is carried out by observing and studying how the system is used by all the user groups. In this step, detailed notes are taken and additional explanations from the users are often required regarding the meanings, purposes of and reasons for certain operations. The human–machine interactions include not only screenshots and keyboard inputs, but also other kinds of interactions, for example email. Figure 12.2 shows an email received from the university email system recalling a borrowed book.

Semantic analysis

Semantic analysis clarifies and captures the meanings of concepts, terms and functions. Using semantic analysis, we can organise these concepts and terms into a semantic model – an ontology chart. An ontology chart describes the patterns of

Date/Address
User Name: *********** ID: *********
Department: *********

Dear ****:

URGENT RECALL NOTICE

The following item has been requested by another user.
Please return it as soon as possible and no later than the new due date printed on this notice.
Thank you.

Book Name: **********/ Author(s): ***********
Call number:********** ID:***********
original date due: 18/2/2003,23:59
NEW date due: 21/1/2003,23:59

FIGURE 12.2 An email to recall a book

behaviour of human actors and IT systems, and defines the relationships between concepts and terms that correspond to the patterns of behaviour. Figure 12.3 shows an example of how the terms used in the recall notice can be organised using the method of semantic analysis.

The ontology chart in Figure 12.3 can be interpreted as follows. A user has attributes such as a name and ID; a user is affiliated to a department; an item exists

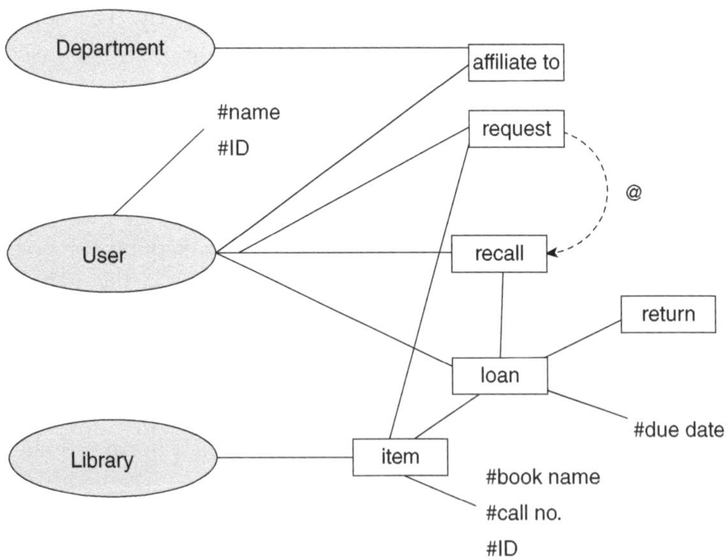

FIGURE 12.3 Semantic analysis of the library recall notice

within the context of the library, and has attributes such as a book name, call number and ID; a user can take an item out on loan, and the existence of the user and the item is the prerequisite for the behaviour 'loan' to be meaningful. Once the loaning has been realised, an attribute 'due date' is attached to the loan. A user can request an item, and if that item is on loan, the system can generate a 'recall' on the 'loan'. The ontological dependency between 'loan' and 'recall' is important because 'loan' forms the context for the behaviour 'recall'. For an item that is not at that point in time on loan, such behaviour is meaningless. The dotted line with the '@' sign in Figure 12.3 represents a semiological relationship (as opposed to an ontological one), which means that a request may or may not lead to a recall, depending on the decision of some authority (e.g. a librarian).

It is important to know who the actor is for each behaviour. Semantic analysis meets these conditions by specifying (a) who does what, for example a user takes an item out on loan, a user returns a loan or the library recalls an item; and (b) in what circumstances the above affordances could come into existence – for example, an item must be on loan to a user before it can be returned, and a recall can be made during the loan. These contexts may at first seem straightforward. However, when systems grow larger and more complex, such clearly defined contexts will be necessary as they build a rigorous representation of understanding of the information systems.

The information collected from the context analysis, human–machine interaction and semantic analysis can be incorporated into a semantic process model. In other words, the interactions between the user and the system can be described in a process model, while the concepts and terms used in the process models are defined in semantic models. Role-activity diagrams (Ould 1995) are chosen as a base technique for representing processes as they can be easily enriched by the semantic analysis method to clarify the meanings.

Stage 2: Dynamic behaviour modelling

The analysis at this stage takes a process perspective, which places an emphasis on the sequences of actions and interactions between human and machine. Information items relating to business concepts and operations, actions performed by the user and the system, and governing norms for these actions are the objects of study at this stage (as seen in Figure 12.1).

Scenario analysis

Scenarios are widely used in the software engineering community as a means of representing the problem domain to elicit, represent and analyse the requirements. There are at least four recognised views of the contents and the use of scenarios (Filippidou 1998):

- *Process view*: Scenarios describe the sequences of 'actions' or 'events', rather than individual acts.
- *Situation view*: A scenario represents a situation or an 'episode' with a temporal component.
- *Choice view*: Scenarios represent alternative options that can be selected for further design or implementation.
- *Use view*: Scenarios enable users (e.g. end users or designers) to focus on the target artefacts from outside the system's boundary.

We adopt the process view here, supplementing it with a temporal component. Scenarios represent the stakeholders, actions and events in a process-oriented model within an explicit time-based framework.

Norm analysis

Norm analysis (Stamper *et al.* 2000) enables us to elicit and represent business rules that have an effect on the system. Norm analysis recognises various types of rules in a broad sense, which may be embedded either in the system or in the procedures for using the system:

- rules that can be specified explicitly as conditions and constraints for system operations;
- rules defining responsibilities and authorities;
- rules for reasoning and decision-making specified by possible conditions and resulting consequences;
- ethical values, socially acceptable practices and business standards.

Norms governing a business give us access to requirements. Norms are associated with purpose in an organisation. Using norm analysis, norms can be specified to identify the controlling relationships with certain system actions. Take the loan recall process as an example. Norms can be expressed as follows:

> whenever <an item is on loan>
>
> if <a user who does not loan this item needs this item>
>
> then <this user>
>
> is <permitted to>
>
> to <place a request to the item>

Enriched semantic scenario

Modelling the dynamic behaviour of a system has been widely used in reverse engineering and requirements capturing. However, as argued by Systa (1999), the static model is also very useful and complements the dynamic model. Although Systa refers the static model mainly to a class/object structure, the same principle applies to requirements recovery, in which the static model refers to semantics and the dynamic model refers to scenarios. As well as describing the systems from both views, combining them into a single view will check the consistency and allow them to enrich each other. The outcome, the enriched semantic scenarios, consists of the process models, sharing clear connections to the norms that govern the changes of state and the control over the actions. Details of information items, data fields and formats and screen layouts may be relevant in some cases.

Stage 3: Requirements derivation

Having created descriptions of the system, the task is now to derive the requirements. This may require a number of iterations through the activities of deriving requirements on the basis of technical evidence on the system, the synthesis of the derived requirements with requirements postulated by the users, and a validation of the requirements against the running system in a form of user acceptance testing.

The first two stages of the AMBOLS approach create a technical representation of the running system in a variety of complementary representations. This final requirements derivation stage creates requirements that explain the various properties of the running system.

The explanation of system capabilities by user requirements is bi-directional. We conjecture the existence of a particular requirement because of some function. We also consider the functions that might arise from some conjectured requirement. Such requirements derive from knowledge of the domain or domains of the system. These domains may be deduced from the terms (ontology) used by users to describe the system. We find these condensed in the ontology charts created through the semantic analysis related to the organisational semiotics approach. So we reason both from capabilities to requirements, and from requirements to capabilities. This requires the use of mixed reasoning such as induction, deduction and abduction.

Plausible users requirements

We cannot claim to derive the actual user requirements for a current system. We cannot (because of our assumption that there is no documentation extant for the system) prove that any user requirements we derive were original user requirements. In reality, we can only derive plausible user requirements from existing systems. These will be plausible in the sense that the existing system is a solution to the problem posed by those user requirements. Those user requirements give rise to everything in the system that is visible. We do not give ourselves the luxury of studying the code to determine if there is anything that is not visible. So the plausible user requirements should be a necessary and sufficient set to explain the existence of the operational system as we observe it.

We can undertake a verification of the plausible user requirements through the task of user acceptance. Here the operational system is verified against (a set of tests derived from) the user requirements to demonstrate compliance with users' needs. In our context, a successful user acceptance test would verify that our derived user requirements were plausible.

We need to be precise about user requirements. Systems have an operational (business) purpose expressed through the objectives or needs of the acquiring organisation. Dardenne *et al.* (1991) describe the needs as goals. These goals are generally too imprecise to form the basis of a development. They must be expressed in a more detailed form that includes the means of assessing the degree to which the goal is met. This detailed form is what we call the user requirements, each requirement expressing a particular aspect of the need and its verification criteria. Our interest is not, however, confined to user requirements; we also wish to derive goals and purposes.

'There is a well known axiom in anthropology that what people say and do are not the same' (Blomberg *et al.* 1990). This and our preceding analysis indicate the need to utilise both elicitation and observation, combined with verification through the usual user acceptance techniques. Our process must then take into account the need to elicit ideas of purpose and goals from those with intimate knowledge of the domain under study. It is not sufficient to ask the stakeholders of the system what (in their opinion) it does; we must also ask what (in their opinion) it is for. The capabilities can be elicited from users and operators, and derived from observation. These give an assessment of capability from which plausible purposes, goals and requirements can be deduced. The validation of user requirements against capability by various means, including techniques of user acceptance testing, will indicate the degree of plausibility. We may have to return to elicitation and observation to identify misinterpretation, oversight or other causes of the mismatch.

Requirements management and validation

The management of requirements is important given the need for iteration, traceability and visibility. The project has chosen to use the Rational Dynamic Objected Oriented Requirements Systems (DOORS) requirements management tool (Box 12.1).The DOORS meta-model is flexible, enabling tailoring for the specific AMBOLS data structures to be represented. The data model represents the requirements and the constraints (non-functional requirements) pertaining to tracing the requirements over previous time periods, together with the higher level purposes and needs from which they derive.

Box 12.1 DOORS – requirements management with traceability

IBM's Rational Dynamic Objected Oriented Requirements Systems (DOORS), originally produced by Telelogic before it was acquired by IBM, is a requirements management toolkit that supports requirements engineering. A key feature of DOORS is its ability to trace evolution requirements. It enables users to find the origin of each requirement and track every change to this requirement.

Requirements are represented in the systems analysis and artefact design, and are finally verified through implementation; the artefacts tied to the later stages should be traced back to the requirements as well. Using a mechanism like this, the justification and responsibility for the changes are clear, and verification, rectification and fall-back are possible to ensure the quality of the requirements.

Validation is intended to uncover any discrepancy between the requirements recovered and the running system. Traceability links between the user requirements and the technical models of the system provide an initial check. Every element of the technical models must be explicable in terms of user requirements, and a requirement is only valid if it explains an element of the technical models. We may also consider user acceptance testing, in which the system is tested for conformance against validations derived from the requirements. We may need to reiterate earlier stages of the analysis if mismatches are uncovered. By using DOORS as the assisting tool, the process of the management and validation of requirements can be specified and implemented.

Case study: the library

One of the case studies we conducted was on a multisite university library system. This had a relatively new computer system that was bought in 1995, but there had been ongoing alterations of the system performed by a system teams from the university library. The library system distributes across several geographical locations to serve customers on the university's campuses and in those federated institutions. The different requirements of the federated institutions have to be allowed for, and, in addition, the local customisation of some system functions has to be accommodated. All these make the university library system not as simple as it first seems.

Behaviour capture

As shown in Figure 12.1 above, this stage of the AMBOLS approach focuses on the observation and analysis of the system's behaviour, starting from the context and interfaces and moving into the system processes.

Context analysis

There are multiple stakeholders who take an interest in and benefit from the library system, as identified in the Table 12.1. The method adopted here is PAM, which categorises stakeholders based on the strength of their influence on (or 'distance' from) the core system. The stakeholders are identified in each category according to this distance:

- the principals and actors who have a direct involvement in the use of, and the power to make decisions about, the system;
- the clients and providers who are either directly affected by or have a direct impact on the system;
- the collaborators and competitors;
- finally, most distant but still relevant, bystanders and legislators.

Stakeholders have roles to play, which are described in our analysis as responsibilities. Understanding these roles and responsibilities helps to capture their different views and the requirements of the retail store system. The analysis of stakeholders also helps us identify the major categories of business activities supported, and relate the system's functions to the stakeholders. Use cases are used to identify the major scenarios, such as usage, administration, lending, returns, cataloguing and so on.

The context analysis gives us an understanding of the different views of the system and its major functional areas.

TABLE 12.1 The library system's stakeholders and responsibilities

Stakeholder	*Category*	*Responsibility*
University	Principal	Ensure the library provides sufficient facilities for education and research
Librarian, deputy librarian	Actor	Responsible for library system, media services, acquisition, cataloguing, video unit, counter services
Systems manager	Actor	Ensure system works properly and respond to problems. Communicate with the systems and supplier
Cataloguing librarian	Actor	Maintain catalogue enquiry facility online public access catalogue
Senior technician	Actor	Manage the video/media unit of the library
Acquisition manager	Actor	Order new books for library
Library administrator	Actor	Manage finance and resources
Principal technician	Actor	Manage media services
Senior tutor librarian	Actor	Provide consultation, teaching, and liaison with schools, assess books for purchasing
Library assistant, information service assistant	Actor	Issue and renew library items, and deal with queries and inter-library loan requests
Library user (University staff, student, library member from other organisations)	Client	Use facilities offered by the library including borrowing library materials, inter-library loan, photocopy, faxing and the reservation and renewal of library materials.
Members of the public	Client	Access newspapers, journals, books – no right of borrowing
Publisher	Provider	Supplies library materials such as books and journals
System suppliers	Provider	Supply software for upgrading and carry out major maintenance.
Other libraries in the UK	Collaborator	Lend and borrow materials
Local and central government	Legislator	Make policies and regulations

Human–machine interactions

The analysis at this stage is carried out by observing how the system is used in daily operations. Screenshots are captured and organised in the same order as they are displayed on the running system. After initial investigation, the main categories of the system's functions are documented. In this case study, functions such as borrowing (or check-out), return (or check-in), user administration and cataloguing are most readily visible.

So far, we have conducted our investigation using interviews and observations of system screens and the system's behaviour in operation. The analysis in the next step uncovers the information required for these operations, without being too greatly concerned with the syntactic structure of the information.

Semantic analysis

The focus of a semantic analysis is to identify the concepts and terms involved in the system's operations. This analysis aims to reveal the items of information that constitute the information model for the system. The semantic analysis involves the analyst and other stakeholders of the system in generating and verifying the model.

The semantic model (ontology chart, as shown in Figure 12.4) defines the behaviour of the system by describing the roles and responsibilities of the human actors involved. The relative left–right position of the entities linked by a line is significant. An entity at the left of a line is the antecedent of the entity on the right. For example, *society* is the antecedent for a *person*, the *university* and an *organisation*. All these three entities can only exist and be meaningful within the context of the society.

The entities in ellipses are agents who can take actions and can be responsible for their actions: *society*, *person* and *organisation*. *Student* and *employee* are role names (placed along a line) determined by the activities they are involved in (i.e. enrolled at the university and employed by the university). The entities within a box are specifics of a certain type: e.g. *members* and the *public* are specifics of the user. The dotted line with the '@' sign denotes an authorisation: for example, a contract governs the employees' use of the library.

The information captured in this ontology chart defines the semantics of the concepts and terms used in the problem domain. It also serves as a foundation for describing the behaviour of the information system.

System environment

The university has three main libraries situated at different locations. Their major services are to lend materials, such as books, archived collections of old magazines, dissertations, company annual reports and audio and video cassettes. Other services are interlibrary loans, online enquiries, reservations and renewals of borrowed materials. They also offer facilities for faxing and photocopying. The university

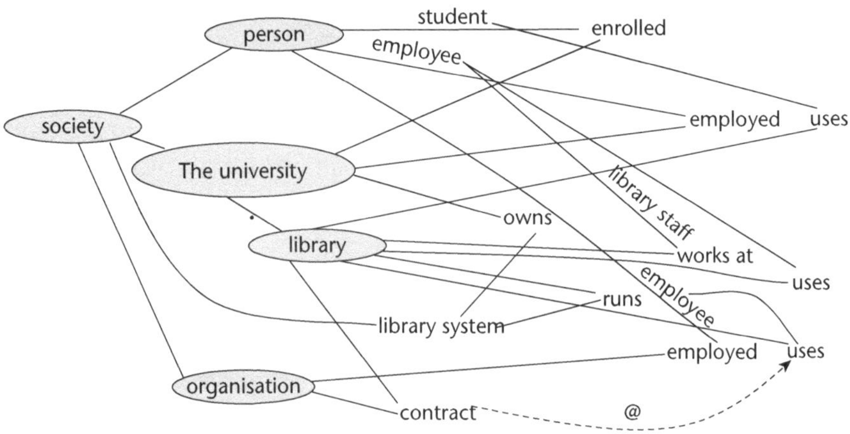

(a) Actors involved in library operations

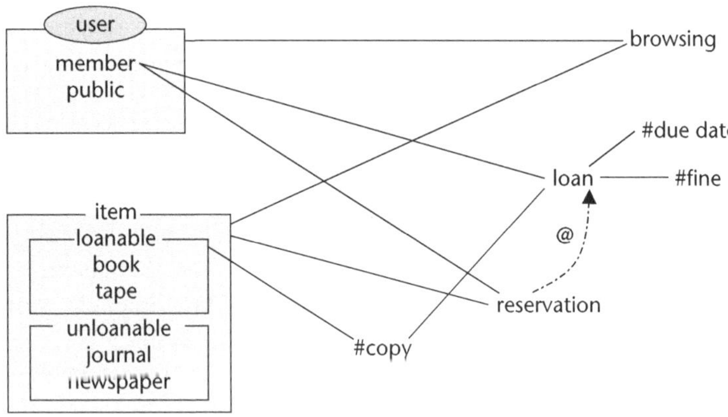

(b) Loan and return of a library item

FIGURE 12.4 Semantic model of the library system

libraries also have a relationship with a number of other libraries in affiliated institutes. The main categories of customers are the students and staff of the university, members of the affiliated colleges and institutes, and members of other organisations. The libraries are also open to the public, although access to the service and facilities depends on whether a member of the public is a registered member.

The three university libraries use one computer library system called Horizon, which handles all the online services. This system is connected with libraries at affiliated institutes, although the services provided to them are limited. The library system communicates with affiliated colleges and national libraries via the internet. The library system is also connected to other university libraries and national libraries governed by agreements such as those for interlibrary loans.

The visible system components are electronic tills, bar code readers, displays on the screen and inputs from keyboards. Transactions at different tills can clearly interact with each other, so they are connected in some way. It is not plausible to suppose that every till is connected to every other till. It is instead reasonable to suppose some central system (within one library or elsewhere) that mediates the communication. We see that we can reason about the observation in order to deduce plausible actors, functions and components. Blocking a library assistant from the concurrent use of two tills is another indication of central control.

The information relating to the hardware and software platform is relevant for us to understand the non-functional and other requirements of the business, such as the service level, access level, system performance and security issues. It helps us in reasoning about the derivation and validation of requirements from another perspective in the requirements recovery process.

Semantic process models

A business process, which involves actors and a computer system, is described using a role-activity diagram. Figure 12.5a shows the process of checking out an item such as a book. This process model and the semantic model complement each other as the former concentrates on the processes, while the latter defines the roles, responsibilities and meanings of the terms used in the process model.

Dynamic behaviour modelling

The investigation at this stage focuses on the behaviour of the system and the interaction between human users and the system.

Scenarios

Scenarios have been widely used for capturing requirements and for software engineering. There are many varieties of methods and techniques, each of which has its advantages and suits specific purposes (Rolland *et al.* 1998). We use scenarios to organise the information on actors and activities in a time-based framework.

The scenario shown in Figure 12.5b describes the dynamic aspect of the checking-out process for a loan item. This provides an overview of actions, with supplementary details from other models: context, interaction and semantic models. Figure 12.5a shows the activitives conducted by the two typical roles (i.e. the library assistant and the borrower). A dark box indicates an activity by that role alone, while a grey box represents an activity that has a connection with another role. The white boxes represents a dummy activity (or a passive activity). Figure 12.5c uses the state diagram technique to describe the sequence of the system interfaces and actions (indicated along the lines). As can be seen in the figure, an action is possible when an interface is displayed, and it will lead to a new interface. Figure 12.5 documents the observation of the system's behaviour. As discussed

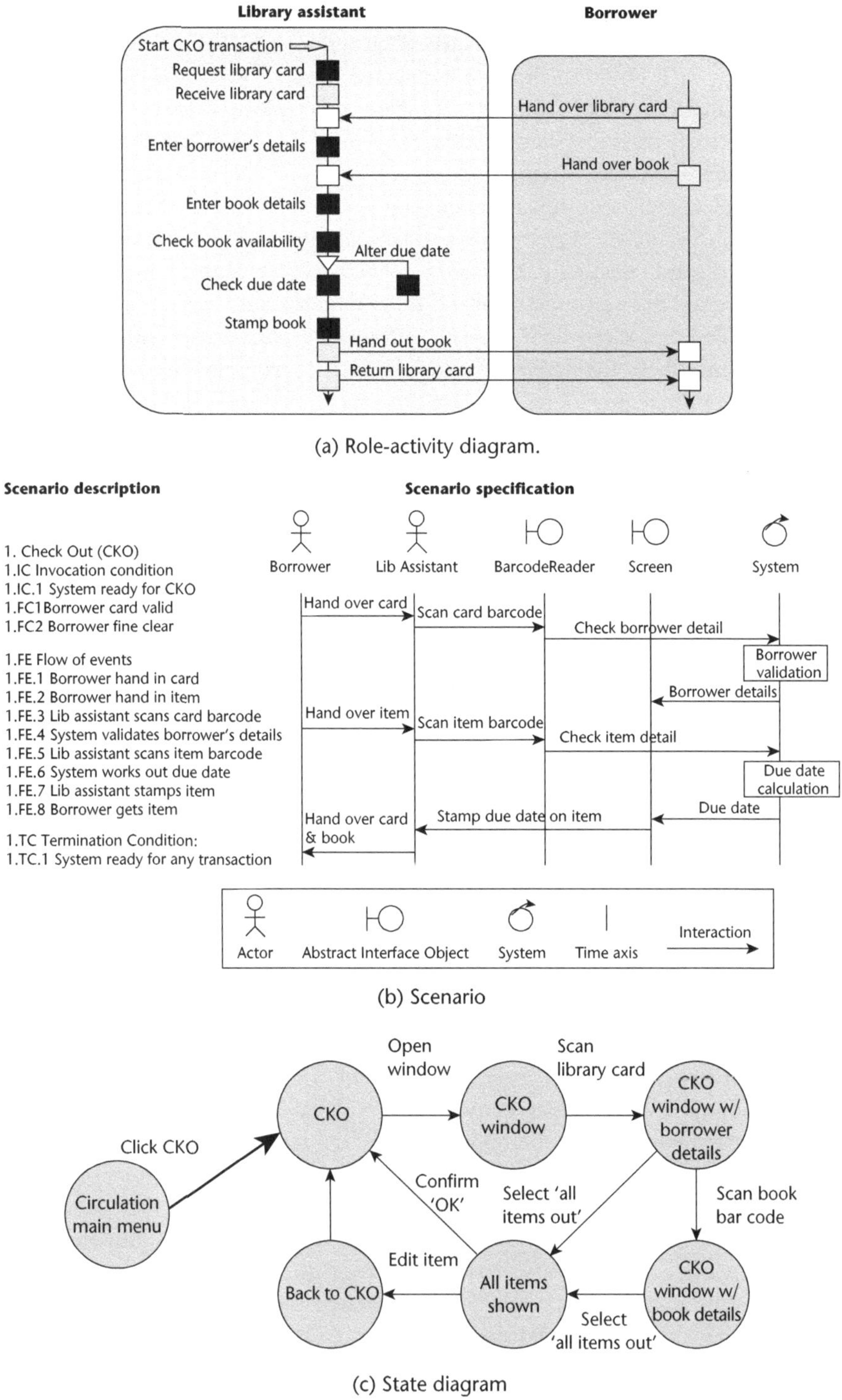

FIGURE 12.5 The process of checking out a book

earlier, a context model identifies the stakeholders, an interaction model describes the human–machine interfaces, and a semantic model defines the concepts and terminology used in modelling.

Norm analysis

In a system's operation, there are conditions to be satisfied for the invocation of a process and for events to take place. These conditions are described in the norms. The norms determine whether and when a certain activity takes place; they also determine the behaviour of the system in performing certain tasks. The business rules must be collected and specified, and the norm analysis assists with this task.

The norm analysis uses the results of the semantic analysis. Each concept in a semantic model represents an object (which may be an entity, an action or an event). Each has a lifespan marked by a start and a finish, which is controlled by a set of norms. For example, the acceptability of a library card is determined by satisfying certain conditions including an expiry date. A variety of norms can be identified, of which two types are most relevant in the library application:

- *Definitional norms* define meanings, boundaries, responsibilities, authorities and status.
- *Action norms* indicate when and which actions are taken.

We can provide examples of norms derived from the semantic model and the library regulations:

- Borrowed items must be returned by the due date.
- Borrowers must not exceed their allowance of items on loan at any one time.
- No items will be issued to a borrower who has items overdue or an unpaid fine.

As mentioned in Chapter 3, a norm specification covers the following elements: condition, state, actor, modality and action, as shown below:

(condition)	When an item is issued to a borrower
(state)	If there is an overdue item or unpaid fine
(actor)	The library assistant
(modality)	Is obliged
(action)	To stop the issuing process.

This norm requires a series of procedures (such as library security) and facilities (such as tills, bar codes and library cards) to implement it. There can also be a norm to define how to calculate any payment, which can be applied in conjunction with this norm.

Enriched semantic scenarios – integrating norms

Each business process is described by a scenario, which captures the actors, actions and behaviour of the system. Semantic analysis defines the meanings of the concepts and terms in the scenario, and norm analysis specifies the rules and conditions that control the actions and events. An abstract interface object in a scenario may suggest the use of one or many data objects in the system. Norms and system interactions with the users represent the system's behaviour, which is an aggregation of the behaviour of all the sub-systems and program components. The integration of these analyses represents the system's behaviour from different perspectives, each complementing and validating the entire understanding of the system. The final view of the system's behaviour and major data objects can be obtained by using several iterations in which hypotheses are set, discarded or altered, and validated.

Requirements derivation

Deductions from domains involved

When we know the domain is the library, the domain knowledge we have helps in deriving the missing parts of the requirements models, as well as in validating the results. If, however, an investigation is in an unfamiliar domain, a study of the domain and operating context becomes crucial before any requirements recovery is attempted.

In our case, we can deduce the meaning of 'borrow', 'loan item', 'due date' and 'fine'. Our understanding of the connotation of these concepts enables us to derive the associated actions and processes taking place though human users and within the computer systems. 'Log on' and 'denied access' imply security, 'checking out' means a certain standard process and so on. We can now look at each domain or context from the knowledge of what it implies in a broader view. Library services entail the law of intellectual properties, the use of library cards entails the law of an individual's rights and so on. Admitting the public and employing staff imply health and safety requirements. We can see the effects of these requirements in the observation.

Deductions from system components

We can note here the use of library card readers and bar code wands. These provide accuracy and speed of operation. Accuracy of recording is important to both the library and the customer. Speed of operation enables queue sizes to be minimised during peak hours, an important system attribute when customers can be discouraged by the queuing time. Transaction times must be low. Bar code readers, electronic tills, printers and library card readers are all technologies that will increase the speed of the transaction.

We can infer that the tills are linked to the library system. We know that the tills are linked to the library membership database and catalogue, and there are means of interacting with these databases and sub-systems at different sites.

Deduction from artefacts

The existence of a library card and the bar code of a loan item show what sort of information is needed by the operation and is stored in the system. By examining the library card and various forms (e.g. the membership application form and book purchase form), we know more about the items of information and even about possible formats of data kept in the system. The library has security gates that sense any item taken through them and set off an alarm. These indicate a requirement to prevent theft.

Deductions from norms

Staff must log on to a till to make it operable. One assistant may be logged on to at most one till at a time, and each till can deal with only one transaction at a time. A till cannot start the next transaction until the previous one has finished either by normal completion of the transaction or by voiding it. These norms relate to the avoidance of fraud and theft on the part of both staff and customers. Transactions may not be completed manually. This information indicates automated ledger activities. Only correctly labelled items can be lent, and the use of the correct codes indicates a computer-assisted catalogue control.

Box 12.1 outlines a summary of some plausible derived goals and requirements that cover both the business and system sides of the process.

Box 12.2 Some plausible goals and requirements

Goal: Operate properly to provide library services
Sub-goal 1: Operate correctly in loan operations
- **Sub-goal 1.1:** Check members' legitimacy (identity, membership grade, fine statues, etc.)
- **Sub-goal 1.2:** Check statues of items (loanability, not reserved by others, etc.)
- **Sub-goal 1.3:** Lend items
- **Sub-goal 1.4:** Process transaction correctly and quickly

Sub-goal 2: Operate correctly in return operations
- **Sub-goal 2.1:** Record returned items
- **Sub-goal 2.2:** Check whether overdue and calculate fine, if appropriate
- **Sub-goal 2.3:** Update loan record of the members

Sub-goal 3: Maintain membership information correctly
Sub-goal 4: Maintain the catalogue of all items.
- **Sub-goal 4.1:** Keep catalogue up to date

Sub-goal 5: Avoid loss due to theft, fraud, and so on
Sub-goal 6: Maintain library information integrity

Validation of requirements

The validation of the requirements is important. This is achieved in several ways. First, the semiotic approach adopted in this project offers us a way to employ the abduction approach throughout the exercise of recovering the requirements. Together with induction and deduction, abduction allows the research team to formulate a hypothesis and verify it using further observation and investigation. As explained in Chapter 2, abduction departs from some surprising facts in observation and formulates a hypothesis; the hypothesis is further tested for adjustment or refinement. We are clearly aware that the requirements recovery is never a one-run activity but demands a series of iterations in which the hypothesis is constantly tested and adjusted.

For example, in our analysis in this case study, we had initially failed to observe system artefacts related to health and safety. However, when our analysis indicated the presence of the public, our knowledge of the existence of the related health and safety domain prompted us to return to the library. As expected, we found fire exits, fire hydrants, signs, safety notices and other artefacts related to that domain.

The second means of validation is that we conduct the analysis from multiple angles. This results in a redundancy of information, which is useful in validating the analysis. For example, although the process of checking out a book is modelled in Figure 12.5a using a role-activity diagram, the same process can be studied by observing operations at the till in the library, represented as a state diagram (see Figure 12.5c). The state diagram is constructed independently without using the information on the role-activity model, which allows cross-checking between the two models.

Management of requirements

The requirements recovery involves large amounts of information collected from various sources and produced at different stages. We record the interview transcripts, and we record our observations as observational notes. These two documents are our main sources of information. The information produced involves case diagrams on usage, role-activity diagrams, scenario analysis, norm analysis, analysis of human–computer interaction and semantic analysis. The documents generated in the AMBOLS project are held in different formats, such as graphics and text. The results of analyses from the different stages must be managed, and cross-referencing is set up between different analyses.

The requirements management tool DOORS gives the support required here. It provides a high level of customisability, version control features, import and export links, and flexible reporting features. In DOORS, files and requirements models are defined 'objects', which are grouped into modules within a project. It defines three kinds of modules, each with a different purpose: (a) a descriptive module represents unstructured, read-only input documents; (b) a formal module represents structured documents with sections and sub-sections; and (c) a link module represents any number of relationships of a specific type. Like most requirements tools, all the objects can be created, copied, deleted, edited and moved as required. In addition, DOORS maintains module and requirements histories for auditing purposes; therefore, users can create baseline versions of entire modules for tracking revisions to the module. This has enormously enhanced the usability of the AMBOLS approach.

Discussion and outlook

Recovering requirements is an important activity in the modernisation and replacement of a legacy system. Successful engineering and re-engineering demands good user requirements. To make decisions about a system's future, we must understand its intended purpose.

The impact of the AMBOLS approach continues in research and industry as the re-engineering and integration of legacy systems is still an activity with a high demand for resources. Documentation relating to the system is often unavailable. Even where design documents and source codes are available, they are usually out of date or otherwise inaccurate. Well-documented user requirements, kept in line with changes, are rare even in current practice. In many circumstances, technical expertise about the internal aspects of the system has long disappeared. The system itself and those who use it are the only reliable sources of information about what it does and why.

The theory and methods of organisational semiotics provide the theoretical foundation for the proposed top-down, black-box approach, which organises the observations on the operational systems into structures of agents and affordances interlinked by ontological dependencies and governed by norms. User requirements are deduced from the enriched semantic scenarios.

We currently focus on what can be deduced from the functionality offered by the system. The prime motivations for a system are generally to provide automated capability to assist the business's processes. Our emphasis on descriptive scenarios arises from this observation. The next most telling category of information contains the limitations or restrictions on the system's functions. We capture these as norms. The norms are indicative of the business policy that the system encapsulates, so again they will suggest user requirements. Other constraints on the system, such as performance and the use of particular software and hardware, can, with varying degrees of difficulty and value, be captured and expressed as user requirements. We need to distinguish between the constraints imposed by the technical capabilities at the time of development and those truly expressive of business needs.

An aphorism frequently quoted in reverse engineering is 'You can make sausages from pigs, but not pigs from sausages.' In our scenario, 'only the sausage skins can be inspected'. However, there are experts who can tell a great deal about the origins of a sausage from its size, colour, smell and taste. This gives inspiration to our venture in which we have no desire to reconstruct pigs, but dearly wish to know the requirements for sausages.

Further research will be undertaken to combine the proposed approach with other methods for modernising legacy systems, especially bottom-up, white-box methods, to form an integrated tool package for industrial users. We will also consider the integration of information about the system that is available from its users, in terms of both its capabilities and other technical attributes, and the understanding of user requirements for the system.

Questions and exercises

1. There are legacy systems in organisations in all industries, for example manufacturing, transportation, healthcare and public services. Why are they called legacy systems? Are they valuable? What are appropriate ways to deal with them?
2. What are the problems caused by legacy systems in an organisation? How do they affect the organisation's activities?
3. How do you understand the notion of interoperability between legacy systems and other systems?
4. How can semiotic methods help to access the value of legacy systems?

13

INFORMATION SYSTEMS TO SUPPORT BUSINESS IN THE DIGITAL AGE

There is a clear trend that information systems are becoming critical to organisations in this digital age. Information systems support business at the strategic and operational levels, and transform the business from e-commerce via e-business to e-enterprise. Exploring the emergence of advanced information technology (IT) such as the Internet of Things (IoT; see below) and mobile technology, this chapter will examine how information management using IT can facilitate organisations in transforming their information systems through supply chain management (SCM), value chains and customer relationship management (CRM).

Trends in IT in the digital age

Progress in IT is transformative. Every year, IT brings faster processing speeds, a greater storage capacity, bigger datasets and more advanced software. Ways of connecting, sharing, collaborating and doing business become richer, more varied, more powerful and more enabled, expanding their IT capabilities.

It is important for companies to understand how these capabilities are evolving. IT-enabled business trends provide fresh opportunities for companies to create new sources of value – new products, new ways of keeping in touch with their customers, and new tools for improving operating efficiency. They also have the potential to shift profit pools, disrupt markets and commercial relationships, undermine existing market leaders, and shift value to consumers or between producers. Figure 13.1 shows examples of the emerging ITs that have a significant impact in the digital age, some of which will be discussed below.

Pervasive computing

Pervasive computing is the ability to digitally engage and interact (via a mobile device) with enabled objects in the surroundings. As a specific form as the technology

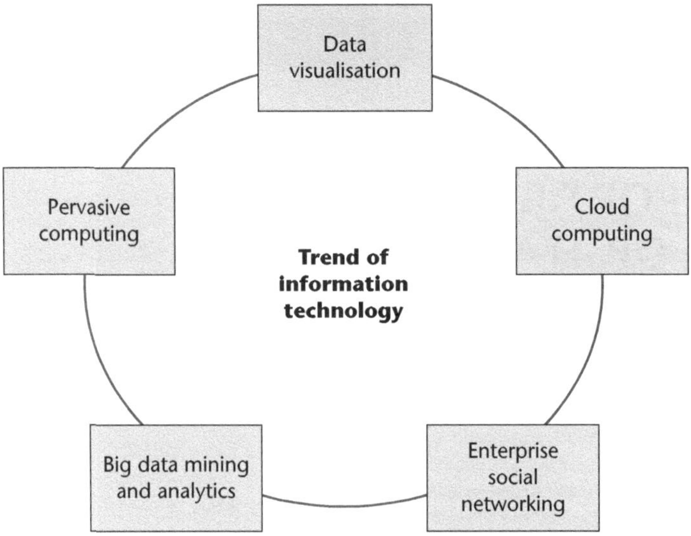

FIGURE 13.1 Significant emerging information technologies (PwC 2013)

of the IoT, pervasive computing will empower humans to pinpoint a wanted object, even being able to find the proverbial needle in the haystack. Instead of users being forced to ferret out relevant mobile apps from the hundreds of thousands available, mobile apps will automatically surf based on situations. In other words, the app will find the user and provide services, rather than the user finding the app.

Data visualisation

As the saying goes, a picture is worth more than a thousand words. Dynamic visualisation techniques (e.g. virtual reality and augmented reality) and advanced display devices (e.g. 4K screens or 'walls', 3D goggles, haptics and gesture-based interfaces) enable use to navigate data in multiple dimensions (3D, plus time, space and even more). Advanced visualisation will provide organisations with a huge 'dashboard' with which to layer and manipulate multiple sources of information on gigantic floor-to-ceiling high-definition monitors in order to analyse past events and explore future scenarios (e.g. economics, competition, technology or customer adoption).

Big data mining and analytics

Big data is more than managing dizzying amounts of data in a faster and cheaper way. Big data are about making better business decisions. Maximising the full potential of big data requires the use of advanced analytics to cull and leverage data from inside and outside the organisation. To benefit from the big data, organisations must foster data-driven decision-making cultures, including seeking more data scientists, to harvest and harness big data.

Cloud computing

Cloud computing changes the way many companies do business. Enterprises are migrating their services to private or public 'clouds' – shared pools of computing resources such as networks, servers, storage facilities and applications that can be rapidly and conveniently provisioned. This allows companies to pay only for the IT resources they consume, as well as delivering software through new as-a-service models, potentially producing substantial savings on their IT spending and increasing convenience for their end consumers.

Enterprise social networking

Workers in the global workforce are becoming increasingly familiar and comfortable with social networking. For most businesses, there is a growing expectation that social networking tools will be used in a business context. Furthermore, there are now proven models to drive the adoption of enterprise social networks and achieve value through their deployment. Organisations that succeed in becoming social organisations may achieve tremendous advantages over their competitors.

Internet of Things versus internet

The IoT (Box 13.1) is an integrated part of the future internet, including existing and evolving internet and network developments. It can be conceptually defined as a dynamic global network infrastructure with self-configuring capabilities based on standard and interoperable communication protocols in which physical and virtual 'things' have identities, physical attributes and virtual personalities. With intelligent interfaces for objects, the network is seamlessly integrated for information-sharing, collaboration and action. Unlike the internet, which provides links only within the sign-based, informational or semiological space, the IoT brings the semiological and physical spaces together to realise the sharing of information as well as connectivity with objects through the use of signs.

Box 13.1 The Internet of Things

The 'Internet of Things' (IoT) refers to uniquely identifiable objects and their virtual representations in an internet-like structure. The term was proposed by Kevin Ashton in 1999 (Ashton 2009). The concept of the IoT first became popular through the Auto-ID Centre at MIT and related market analyst publications (Auto-ID Labs 2014).

Radiofrequency identification is often seen as a prerequisite for the IoT. If all objects and people in daily life were equipped with identifiers, they could be managed and inventoried by computers. Equipping all objects in the world with minuscule identifying devices could be transformative for daily life. It would realise a connectivity from anytime and anyplace to anything for anyone.

Internet of Things versus business

In the IoT, 'things' are expected to become active participants in business, information and social processes, where they are enabled to interact and communicate between themselves and with the environment by exchanging data and information 'sensed' about the environment. IoT tries to react autonomously to 'real/physical world' events and influence them by running processes that trigger actions and create services with or without direct human intervention. Services will be able to interact with these 'things' using standard interfaces that will provide the necessary link via the internet, to query and change their state and retrieve any information associated with them, while security and privacy have been taken care of.

Evolution of business driven by IT

IT has driven the evolution of business modes in a remarkable manner. Business evolves with the development of technology, and many companies have gone through the major phases of evolution: from e-commerce, via e-business and m-business to e-enterprise.

e-Commerce

The global availability of the internet for the exchange of transactions between buyers and sellers has fuelled the growth of e-commerce. E-commerce is the process of buying and selling goods and services electronically by computerised business transactions using the internet, networks and other digital technologies. It also encompasses activities supporting those market transactions, such as advertising, marketing, customer support, delivery and payment.

By replacing manual and paper-based procedures with electronic alternatives, and by using information flows in new and dynamic ways, e-commerce can

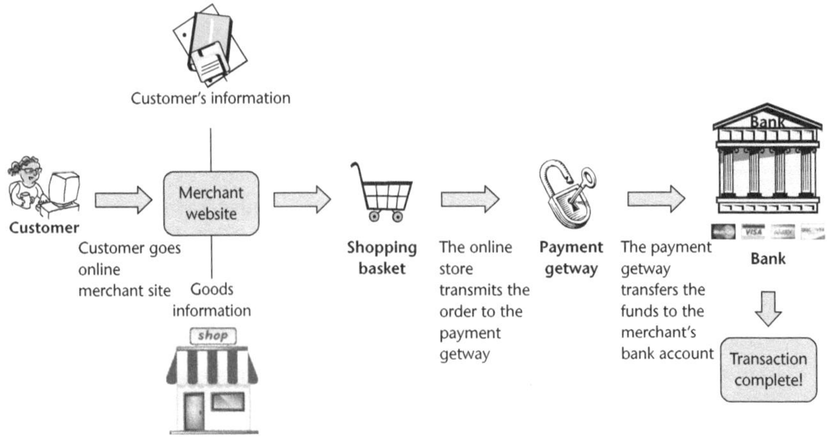

FIGURE 13.2 An e-commerce scenario

accelerate ordering, delivery and payment for goods and services while reducing companies' operating and inventory costs. Figure 13.2 shows a typical scenario in e-commerce, with services, products and communication transactions conducted via the internet.

e-Business

e-Business results from the transformation of an organisation's processes to achieve additional value through the application of technologies, philosophies and computing paradigms within the company as well as externally (Zorayda 2003).

e-Business and e-commerce are distinct in a few ways. In e-commerce, IT is used mainly to facilitate communication and interactions between the company and its customers; the key focus is enhancing the efficiency of business-to-consumer (B2C) transactions (transactions between organisations and individuals). In e-business, however, IT is not only used to enhance communications and transactions with customers, but is also applied within the organisation with an emphasis on the improvement or engineering of the business itself, by changing the organisational structure, business models and processes.

Three primary processes are enhanced through the transformation to e-business, which involve an organisation in internal and external change:

- *production processes*, which include the procurement, ordering and replenishment of stocks, processing of payments, electronic links with suppliers, and production control processes, among others;
- *customer-focused processes*, which include, for example, promotional and marketing efforts, selling over the internet, processing customers' purchase orders and payments, and customer support;
- *internal management processes*, which include aspects such as employee services, training, internal information-sharing, video-conferencing and recruiting, workgroup communications and electronic publishing. Electronic applications enhance the information flow between production and sales forces to improve the productivity of the sales force.

Figure 13.3 illustrates an organisation making intensive use of internet and digital technology for e-commerce and e-business. Information can flow seamlessly between different parts of the company and between the company and external entities: its customers, suppliers and business partners.

Types of e-business

There are many different types of e-business (which are often interchangeably termed e-commerce): business-to-business (B2B), business-to-customer (B2C), business-to-government (B2G), consumer-to-consumer (C2C) and mobile commerce (m-commerce).

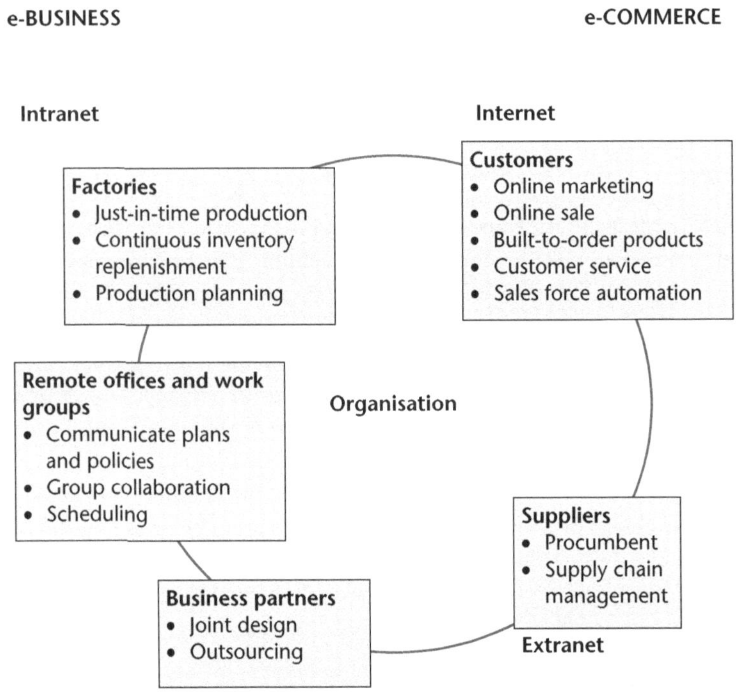

FIGURE 13.3 Schema of an organisation making intensive use of internet and digital technology for e-commerce and e-business

Business-to-business

B2B e-business (or e-commerce) occurs between companies. This type of e-business deals with the relationships between and inside businesses. About 80 percent of e-business is of this type, and most experts predict that B2B e-commerce will continue to grow faster than the B2C segment. Most B2B applications, such as supplier management, inventory management, distribution management, channel management and payment management, are extranet based so they can be accessed by an organisation's partners.

Business-to-consumer

B2C e-business, or e-commerce, between companies and consumers involves customers gathering information, purchasing physical goods (i.e. tangibles such as books or consumer products) or informational goods (or goods of electronic material or digitised content, such as software or e-books) and, for informational goods, receiving products via an electronic network.

This is the second largest and the earliest form of e-commerce. Its origins can be traced to online retailing (or e-tailing). Thus, the more common B2C business models are those of online retailing companies such as Amazon.com, Alibaba.com and Toysrus.com. Other B2C examples involving informational goods are the companies E*Trade and Travelocity.

Consumer-to-consumer

C2C e-commerce is simply commerce between private individuals or consumers. This type of e-commerce is characterised by the growth of electronic marketplaces and online auction sites, particularly in vertical industries where firms and businesses can bid for what they want from among multiple suppliers. Popular C2C sites such as eBay and Napster indicate that this market is quite large: these sites produce millions of pounds in sales every day.

Consumer-to-business

Consumer-to-business (C2B) transactions are featured by reverse auctions, which empower the consumer to drive the transactions. An example of this is when several airlines have to decrease their ticket prices if they wish to meet the price the traveller has been quoted by the competing suppliers. In doing this, the price goes downwards instead of upwards, as it would in a traditional auction.

m-Commerce

m-Commerce is another type of e-business model. It refers to a transaction if it involves the transfer of ownership or rights to use goods and services, and is initiated and/or completed by using mobile access to computer-mediated networks with the help of an electronic device (Tiwari 2006).

The term 'mobile commerce' was coined in the late 1990s to mean the delivery of e-commerce capabilities directly into the consumer's hand, anywhere, via wireless technology. m-Commerce opens up new business opportunities by enabling innovative, location-based services that the 'immobile' internet cannot offer. For instance, the location of the nearest ATM in real time can only be provided by determining the user's current geographical position.

Features of m-commerce

m-Commerce is characterised by some unique features that equip it with certain advantages against conventional forms of commercial transactions, including e-commerce:

- *Ubiquity*: Users can make use of services and carry out transactions largely independent of their current geographical location (the 'anywhere' feature). This feature can be useful in many situations, for example to cross-check prices while standing in a supermarket or while on the move.

- *Immediacy*. Closely related to ubiquity is the possibility of real-time access to services (the 'anytime' feature). This feature is particularly attractive for services that are time-critical and demand a fast reaction, for example stock market information for a broker. Additionally, consumers can buy goods and services as and when they feel the need. The immediacy of transaction helps to capture consumers at the moment of intention so that sales are not lost in the hiatus between the point of intention and the point of actual purchase.
- *Localisation*: Positioning technologies, such as the Global Positioning System (GPS), allow companies to offer goods and services to users that are specific to their current location. Location-based services can thus be offered to meet consumers' needs and wishes for a localised content and services.
- *Instant connectivity*: Ever since the introduction of the General Packet Radio Service (GPRS), mobile devices are constantly online, that is, in touch with the network. This feature brings convenience to the user, as time-consuming dial-up or boot processes are not necessary.
- *Proactive functionality*: By virtue of its ability to be immediate, local and personal, m-commerce opens new avenues for push marketing, such as content and product offers. Services like 'opt-in advertising' can be offered, so that users may choose those products, services and companies that they want to be kept informed about. The Short Message Service (SMS) can be used to send brief text messages to consumers, informing them of relevant local offerings that best suit their needs. This feature ensures that the 'right' (relevant) information can be provided to users in the 'right' place at the 'right' time. Similarly, users do not have to fear missing some potentially crucial information or getting it too late.

Service and applications

Mobile commerce has been applied in diverse business areas to provide a rich range of services, as elaborated below and summarised in Table 13.1:

- *Mobile banking*: This application makes it possible to complete bank-related transactions, for example checking account statuses, transferring money and selling stocks, via mobile devices independent of the user's current location.
- *Mobile entertainment*: This application contains services that provide the user with digital data with entertainment value on mobile devices; this can be ringtones, music or videos. It also opens up an array of interactive services, such as betting, gaming, dating and chatting.
- *Mobile information services*: This term refers to mobile services that provide subscribers with content of an informational character. Examples of such services are news updates of any nature (e.g. finance, politics and sports), travel information, access to search engines and mobile office capability (emails, appointments, etc.).

TABLE 13.1 m-commerce service and applications

Application	*Examples of services offered*
Mobile banking	Mobile accounting Mobile brokerage Mobile financial information
Mobile entertainment	Mobile gaming Downloading of music and ring tones Downloading of videos and digital images Location-based entertainment services
Mobile information services	Current affairs (financial, sport and other news) Travel information Tracking services (persons and objects) Mobile search engines and directories mobile office
Mobile marketing	Mobile couponing Direct (context-sensitive) marketing Organisation of mobile events Mobile newsletters
Mobile shopping	Mobile purchasing of goods and services
Mobile ticketing	Public transport Sports and cultural events Air and rail traffic Parking
Telematics services	Remote diagnosis and maintenance of vehicles Navigation services Vehicle tracking and theft protection Emergency services

- *Mobile marketing*: This refers to services based on mobile communication technologies that provide firms with new, innovative instruments, for example to increase sales, win and retain customers, improve after-sales services, build and sustain a positive and modern image/brand and carry out market research. In this way, mobile devices serve as simple and relatively inexpensive channels of interaction.
- *Mobile shopping*: This application bundles services that allow for the mobile processing of transactions involving the purchase of goods that are in common daily use. Users can purchase (mostly standardised) products by choosing them from a catalogue accessible from a mobile device.
- *Mobile ticketing*: All services that must be paid for before the lawful utilisation of a service can take place are suitable for mobile ticketing, for example travel by public transport or entry to a cultural event or cinema. This application ensures that users can purchase a right to utilisation or entry (i.e. a ticket) via a mobile device, replacing the conventional paper ticket.
- *Telematics services*: This refers to innovative technologies that link telecommunication technologies with informatics. The transport segment has been the primary area for this application, which is also known as intelligent transport

systems. The main services involved are navigation systems, remote diagnosis and access to other mobile applications, such as mobile entertainment, mobile content/office, mobile banking and mobile shopping.

e-Enterprise

e-Enterprise marks a new phase of IT-supported business after e-commerce and e-business in the digital era. When a company adopts the e-enterprise model, it enables itself to leverage fully the potential of information, IT and the benefits of the extended value chain.

In an e-enterprise, the whole value chain – from the procurement of raw materials on the supply side to consumer retailing and customer management on the demand side – is extended by combining the traditional bricks and mortar assets with the efficiency of cybermediation with external partners. The optimal benefits can be achieved if the enterprise can interconnect with the business processes of the partner organisations to form a 'coopetitive' virtual relationship, that is, a cooperative competitive relationship with customers, suppliers, distributors, partners and competitors. The competitive advantage of each e-enterprise is embedded in the speed and agility that are gained by establishing e-business models that leverage its existing asset base and the extended value chain.

Fundamentally, e-enterprise is about engineering and re-engineering inward- and outward-facing business processes by leveraging the unique strengths of IT. Traditional industry boundaries will crumble over time; antiquated industries gradually will become extinct, and new industries will be born to take their place. e-Enterprise is a new paradigm in organisational cultures, business models and processes, and is much more than just technologies. It is about repositioning brands and companies, cannibalising distribution channels through disintermediation, establishing new markets on the internet through re-intermediation, segmenting customers' needs, marketing products on a one-to-one basis, empowering customers with customer self-service, and building communities of interest to promote goods and services.

What makes up an e-enterprise?

As shown in Figure 13.4, an e-enterprise integrates supplier-facing systems (e.g. SCM), internal systems (e.g. enterprise resource planning [Box 13.2]) and customer-facing systems (e.g. CRM). With the effective use of information, e-enterprise is able to synchronise the supply and demand in real time, manage the ore processes and interact with customers more smoothly. The following sections will discuss how effective use of information supports the key functions of an e-enterprise.

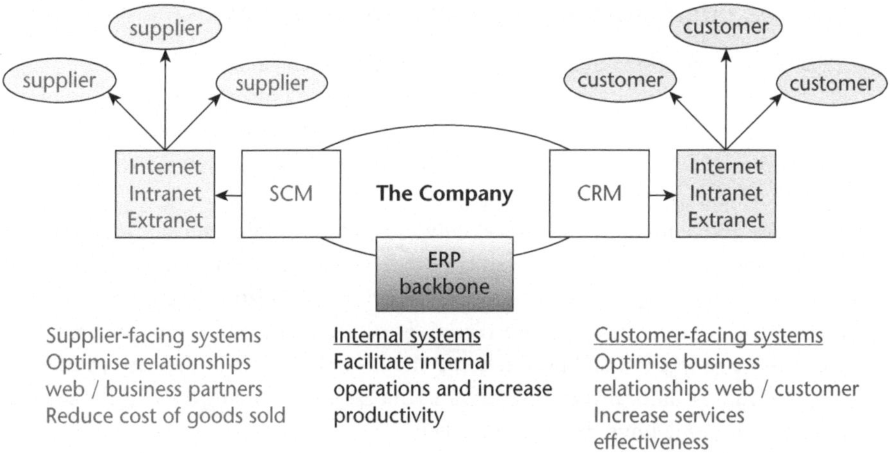

FIGURE 13.4 The typical composition of an e-enterprise. ERP, enterprise resource planning

Box 13.2 What is ERP?

ERP stands for enterprise resource planning. To get a deeper understanding of how ERP solutions can transform a business, it helps to get a better sense of what ERP actually is and how it works.

ERP refers to business management software that consists of a suite of integrated applications to support various business activities and processes. These activities and processes are often essential to running a business, including inventory and order management, accounting, human resources, customer relationship management and beyond. At its most basic level, ERP software integrates these various functions into one complete system to streamline processes and information across the entire organisation.

The central feature of all ERP systems is a shared database that supports the multiple functions used by different business units. In practice, this means that employees in different divisions — for example, accounting and sales — can rely on the same information for their specific needs.

ERP software also offers some degree of synchronised reporting and automation. Instead of forcing employees to maintain separate databases and spreadsheets that have to be manually merged to generate reports, some ERP solutions allow staff to pull reports from one system. For instance, with sales orders automatically flowing into the financial system without any manual rekeying, the order management department can process orders more quickly and accurately, and the finance department can close the books faster. Other common ERP features include a portal or dashboard to enable employees to quickly understand the business's performance on key metrics.

Business informatics in supply chain management

SCM aims to coordinate all the supply activities of an organisation, from its suppliers and partners to its customers. SCM is the close linkage and coordination of activities involved in buying, making and moving a product. It integrates supplier, manufacturer, distributor and customer logistics processes to reduce time, redundant effort and inventory costs.

Figure 13.5 illustrates the major entities in the supply chain and the flow of information upstream and downstream to coordinate the activities involved in buying, making and moving a product. Materials, information and payments flow through the supply chain in both directions. Goods start out as raw materials and move through logistics and production systems until they reach the customers. The supply chain includes reverse logistics in which returned items flow in the reverse direction from the buyer back to the seller.

Relevant activities

The supply chain is a network of organisations and business processes for procuring materials, transforming raw materials into intermediate and finished products, and distributing the finished products to the customers.

Stakeholders

SCM links suppliers, manufacturing plants, distribution centres, conveyances, retail outlets, people and information through processes such as procurement, inventory control, distribution and delivery to supply goods and services from the source through to consumption.

Relevant information

The effective use of information is critical in coordinating activities in the supply chain to improve efficiency. For example, the upstream information includes

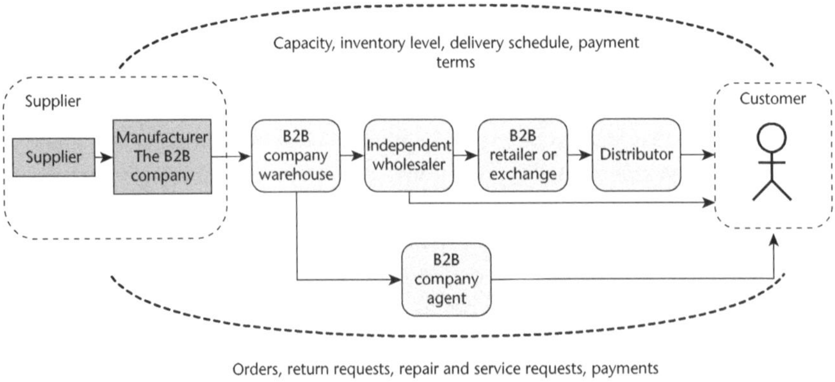

FIGURE 13.5 Supply chain management. B2B, business-to-business

the capacity, inventory level, delivery schedule and payment terms. On the other hand, the downstream information includes orders, return requests, repair and service requests, and payments. The effective use of information therefore helps organisations to get the right amount of products from their source to their point of consumption in the least amount of time and at the lowest cost.

'Push' supply chain models

These are a more traditional type of supply chain. As shown in Figure 13.6, under the push model products are manufactured or procured based on anticipated customer orders. The core assumption is that demand can be anticipated, and that it is more efficient and reliable to mobilise resources in prespecified ways to serve this demand. The aim of push model is to maximise the utilisation of resources, raw materials or infrastructure at the lowest cost.

However, the 'push' model is often associated with long production runs and high inventory levels due to the assumption of anticipated demands that may not reflect sudden fluctuations in the market. In such a supply chain, sensitivity to market demands and the agility to change production are not the central concerns, and information-sharing throughout the supply chain for a swift response to the fluctuation in market demands may not be a key feature. When demands suddenly change, there may be inefficiencies in the supply chain, such as parts shortages, underutilised plant capacity, an excessive finished goods inventory or run-away transportation costs. For example, manufacturers may have to keep ample parts in inventory because it might be hard to know exactly when they will receive their next shipment from their suppliers. In turn, suppliers may order too few raw materials because they do not have precise information on demand. These supply chain inefficiencies can cause significant wastage in a company's operating cost.

An integrated supply chain, which allows its members share information dynamically about inventory levels, schedules, forecasts and shipments, will lead to increased efficiency.

'Pull' supply chain model

In a pull supply chain, procurement, production and distribution are directly driven by customer demands, as shown in Figure 13.7. The pull supply chain model takes customers' demands as the input and, in response, provides products and services specific to those customers. Information about market changes and

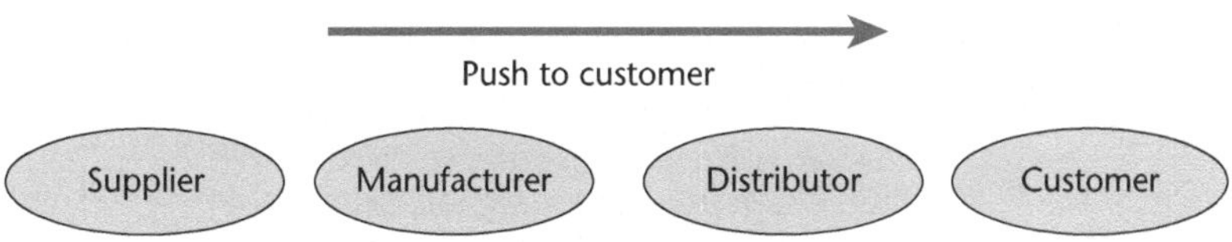

FIGURE 13.6 Push model of supply chain management

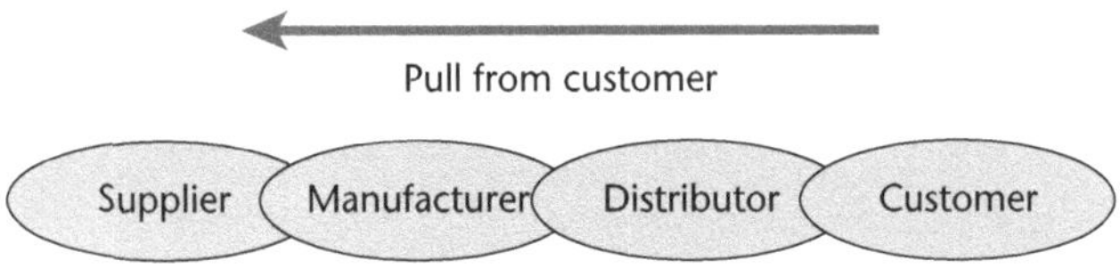

FIGURE 13.7 Pull model of supply chain management

customer demands are drivers in planning the procurement of raw materials, production and distribution. IT is used for market research, and information-sharing between stakeholders is critically important. Therefore, this model has short and flexible production runs as well as low inventories.

How information systems can facilitate supply chain management

Supply chains are often a combination of both the push and pull models, with information systems playing an important role in facilitating the activities. Information systems make SCM more efficient by helping companies to coordinate, schedule and control procurement, production, inventory management and the delivery of products and services. SCM systems can be built using intranets, extranets or special SCM software. Companies can benefit from using information systems for SCM in different ways, for example deciding when and what to produce, store and move, and tracking the status of orders.

Information systems can support the supply chain in two areas: supply chain planning and supply chain execution. Information systems can support organisations to generate demand forecasts for a product and to develop sourcing and manufacturing plans for that product, as in the following examples:

- *Order planning*: Select an order fulfilment plan that best meets the desired level of service to the customer given the existing transportation and manufacturing constraints.
- *Advanced scheduling and manufacturing planning*: Provide a detailed coordination of scheduling based on an analysis of changing factors such as customer orders, equipment outages or supply interruptions. Scheduling modules create job schedules for the manufacturing process and supplier logistics.
- *Demand planning*: Generate demand forecasts from all business units using statistical tools and business forecasting techniques.
- *Distribution planning*: Create operating plans for logistics managers for order fulfilment, based on an input from the demand and manufacturing planning modules.
- *Transportation planning*: Track and analyse the inbound and outbound movement of materials and products to ensure that materials and finished goods are delivered at the right time, in the right place and at the minimum cost.

Information systems can also manage the flow of products through distribution centres and warehouses to ensure that products are delivered to the right locations in the most efficient manner, as below:

- *Final production*: Organise and schedule the final sub-assemblies required to make each final product.
- *Replenishment*: Coordinate the component replenishment work so that warehouses remain stocked with the minimum amount of inventory in the pipeline.
- *Distribution management*: Coordinate the process of transporting goods from the manufacturer to the distribution centres and on to the final customers. Provide online customer access to the shipment and delivery data.
- *Reverse distribution*: Track the shipment and accounting for returned goods or remanufactured products.

Enhancing supply chain management with the Internet of Things

The IoT has been recognised as an effective way to improve the visibility of SCM. By adding radiofrequency identification (RFID) tags to every product, tool, resource and item of materials, each container, pallet, case and item being manufactured and shipped can be uniquely identified and closely tracked. The IoT benefits SCM in the following ways (Wagenaar, 2012).

Improved inventory management

By using the technology of the IoT, stock can be monitored in real time (Box 13.3), which can save overstocking and overproduction. The application of the IoT can decrease the reaction time of a traditional enterprise from being alerted to the customer's requirements to the supply of a commodity from 120 days to a few days (Atzori *et al.* 2010), which allows a significant decrease in stock size, and thus a cost saving. Other advantages include theft and loss prevention, reduced turnaround times and the avoidance of unnecessary handling (Decker *et al.* 2008) (from Wagenaar 2012).

Box 13.3 Mini case study: the Internet of things in real world of supply chain management – American Apparel's 'one size/one style' model

This rapidly expanding specialty apparel chain introduced a pilot item-level radiofrequency identification (RFID) system in one of its Manhattan stores in October 2007. The system included a combination of fixed and mobile RFID readers, and every garment in the store carried a serialised RFID tag.

(Continued)

(Continued)

The results of the pilot programme were dramatic. Inventory accuracy, which had been about 70–75% before RFID, leapt to 99%. The time to count the sales floor was slashed from 30 man-hours to just under 4 man-hours. Better visibility into the location of merchandise in the stock room allowed the store to reduce its average stock levels by 10,000 pieces (roughly 15%) without compromising its in-stock position on the selling floor. American Apparel also began testing 'magic' mirrors on the selling floor.

The pilot scheme offered such a clear return on investment that American Apparel planned to roll out RFID across all of its nearly 150 North American stores, beginning with 17 stores in the New York metro area. In addition to the benefits listed above, once the system had been regionalised, the company was expecting it to increase sales by enhancing the intrastore transfer process.

Real-time supply chain management

One of the major challenges in SCM is reducing the bullwhip effect. A major cause of the bullwhip effect is information distortion (Lee *et al.* 1997). For a better information flow, the IoT is able to trigger all the relevant actors in the supply chain upon the sale of a product (He *et al.* 2010). In traditional processes, information on demand was only passed to the direct downstream partner instead of being shared with the whole chain. The new sophisticated RFID chips used in the IoT allow the recording of all kinds of manufacturing information, production date, expiry date, warranty period, after-sales details and so on, allowing real-time and more efficient SCM (Agrawal and Das 2011).

Increased logistic transparency

The IoT embeds the load carried by a logistics operator with smart objects, which can make information about transport (destination, identification, transport conditions, etc.) available to the entire supply chain, making the chain more transparent (Decker 2008). The smart items monitor the goods and proactively raise an alert if transport conditions are no longer appropriate, so the carrier is alerted and the goods have a higher chance of being saved. This reduces the costs of return and the removal of defective goods, and lowers transport costs due to lower reshipping rate. Because the load is actively providing information, the status of the load is more transparent, so a carrier can accurately be held responsible for the amount of defective goods.

Business process optimisation

With the IoT, we can embed almost everything – trucks, forklifts, pallets, work-in-progress bins, consumer products – within a business process, the result being a more detailed look into business processes, simplifying the detection of conflicts and inefficiencies. The use of the IoT often leads to the discovery of problems that had not at first been uncovered, creating new possibilities to optimise a process (Fleish 2010) (Box 13.4).

Box 13.4 Mini case study: the Internet of Things in the real world of supply chain management – retail giant Falabella restocking high-value menswear

Chile's 118-year old Falabella Group recognised the retail potential of radiofrequency identification (RFID) early, but waited until the technology's second generation had demonstrated high reliability to introduce a 4-month pilot programme in one of its Santiago department stores. The system includes handheld and mobile readers mounted on carts; RFID tags were affixed to two popular lines of men's apparel, including tailored garments as well as trousers, shirts, sweaters and other items perceived to have high value to the store's customers.

The readability of RFID tags was quickly proven to be 99.7% accurate. With high confidence in the data that would be recorded, Falabella began daily inventory counts. This had been a monthly or even quarterly process, requiring as many as fifty employees working over two full nights while the store was closed. With RFID, a single associate could walk the floor pushing a mobile reader cart before the store opened each day. Using this system, hundreds of man-hours were reduced to a few hours while achieving 98.4% inventory accuracy. Routine daily reports gave store managers the data needed to set new key performance indicators on issues such as shrinkage and the dwell-time of merchandise in the back room, on the sales floor or in transit between the two.

Business informatics in customer relationship management

Instead of treating customers as exploitable sources of income, businesses now view them as long-term assets to be nurtured through CRM. CRM focuses on managing in all the ways that a firm deals with its existing and potential customers.

CRM is both a business and a technology discipline that uses information systems to coordinate all of the business processes surrounding the firm's interactions with its customers in terms of sales, marketing and service. In particular, the effective use of CRM solutions supports business decisions related to the identification of new market segments, the determination of the lifetime value of customers, the prioritisation of prospecting efforts as well as the creation of new products and services. The ideal CRM system provides end-to-end customer care from the receipt of an order through to product delivery and service.

In CRM, *customer lifecycle* is a term used to describe the progression of steps a customer goes through when considering, purchasing, using and maintaining loyalty to a product or service. However, most CRM systems address only a single phase of the lifecycle, such as the customer acquisition process or after-sales support. But customers require care during every step, and not just during those phases supported by narrowly defined CRM applications.

The effective use of information to support the whole customer lifecycle

As CRM applications become more pervasive throughout industry, customers come to expect the efficient service they enjoy in a truly customer-oriented manner. No company's customers will tolerate the inefficiency and annoyance of having to repeatedly provide information to customer service representatives if they have dealt with the company before. This means that no company can effectively service their customers without streamlining and integrating all the phases of the customer lifecycle. As customer-oriented companies realise the benefits of integrated CRM technology, they push their technology vendors to add more customer-oriented functionality and to address a greater part of the customer lifecycle. Yet CRM vendors that provide applications in support of only some segments of the customer lifecycle can never support the streamlined vision these companies need.

As shown in Figure 13.8, the customer lifecycle actually consists of five phases: perceiving, acquiring, fulfilling, sustaining and enhancing. While they are described here as if each phase occurs sequentially, in the real world the phases are more like a circle or an endless continuum.

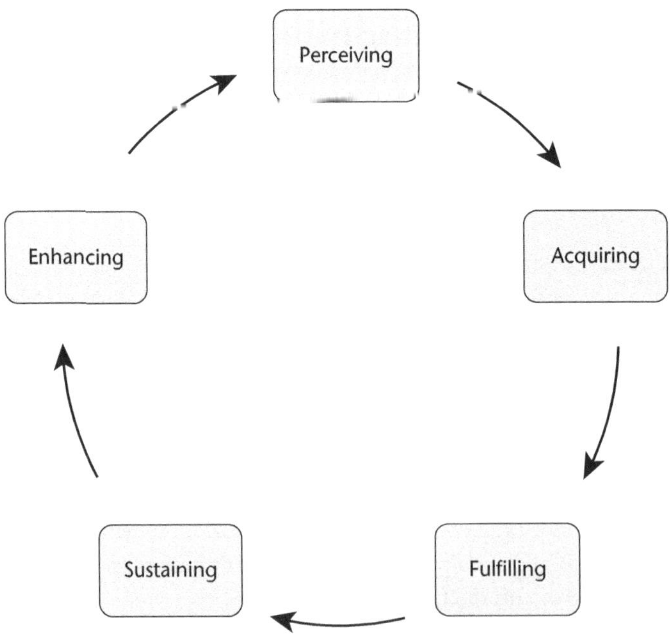

FIGURE 13.8 The customer lifecycle

Phase 1: Perceiving

The perceiving phase is a discovery process to find out who the potential customers are, what the customers need and which of the company's offers meet their needs. The effective use of information can help in perceiving customers in a number of ways.

Business intelligence

Business intelligence has become an increasingly important approach to learn about and perceive customers. The ability to predict which customers will be most profitable, or which products or offers will appeal to certain segments of the market, has a huge impact on the company's bottom line. By focusing a company's marketing efforts, integrated business intelligence results in a faster return on investment through shortened sales cycles, less chasing of unqualified accounts, larger orders and more repeat orders.

Sales force automation and lead management

A sales force automation and lead management system will help to integrate the data from the rest of the company's business systems. This prevents the duplication of contact information or the inappropriate contact of existing customers, and creates an essential repository for any knowledge gained in the preliminary discussion phases – which is vital to effective customer lifecycle management.

Phase 2: Acquiring

The acquiring phase of customer lifecycle management includes the activities and techniques used to gain new customers. Communication is important in acquiring new customers. Communicating with customers may encompass marketing campaigns, advertising and other branding efforts and communications from the sales force or other company employees. The use of information is vitally important in establishing a two-way communication with customers and prospects in order to understand their problems and to explain how the company's products or services can help to resolve them. This ensures that prospects are being targeted with the most effective offers at the most effective intervals. Customer feedback helps companies to create better products and services that meet their needs better than those of the company's competitors. The effective use of information can be achieved in several ways:

- *Marketing automation*: Marketing automation can, for example, select from dozens of campaigns or even create a new one on the fly, to determine the most appropriate version for a specific individual or company.
- *Analytic applications*: These present the success rates of various formats or campaigns, and allow a virtually unlimited variety of demographic 'slicing and dicing'.
- *Customer self-service*: Self-service is another key communication method. Customers enjoy the chance to browse products and learn about new features or offerings without the pressure of a live interaction.

Phase 3: Fulfilling

This phase ensures that the product is planned for delivery to meet the customer's needs, along with their approval of price and other terms and conditions of the order. Sales order entry, product configurators and quotation management are critically important pieces of the technology required to support this phase. Demand information comes through many channels. Companies often have both a direct sales force and a network of distribution partners. In any case, the field representation for any company is usually geographically scattered and may have varied communication capabilities. In addition, customers may provide input directly through storefronts or collaboration portals. The effective use of demand information can be realised in a number of ways.

Integration of information

The ability to aggregate the information from all these different sources into a single, cohesive picture of the demand for a company's products can prove invaluable in ensuring a consistent supply and an efficient value chain. This aggregation of information is best achieved through a solution that provides access across every channel and is also integrated with the company's back-office systems. The efficient aggregation of information frees up expensive sales personnel and a channel partner to focus on what really counts – getting the order.

Multiple communication channels

It is imperative that the fulfilling phase is supported through every possible channel, for example via a customer contact centre, web storefronts and customer self-service portals, from a company's channel partners or by its own sales force. By supporting all these channels, IT can help a company to effectively segment its market and deploy the right solution rapidly. This enhanced access to information reduces the cost of servicing a customer, regardless of the channel utilised, by reducing wasted efforts and shortening sales cycles.

Phase 4: Sustaining/retaining

The sustaining phase involves activities and techniques that are designed to maintain relationships with existing customers. The key to customer retention is more than remembering a customer's name. Customers are loyal when you deliver the right product at the right time and at the right price. True customer orientation is about more than just communication. Once a customer has trusted a company by placing an order, the company needs to make good on that trust by fulfilling the order, quickly, efficiently and correctly every time.

But in today's fast-paced business environment, almost about any delay and any error can result in the loss of a customer's repeat business. Speed and excellence of execution at every step is the key to customer satisfaction and provides a true competitive advantage.

The effective use of information to sustain customers can be implemented in integrated systems. Integrated systems for the customer acquisition and fulfilment phases eliminate a major source of delay and error. Faster delivery times lead to happier customers and more repeat orders. Integration with back-office systems also results in greater billing accuracy by eliminating the need for redundant data entry. This results in better Figures for days that sales are outstanding and increased cash flow. Fewer errors also lead to happier customers and more orders. The integration of front-office and back-office systems is a key to providing excellent – rather than merely adequate – customer service. Having stand-alone or cobbled-together systems in these critical areas is an invitation to achieve unhappy customers and a resulting loss of business.

Phase 5: Enhancing

The enhancing phase involves activities and techniques to encourage customers to increase their involvement with an organisation. The job is not done yet when the order has shipped. Truly customer-oriented companies recognise that every customer interaction is an opportunity. Customers often require installation, training or repair services related to products and equipment.

The effective use of customer activity information can be achieved by information systems applications. It vital that a company has a record of exactly what was shipped to a customer and any modifications that have been made to it since the original configuration. This enables the company to despatch the technician with the right skills and the right materials to service the customer quickly, cost-effectively and efficiently. Understanding warranties and service contracts, and having that information readily available to the service group, ensures that customers are not billed for warranty work or billed incorrectly under the terms of their service contract.

Yet if servicing is managed within a disparate separate system, this information must be laboriously re-entered or mapped to the other system, introducing a source of error, delay and potential customer dissatisfaction. This will quickly lead to declining customer loyalty, fewer future orders and, ultimately, decreasing competitive advantage. The integrated customer information streamlines the information process and helps to eliminate billing errors. By offering self-service options along with a contact centre, warranty management and field service applications, the effective use of information allows a company to service the customer cost-effectively in the most optimal way.

Social media, mobile technology, radiofrequency identification and customer relationship management

Social CRM is a recent development within CRM. Integrating social media with CRM strategies seems to be the next frontier for organisations that want to optimise the power of social interactions to get closer to their customers. With the worldwide explosion of social media usage, businesses are feeling extreme pressure to be where their customers are. Social media holds enormous potential for companies to get closer to their customers and, by doing so, facilitate increased revenue, cost reduction and greater efficiencies. Social media initiatives are quickly springing up across organisations.

Many companies offer commerce opportunities delivered through third-party social platforms such as Facebook (Box 13.5). In 2009, 1-800-FLOWERS.COM was among the first to enable customers on Facebook to select products and purchase directly from a Facebook page. In 2010, Delta Airlines launched a 'social media ticket window' on Facebook, allowing customers to book a flight without having to go to Delta's website. Delta has indicated that Facebook is used by more customers while in flight than any other website, making it a 'natural launching point' for its initiative.

Box 13.5 Mini case study: Cold Stone Creamery – real value for real friends

Cold Stone Creamery's eGift program on Facebook is an excellent example of social commerce that optimises the unique community aspect of social networking.

Cold Stone Creamery, an ice cream franchiser with 1,500 locations in 16 countries, wanted to find a creative way to engage followers with a valued offering and, at the same time, drive a measurable impact on in-store sales. On Cold Stone's Facebook page, customers can select one or more friends to send gifts to, choose the product they would like their friends to receive, add a personal message and proceed through the security-rich check-out process. Recipients get a Facebook message or email with the eGift and its associated redemption code. By following the instructions provided, recipients can redeem their treat and customise its flavour in any US Cold Stone store location.

The results have been impressive. Cold Stone linked social media interaction with concrete consumer behaviour patterns to increase profitability. They monetised their Facebook presence by facilitating a fun, easy way for followers to send small treats to friends – something they believed their customers would value. They were right – within weeks, eGift had added thousands of dollars in incremental sales to franchisees.

Business informatics in value chain management

A value chain captures the activities that a firm operating in a specific industry performs in order to deliver a valuable product or service to the market (Box 13.6).

Box 13.6 The value chain

The value chain was first proposed by Michael Porter in his 1985 best-seller book *Competitive Advantage: Creating and Sustaining Superior Performance.* It is

(Continued)

(Continued)

a concept that was originally used in business management. The value chain addresses the economic logic of why an organisation exists in the first place.

The value chain aims to address the following questions: How does your organisation create value? How do you change business inputs into business outputs in such a way that they have a greater value than the original cost of creating those outputs?

For example, manufacturing companies create value by acquiring raw materials and using them to produce something useful. Retailers bring together a range of products and present them in a way that is convenient to customers, sometimes supported by services such as fitting rooms or advice from a personal shopper. Insurance companies offer customers policies that are underwritten by larger re-insurance policies.

Understanding how the company creates value and looking for ways to add more value are critical elements in developing a competitive strategy. A value chain for a product or service reflects all the value-adding activities that occur during the product's creation, development, sales and after-sales service. The way in which value chain activities are performed determines the costs and affects the profits, so it can help to understand the sources of value for the organisation. Studying an organisation's value chain will help in exploring how to add value at every activity and also identifying how another company could add more value by teaming up with the firm.

Traditional value chain

Porter describes a chain of activities common to all businesses, and divides them into primary and support activities, as shown in Figure 13.9.

Primary activities

Primary activities relate directly to the physical creation, sale, maintenance and support of a product or service. They consist of the following:

- *Inbound logistics*: These are all the processes related to receiving, storing and distributing inputs internally. Supplier relationships are a key factor in creating value here.
- *Operations:* These are the transformation activities that change inputs into the outputs that are sold to customers. Operational systems create value here.
- *Outbound logistics*: These activities deliver the company's product or service to the customer. These are things like the collection, storage and distribution systems, and they may be internal or external to the organisation.
- *Marketing and sales*: These are the processes the company uses to persuade clients to purchase from them instead of their competitors. The benefits the

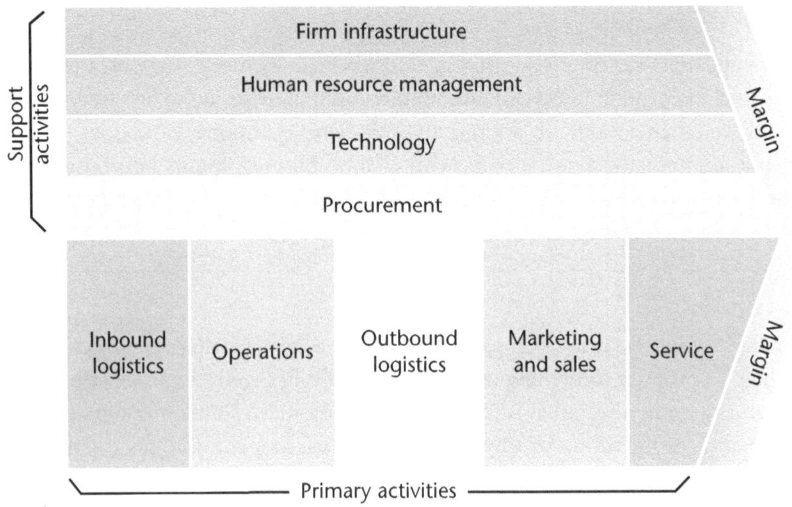

FIGURE 13.9 Porter's value chain model (Porter 1985)

company offers, and how well the company communicates them, are sources of value here.

- *Service*: These are the activities related to maintaining the value of the product or service to customers once it has been purchased.

Support activities

These activities support the primary functions above. In Figure 13.9, support, or secondary, activities in the top part of the diagram play a role in support the primary activities. For example, procurement supports operations with certain activities, but it also supports marketing and sales with other activities.

- *Procurement (purchasing)*: This is what the organisation does to get the resources it needs to operate. This includes finding vendors and negotiating the best prices.
- *Human resource management*: This relates to how well a company recruits, hires, trains, motivates, rewards and retains its workers. People are a significant source of value, so businesses can create a clear advantage with good human resource practices.
- *Technological development*: These activities relate to managing and processing information, as well as to protecting a company's knowledge base. Minimising the IT costs, staying current with technological advances and maintaining technical excellence are sources of value creation.
- *Infrastructure*: These are a company's support systems and the functions that allow a company to maintain its daily operations. Accounting, legal, administrative and

general management functions are examples of the necessary infrastructure that businesses can use to their advantage.

Companies use these primary and support activities as 'building blocks' to create a valuable product or service.

Reversed value chain through effective information management

Like the 'push' supply chain, the traditional Porter's value chain is a one-direction chain to make value by pushing products. It does not particularly highlight the importance of understanding customer needs and innovation. The effective use of information makes it possible to reverse the value chain by an increased focus on the market and the customers. As shown in Figure 13.10, all the activities in the reversed value change are initiated in market research, which is followed by new product design and development, product marketing, product materials, production and selling to fulfilment, as explained below:

- *Market research*: This will collect information on the market potential and users' requirements.
- *New product development*: Only when the demands have been identified and understood can the design and prototyping of the new product be started.
- *Market products*: Marketing campaigns may have started even before the product has been put on the production line. Orders will be taken already before the products have been made available.
- *Product materials/produce products*: Production is taking place when specific orders for the products have been placed. Each product can be customised to meet the specific requirements of the ordering customer, and can be delivered to the customer as soon as it is completed without being held in storage in the factory.
- *Manage selling and fulfilment*: This may include detailed customisation or fine-tuning of the product to meet the personalised requirements, as well as an in-depth after-sales service.

The reversed value chain has many advantages over the traditional value chain. However, one must realise that the effective use of information, supported by highly integrated information systems, is critical in this model. Information

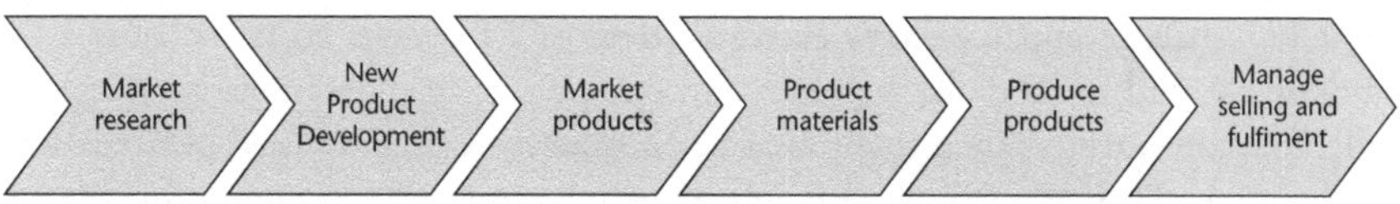

FIGURE 13.10 The reversed value chain model

systems covering each section of the value chain must be interoperable, which allows information-sharing across all the business areas. Effective decision-making and a speedy response to the market and to customer demands are essential.

Optimising value through business informatics

Business informatics is about effective management and the use of information as a resource in business. Information systems enable business users to adopt appropriate value chains, business models and business processes.

In most cases, both traditional and reversed value chain models may be adopted in the same organisation. For example, many automotive firms continue to apply the traditional value chain and subscribe to the push supply chain with their dealers, while others, even in the section of the car industry that is highly specialised to address high-end customers, may find the reversed value chain more appropriate.

Manufacturers of extremely expensive products have to follow the reversed value chain – it would be not so smart for the producer of an Airbus 380 to keep producing and leave a few planes in their stock without having received any orders for more. It should also be noted that computer manufacturer Dell has for many years adopted the pull supply chain: each desktop is not built until an order with technical specifications has been received.

It is appropriate to adopt the push replenishment philosophy when market demand is deemed stable and reasonably known; however, it is more reasonable to adopt the reversed value chain for fluctuating and unpredictable demands because it can synchronise with market variability and rapidly satisfy customer requirements.

The effective use of information facilitates information-sharing between all stakeholders from, for example, research and development, design, engineering, production and transportation to warehousing and customers service. The ability to optimise the logistics, value chain and service levels are affected by the use of information between the firm and its partners. Firms that manage and use information better both within the firm and between themselves and their external stakeholders can hold a competitive advantage in the marketplace (Bardi *et al.* 1994).

Value network

Successful value chain management requires an atmosphere of trust in which all the members of the value chain agree to cooperate and to honour the commitments they have made to each other (Welty and Becerra-Fernandez 2001). In some industries, companies have extended their SCM systems to work more collaboratively with customers, suppliers and other firms in their industry. This is a much broader mission than traditional SCM systems, which focused primarily on managing the flow of transactions between organisations. It focuses on using shared systems and business processes to optimise the value of relationships.

Distributed collaborative value network

Companies are relying on these new collaborative relationships to further improve their planning, production and distribution of goods and services. Therefore, the *distributed collaborative value network* is emerging as a new form of value chain. This value network uses digital technologies to enable multiple organisations to collaboratively design, develop, build, move and manage products and make value collaboratively through their lifecycles.

Stakeholders and relationships in value network

Firms can integrate their systems with those of their supply chain partners to coordinate demand forecasting, resource planning, production planning, replenishment, shipping and warehousing. They can work jointly with suppliers on product design and marketing. Customers can provide feedback for marketers to use to improve the product design, support and servicing arrangements. A firm engaged in collaborative commerce with its suppliers and customers can achieve new levels of efficiency in reducing product design cycles, minimising excess inventory, forecasting demand and keeping partners and customers informed.

Information technology in the enterprise value network

IT is making this level of collaboration possible by providing a platform where systems from different companies can seamlessly exchange information. Web-enabled networks for the coordination of transorganisational business processes provide an infrastructure for collaborative commerce activities (Box 13.7).

Box 13.7 Mini case study – Procter & Gamble's network

Procter & Gamble (P&G), the world's largest consumer goods company, developed an integrated industry-wide system to coordinate grocery store point-of-sale systems with grocery store warehouses, shippers, its own manufacturing facilities and the suppliers of its raw materials. This single industry-spanning system effectively allows P&G to monitor the movement of all its products from raw materials to customer purchase.

P&G uses data collected from point-of-sale terminals to trigger shipments to retailers of items that customers have purchased and that need restocking. Electronic links to suppliers enable P&G to order materials from its own suppliers

(Continued)

(Continued)

when its inventories are low. The system helps P&G reduce its inventory by allowing the company to produce products as they are demanded by retailers. P&G is implementing an Ultimate Supply System that uses internet technology to link retailers and suppliers to its private corporate intranet. By having retailers and suppliers integrate their systems with P&G's own systems, P&G hopes to reduce the product cycle time by half, inventory costs by $4.5 billion and systems costs by $5 billion.

IT permits firms and their business partners to share information such as product design and development, marketing, inventory and production scheduling, including the transmission of graphics, emails and computer-aided design drawings. Many of these networks are 'owned' and managed by large companies who use them to coordinate purchases, orders and other activities with their suppliers, distributors and selected business partners.

Similarly, Safeway U.K. (taken over by Morrisons in 2004) has electronic links to suppliers where it can share information about forecasts, shelf space and inventory in its supermarkets so suppliers can track the demand for their products, adjust their production, and adjust the timing and size of their deliveries. The suppliers can download Safeway's information into their enterprise systems or production planning systems. Suppliers send Safeway information about product availability, production capacity, and inventory levels.

Information technology in transenterprise applications

Some collaborative value chains can encompass an entire industry, coordinating the business processes for the key players in that industry, including suppliers, transporters, production firms, distributors and retailers. For example, the Oasis Systems websites link US electrical utility companies in regional power pool groups to sell their surplus power to wholesalers, and to locate the transmission facilities for moving the power between its source and the customers.

A few industrial networks have been built to support collaboration between firms in multiple industries. General Mills, Kellogg's, Land O'Lakes and Monsanto have used a common system based on internet technology to share their excess shipping capacity. The system uses a private network to coordinate underutilised shipping capacity in container trucks and railroad cars to reduce logistics costs for the participating members.

Questions and exercises

1. Identify applicable information systems and the functions of these systems in support of each aspect of the virtual value chain. Discuss how these systems enhance organisational performance in each aspect of the virtual value chain.

2. Is an enterprise resource planning system required to implement SCM and/or CRM systems, or vice versa?
3. Identify recent technologies that further support e-enterprises, and discuss how they contribute to them.
4. Identify the characteristics of the virtual value chain in comparison with the traditional value chain.
5. What is flattening the structure of the organisation? Discuss how the organisational structure evolves with the development of IT and e-enterprise.

BIBLIOGRAPHY

Accenture, 2010, Information Management In Policing – Improving Efficiency and Performance by Unlocking the Value of Information. Institute for Health & Public Service. http://www.accenture.com/sitecollectiondocuments/pdf/accenture_information_management_in_policing.pdf.

Accenture, 2013, Preparing Police Service for the Future. http://www.accenture.com/sitecollectiondocuments/pdf/preparing-police-services-future.pdf.

Ackoff, R., 1967, Management Misinformation Systems. *Management Science*, 14(4), 147–156.

Adema, J. J., 1990, Models and Algorithms for the Construction of Achievement Tests. Doctoral Thesis, University of Twente, Enschede.

Ades, Y. M., 1989, *NAMAT System User Manual*. SIS Project, University of Qatar.

Agrawal, S., Das, M., 2011, Internet of Things – A Paradigm Shift of Future Internet Applications. In *Nirma University International Conference on Engineering*.

Aho, A. V., Sethi, R., Ullman, J. D., 1986, *Compilers: Principles, Techniques, and Tools*. Addison-Wesley, Reading, MA.

Allen, L. E., Saxon, C. S, 1986, Analysis of the Logical Structure of Legal Rules by a Modernized and Formalized Version of Hohfeld's Fundamental Legal Conceptions. In Martino, A. A., Natali, F. S. (Eds.), *Automated Analysis of Legal Texts: Logic, Informatics, Law*. Elsevier Science, Amsterdam.

Alshehri, M., Drew, S. J., 2011, E-Government Principles: Implementation, Advantages and Challenges. *International Journal of Electronic Business*, 9(3), 255–270.

Andersen, P. B., 1991, A Semiotic Approach to Construction and Assessment of Computer Systems. In Nissen, H. E., Klein, H. K., Hirschheim, R. (Eds.), *Information Systems Research: Contemporary Approaches and Emergent Traditions*. Elsevier Science, Amsterdam.

Andersen, P. B., 1997, *A Theory of Computer Semiotics. Semiotic Approaches to Construction and Assessment of Computer Systems*. Cambridge University Press, Cambridge.

Åqvist, L., 1984, Deontic Logic. In Gabbay, D., Guenthner, D. (Eds.), *Handbook Of Philosophical Logic*, Vol. II. D. Reidel, Dordrecht, Holland.

Ashton, K., 2009, That 'Internet of Things' Thing. *RFiD Journal*, 22, 97–114.

Association for Computing Machinery (ACM), 2013, Curricula Recommendations,.http://www.acm.org/education/curricula-recommendations.

Atkinson, M., Bancilhon, F., Dewitt, D., Dittrich, K., Maier, D., Zdonik, S., 1990, The Object-oriented Database System Manifesto. In Kim, W., Nicolas, J.-M., Nishio, S. (Eds.), *Deductive and Object-Oriented Databases*. Elsevier Science, Amsterdam.

Atzori, L., Iera, A., Morabito, G., 2010, The Internet of Things: A survey. *Computer Networks*, 54(15), 2787–2805.

Auramäki, E., Lehtinen, E., Lyytinen, K., 1988, A Speech-act-based Office Modeling Approach. *ACM Transactions on Office Information Systems*, 6(2), 126–152.

Austin, J. L., 1980, *How To Do Things With Words. The William James Lectures Delivered At Harvard University in 1955*. Oxford University Press, Oxford.

Auto-ID Labs, 2014, Advancing the Internet of Things for Global Commerce. http://www.autoidlabs.org/.

Avison, D. E., Fitzgerald, G., 2006, *Information Systems Development: Methodologies, Techniques, and Tools*, 4th Ed. McGraw-Hill, New York.

Avison, D. E., Nandhakumar, J., 1995, The Discipline of Information Systems: Let Many Flowers Bloom! In *Proceedings of the IFIP International Working Conference on Information System Concepts: Towards a Consolidation of Views*. Chapman & Hall.

Bandura, A., 2001, Social cognitive theory: An agentic perspective. *Annual Review of Psychology*, 52(1), 1–26.

Barbic, F., Pernici, B., 1985. Time Modeling in Office Information Systems. In *Proceedings of the 1985 ACM SIGMOD International Conference On Management Of Data (SIGMOD '85)*. ACM, New York.

Barbosa, S. D. J., Souza, C. S. D., 2001, Extending software through metaphors and metonymies. *Knowledge-Based Systems*, 14(1–2), 15–27.

Bardi, E. J., Raghunathan, T. S., Bagchi, P. K., 1994, Logistics information systems: The strategic role of top management. *Journal of Business Logistics*, 15(1), 71–85.

Barr, P., Noble, J., Biddle, R., 2004, *A Semiotic Model of User-Interface Metaphor. Virtual, Distributed and Flexible Organisations Studies in Organisational Semiotics*, Springer, Dordrecht.

BBC, 2013, Costs of Failed NHS IT Project Continue To Rise. Http://Www.Bbc.Co.Uk/News/Health-24140967.

Beck, K., Cunningham, W., 1989, A laboratory for teaching object oriented thinking. *SIGPLAN Not*, 24(10), 1–6.

Benyon, D., 1994, A functional model of interacting systems: A semiotic approach. In Connolly, J. H., Edmonds, E. A. (Eds.), *CSCW and Artificial Intelligence*, Springer-Verlag, London.

Beynon-Davies, P., 2009, *Business Information Systems*. Palgrave Macmillan, London.

Bickerton, M., Siddiqi, J., 1993, The classification of requirements engineering methods. *Proceedings RE'93, IEEE International Symposium On Requirements Engineering*. IEEE, San Diego.

Bloch, M., Blumberg, S., Laartz, J., 2012, Delivering Large-scale IT projects on Time, on Budget, and on Value. McKinsey Insights and Publications. http://www.mckinsey.com/insights/business_technology/delivering_large-scale_it_projects_on_time_on_budget_and_on_value.

Blomberg, J., Giacomi, J., Mosher, A., Swenton-Wall, P., 1990, Ethnographic Field Methods and the Relation to Design. *Proceedings of the 1st Participatory Design Conference*, Seattle, WA.

Boehm, B., 1981, *Software Engineering Economics*. Prentice-Hall, Englewood Cliffs, NJ.

Boekkooi-Timminga, E., 1989, Models for Computerised Test Construction. Doctoral Dissertation, University Of Twente, Netherlands..

Boekkooi-Timminga, E., Sun, L., 1991, Contest: A Computerised Test Construction System. In Hoogstraten, J., Linden, W. J. V., (Eds.), *Proceedings of Dutch National*

Conference on Educational Research 'Onderwijs-Researchdagen'91'. Stichting Centrum Voor Onderwijsonderzoek, Van De Universiteit, Amsterdam.
Booch, G., 1993, *Object Oriented Design, with Applications*. Benjamin/Cummings, Redwood City, CA.
Booch, G., Rumbaugh, J., Jacobson, I., 1998, *Unified Modelling Language User Guide*. Addison-Wesley, Reading, Massachusetts.
Booch, G., Maksimchuk, R. A., Engle, M., Conallen, J., Houston, K., Young, B., 2007, *Object-oriented Analysis and Design with Applications*. Pearson Education, India.
Boustred, C., 1997, ATSI Seminars. http://www.strategize.com/presentations/paradigm/sld014.htm.
Brachman, R. J., 1979, On the epistemological status of semantic networks. In Findler, N. V. (Ed.), *Associative Networks: Representation and Use of Knowledge by Computers*. Academic Press, New York.
Brachman, R. J., Levesque, H. J. (Eds.), 1985, *Readings in Knowledge Representation*. Morgan Kaufmann, Los Altos, CA.
Bradley, R., Swartz, N., 1979, *Possible Worlds: An Introduction to Logic and its Philosophy*. Basil Blackwell, Oxford.
Brkic, J., 1970, *Norm And Order – An Investigation into Logic, Semantics, and the Theory of Law and Morals*. Humanities Press, New York.
Brynjolfsson, E., 1993, The Productivity Paradox of Information Technology. *Communications of the ACM*, 36(12), 66–77.
Burrell, G., Morgan, G., 1979, *Sociological Paradigms and Organisational Analysis*. Heinemann, London.
Buse, S., 2002, Der Mobile Erfolg – Ergebnisse Einer Empirischen Untersuchung In Ausgewählten Branchen, In Keuper, F. (Ed.): *Electronic Business und Mobile Business*. Gabler, Wiesbaden.
Carmel, E., Becker, S., 1995, A process model for packaged software development. *IEEE Transactions Of Engineering Management*, 41(5), 50–61.
Chakraborty, A., Baowaly, M. K., Arefin, A., Bahar, A. N., 2012, The role of requirement engineering in software development life cycle. *Journal of Emerging Trends in Computing and Information Sciences*, 3(5), 723–729.
Chandler, D., 2007, *Semiotics for Beginners* (2nd Ed.). Routledge, London.
Checkland, P. B., 1981, *Systems Thinking, Systems Practice*. John Wiley, Chichester.
Chellas, B. F., 1980, *Modal Logic: An Introduction*. Cambridge University Press, Cambridge.
Chen, P. P., 1976, The entity-relationship model, towards a unified view of data. *ACM Transactions on Database Systems*, 1(1), 9–36.
Clarke, R. J., 2001, Social semiotics contributions to the systemic semiotic workpractice framework. *Sign System Studies*, 29, 587–605.
Clarke, R. J., Nilsson, A. G., 2008, Business services as communication patterns: A work practice approach for analysing service encounters. *IBM Systems Journal*, 47(1), 129–141.
Clifford, J., Tansel A. U., 1985, On an Algebra for Historical Relational Databases: Two Views. In *Proceedings of the 1985 ACM SIGMOD International Conference on Management of Data (SIGMOD '85)*. ACM, New York.
Coad, P., Yourdon, E., 1990, *Object-oriented Analysis*. Prentice Hall, Englewood Cliffs, NJ.
Codd, E. F., 1970, A relational model of data for large shared data banks. *Communications of the ACM*, 13(6), 377–387.
Coffey, R., Richards, J., Remmert, C., Leroy, S., Schoville, R., Baldwin, P., 1992, An introduction to critical paths. *Quality Management in Health Care* 14(1), 45–55.
Cooper, R., Foster, M. (1971). Sociotechnical systems. *American Psychologist*, 26, 467–474.

Cunningham, D. J., 1992, Beyond educational psychology: Steps toward an educational semiotics. *Educational Psychology Review*, 4, 165–194.

Dahalin, Z. M., Razak, R. A., Ibrahim, H., Yusop, N. I., Kasiran, K. M., Malaysia, U., 2010, An enterprise architecture methodology for business–IT alignment: Adopter and developer perspectives. *Communications of the IBIMA*, 2010, 1–14.

Dardenne, A., Fickas, S., van Lamsweerde, A., 1991, Goal Directed Concept Acquisition in Requirements Elicitation. *Proceedings of the 6th International Workshop on Software Specification and Design*, Como, Italy.

Date, C. J., 1990, *An Introduction to Database Systems*, Vol. I (5th Ed.). Addison-Wesley, Reading, MA.

Decker, C., Berchtold, M., Chaves, L., Beigl, M., Roehr, D., Riedel, T. *et al.*, 2008, *Cost Benefit Model for Smart Items in the Supply Chain*. Lecture Notes in Computer Science. Akihabara, Tokyo.

Derry, S. J., 1999, A Fish Called Peer Learning: Searching for Common Themes. In A. M. O'Donnell, A. King (Eds.), *Cognitive Perspectives on Peer Learning*. Lawrence Erlbaum, Mahwah, NJ.

Devlin,K.,1991, *Logic and Information*. Cambridge University Press, Cambridge.

Dietz, J. L. G., 1992, Subject-oriented Modelling of Open Active Systems. In Falkenberg, E.D., Rolland, C., El-Sayed, E. N. (Eds.), *Information System Concepts: Improving the Understanding*. Elsevier Science, Amsterdam.

Dietz, J. L. G., Widdershoven, G. A. M., 1991, Speech Acts or Communicative Action? In Bannon, L., Robinson, M., Schmidt, K. (Eds.), *Proceedings of the Second European Conference on Computer-Supported Cooperative Work (CSCW'91)*. Kluwer, Dordrecht.

Dijk, T. A. V., 1981, *Studies in the Pragmatics of Discourse*. Mouton, The Hague.

Dik, S. C., 1978, *Functional Grammar*. North-Holland, Amsterdam.

Dik, S. C., 1989, *The Theory of Functional Grammar*, Part 1, *The Structure of the Clause*. Foris, Dordrecht.

Eco, U., 1976, *A Theory of Semiotics*. Indiana University Press, Bloomington, IN.

Eemeren, F. H. V., Grootendorst, R., 1984, *Speech Acts in Argumentative Discussions*. Foris, Dordrecht.

Embley, D. W., Kurtz, B. D., Woodfield, S. N., 1992, *Object-oriented Systems Analysis, A Model-Driven Approach*. Prentice Hall, Englewood Cliffs, NJ.

Engeström, Y., 1987, *Learning by Expanding: An Activity-theoretical Approach to Developmental Research*. Orienta-Konsultit,, Helsinki.

Ernest, P., 1999, *Social Constructivism as a Philosophy of Mathematics: Radical Constructivism*, SUNY Press, Albany, NY.

Everaert-Desmedt, N., 2011, Peirce's Semiotics. http://www.signosemio.com/peirce/semiotics.asp.

Falkenberg, E. D., Hesse, W., Lindgreen, P., Nilsson, B. E., Oei, J. L. H, Rolland, C. *et al.*, 1998, A Framework of Information System Concepts. The FRISCO Report (Web Edition), ftp://fip.leidenuiv.nl/pub/rul/fri-full.zip.

Federation of EA Professional Organizations, 2013, Common Perspectives on Enterprise Architecture. *Architecture and Governance Magazine*, (9-4).

Feng, X., Liu, K., Jiang, G. (Eds.), 2009, *Information Systems in the Changing Era: Theory and Practice. Proceedings of the 11th Conference on Organisational Semiotics*. Aussino Academic Publishing House, Beijing.

Filippidou, D., 1998, Designing with scenarios: A critical review of current research and practice. *Requirements Engineering*, 3(1), 1–22.

Fiske, J., 1990, *Introduction to Communication Studies*. Routledge, London.

Fleisch, E., 2010, *What is the Internet of Things? When Things Add Value*. Auto-ID Labs White Paper WP-BIZAPP-053. Auto-ID Labs, St Gallen, Switzerland.

Flores, F., Graves, M., Hartfield, B., Winograd, T., 1988, Computer systems and the design of organisational interaction. *ACM Transactions on Office Information Systems*, 6(2), 153–172.

Follesdal, D., Hilpinen, R., 1971, Deontic Logic: An Introduction. In Hilpinen, R. (Ed.), *Deontic Logic: Introductory and Systematic Readings*. Reidel, Dordrecht.

Franke. R., 1987, Technological revolution and productivity decline: Computer introduction in the financial industry. *Technological Forecasting and Social Change*, 31, 143–154.

Freeman, C., 1991, Innovation, Changes of Techno-Economic Paradigm and Biological Analogies in Economics. *Revue économique*, 42(2), 211–231.

Gadia, S. K., Vaishnav J. H., 1985, A Query Language for a Homogeneous Temporal Database. *Proceedings of the Fourth ACM SIGACT-SIGMOD Symposium on Principles Of Database Systems*.

Galliers, R. (Ed.), 1987, *Information Analysis – Selected Readings*. Addison-Wesley, Wokingham, Sydney.

Gibbs, J. P., 1981, *Norms, Deviance, and Social Control – Conceptual Matters*. Elsevier, New York.

Gibson, J. J., 1968, *The Ecological Approach to Visual Perception*. Houghton Mifflin, Boston.

Goguen, J., 1992, The "Dry" and the "Wet". In Falkenberg, E. D., Rolland, C., El-Sayed, E. N. (Eds.), *Information System Concepts: Improving the Understanding*. Elsevier Science, Amsterdam.

Gomes, A., Gudwin, R., Queiroz, J., 2003, Towards meaning processes in computers from peircean semiotics. *Semiotics, Evolution, Energy, and Development*, 3(2), 69–79.

Gonzalez, R., 1997, Hypermedia data modeling, coding, and semiotics. *Proceedings of the FEEE*, 85(7), 1111–1140.

Gornik, D. (2004). IBM Rational Unified Process: Best Practices for Software Development Teams. Rational Software White Paper TP026B, Rev, 11(01).

Gredler, M. E., 1997, *Learning and Instruction: Theory Into Practice* (3rd Ed.). Prentice-Hall, Upper Saddle River, NJ.

Groot, C. De, 1992, Pragmatics in Functional Grammar. *Proceedings of Workshop of TWLT 4*. University Of Twente, Enschede.

Gudwin, R., Queiroz, J., 2005, *Towards an Introduction to Computational Semiotics, Proceedings of the 2005 IEEE International Conference on Integration of Knowledge Intensive Multi-Agent Systems (KIMAS' 05)*. Waltham, MA.

Gudwin, R., Queiroz, J. (Eds.), 2007, *Semiotics and Intelligent Systems Development*. IGI Global, Hershey, PA. Gurung, A., 2005, *A Survey of Information Technologies in Logistics Management*. IGI Global, Hershey, PA.

Gust, H., Kühnberger, K. U., 2008, *Universität Osnabrück Computational Logic And Cognitive Science: An Overview*. ICCL Summer School, Technical University of Dresden.

Haack, S., 1978, *Philosophy of Logics*. Cambridge University Press, Cambridge.

Hall, E. T., 1959, *The Silent Language*. Doubleday, New York.

Handler, R. A., 2013, *To Improve IT Project Success, Focus on Partnership, Requirements and Resources*. Gartner, USA.

Hartshorne, C., Weiss, P. (Eds.), 1974, *Collected Papers of Charles Sanders Peirce*, Vols. III and IV (4th Printing). Belknap Press Of Harvard University Press, Cambridge, MA.

Hawkes, T., 1977, *Structuralism and Semiotics*. Routledge, London.

He, M., Ren, C., Wang, Q., Shao, B., Dong, J., 2010, The Internet of Things as an Enabler to Supply Chain Innovation. In *IEEE 7th International Conference e-Business Engineering*.

Hedman, J., Lind, M., 2009, *Is There Only One Systems Development Life Cycle?* Springer US.

Heil, J., (Ed.), 2013, *Philosophy of Mind: A Contemporary Introduction*. Routledge, Oxford.

Hilpinen, R. (Ed.), 1971, *Deontic Logic: Introductory and Systematic Readings*. Reidel, Dordrecht.

Hirschheim, R., 1985, *Office Automation: A Social and Organizational Perspective*. John Wiley, Chichester.

Hirschheim, R., Klein, H. K., 1989, Four paradigms of information systems development. *Communications of the ACM*, 32(10), 1199–1216.

Hirschheim, R., Klein, H. K., Lyytinen, K., 1995, *Information Systems Development and Data Modelling: Conceptual and Philosophical Foundations*. Cambridge University Press, Cambridge.

Hoede, C., 1986, *Similarity in Knowledge Graphs*. Department of Applied Mathematics, University of Twente, Enschede.

Holy, L., Stuchlik, M., 1983, *Actions, Norms and Representation, Foundations of Anthropological Inquiry*. Cambridge University Press, Cambridge.

Hoque, F., 1999, E-Enterprise: Where Are You Today? White Paper.

House of Commons Committee of Public Accounts, 2011, The National Programme for IT in the NHS: An Update on the Delivery of Detailed Care Records Systems. Forty-Fifth Report Of Session 2010–12. http://www.publications.parliament.uk/pa/cm201012/cmselect/cmpubacc/1070/1070.pdf.

Howe, D. R., 1989, *Data Analysis for Database Design*. Routledge, Chapman & Hall, London.

Huang, K., 1998, Organisational Aspect of EDI: A Norm-Oriented Approach. PhD Thesis, University of Twente, Enschede.

Hull, E., Jackson, K., Dick, J., 2005, *Requirements Engineering*. Springer, London.

IBM, 2011a, From Social Media to Social CRM – Reinventing The Customer Relationship. Part 2, Executive Report. http://www-935.ibm.com/services/uk/cio/pdf/social_media_part_executive_report.pdf.

IBM, 2011b, From Social Media to Social CRM – What Customers Want? Executive Report. http://public.dhe.ibm.com/common/ssi/ecm/en/gbe03391usen/gbe03391usen.pdf.

Iivari, J., Hirschheim, R., Klein, H., 1998, A paradigmatic analysis contrasting information systems development approaches and methodologies. *Information Systems Research*, 9(2), 164–193.

Informatics Research Centre (IRC), 2013, Introduction to the Centre. http://www.henley.ac.uk/research/research-centres/informatics-research-centre/.

International Labour Organization (ILO), 2006, Report of the Director-General: Changing Patterns in The World Of Work. International Labour Conference 95th Session 2006, Geneva.

International Telecommunication Union, 2013, Measuring the Information Society. http://www.itu.int/en/itu-d/statistics/documents/publications/mis2013/mis2013_without_annex_4.pdf.

Jackman, M., Pavelin, C., 1988, Conceptual Graphs. In Ringland, G. A., Duce, D. A. (Eds.), *Approaches to Knowledge Representation*. Research Studies Press., Taunton; John Wiley, New York.

Jackson, M. A., 1983, *Systems Development*. Prentice Hall, Englewood Cliffs, NJ.

Jackson, M., 2001, *Problem Frames: Analysing and Structuring Software Development Problems*. Addison-Wesley, New York.

Jardine, D. A., 1984, Concepts and terminology for the conceptual schema and the information base. *Computers and Standards*, 3(1), 3–17.

Jayaratna, N., 1986, Normative Information Model-Based Systems Analysis and Design (NIMSAD): A framework for understanding and evaluating methodologies. *Journal of Applied Systems Analysis*, 13, 73–87.

Jayaratna, N., 1990, Systems analysis: The need for a better understanding. *International Journal of Information Management*, 10, 228–234.

Jones, A. J. I., 1983, *Communication and Meaning, an Essay in Applied Modal Logic*. Reidel, Dordrecht.

Jones, S., Mason, P., Stamper, R., 1979, LEGOL 2.0: A relational specification language for complex rules. *Information Systems*, 4, 28–48.

Jonkers, H., Lankhorst, M., Van Buuren, R., Hoppenbrouwers, S., Bonsangue, M., Van Der Torre, L., 2004, Concepts for modeling enterprise architectures. *International Journal of Cooperative Information Systems*, 13(3), 257–287.

Ketabchi, S., 2011, Patterns of Semiosis in Requirements Engineering. PhD Thesis, University of Reading.

Kim, B., 2001, Social constructivism. *Emerging Perspectives on Learning, Teaching, and Technology*, 1–8.

Kim, J., Yoo, H., Lee, Y., 1990, Design and implementation of a temporal query language with abstract time. *Information Systems*, 15(3), 349–357.

Kitchiner, D., Bundred, P., 1996, Integrated care pathways. *Archives of Disease in Childhood*, 75(2), 166–168.

Klarenberg, P., 1991, Issues on Design and Implementation of the Normbase Systems. Thesis, University of Twente, Enschede.

Klein, H. K., 1996, Preface: The Potential Contribution of Semiotics and Systems Theory to the Continuing Evolution of Information Systems Research. In Holmqvist, B., Andersen, P. B., Klein, H., Posner R., (Eds.), *Signs of Work: Semiosis and Information Processing in Organisations*. Walter De Gruyter, Berlin.

Kolkman, M., 1993, Problem Articulation Methodology. Doctoral Thesis, University of Twente, Enschede.

Kolkman, M., 1995, Managing Ambiguity and Change with the Problem Articulation Methodology. In Pettgrew A., Hines D. (Eds.), *Globalisation and Process Analysis of the Organisation*. Sage.

Kolkman, M., Liu, K., 1991, *Systems Physiology: An Approach of Norm-Governed Action. Proceedings of Dutch National Conference of Business Research (NOBO)*, Enschede.

Kotonya, G., Sommerville I., 1998, *Requirements Engineering: Processes AND Techniques*. John Wiley, New York.

Kuhn, T. S.,1962, *The Structure of Scientific Revolutions*. University of Chicago Press, Chicago.

Kuhn, T. S., 1970, *The Structure of Scientific Revolutions* (2nd Ed,). University of Chicago Press, Chicago.

Kukla, A., 2000, *Social Constructivism and the Philosophy of Science*. Routledge, New York.

Lacey, A. R., 1976, *A Dictionary of Philosophy*. Routledge & Kegan Paul, London.

Lakatos, I., 1970, Falsification and the Methodology of Scientific Research Programmes. In Lakatos, I., Musgrave, A., (Eds.), *Criticism and the Growth of Knowledge*. Cambridge University Press, Cambridge.

Lankhorst, M. M., 2004, Enterprise Architecture modelling: The issue of integration. *Advanced Engineering Informatics*, 18(4), 205–216.

Lapkin, A., Allega, P., Burke, B., Burton, B., Bittler, R. C., Handler, R. A. *et al.*, 2008, Gartner Clarifies the Definition of the Term 'Enterprise Architecture'. https://www.gartner.com/doc/740712/gartner-clarifies-definition-term-enterprise.

Larson, R. C., 2008, Service science: At the intersection of management, social and engineering sciences. *IBM Systems Journal*, 47(1), 41–51.

Laudon, K. C., Laudon, J. P., 2000, *Management Information Systems* (Vol. 6). New Jersey: Prentice Hall.

Lee, R. M., 1988, Bureaucracies as deontic systems. *ACM Transactions on Office Information Systems*, 6(2), 87–108.

Lee, H., Padmanabhan, V., Whang, S., 1997, Information distortion in a supply chain: the bullwhip effect. *Management Science*, 43(4), 546–558.

Leslie, R. E., 1986, *Systems Analysis and Design*. Prentice-Hall, Englewood Cliffs, NJ.

Li, W., Liu, K., Yang, H., Yu, C., 2013, Integrated clinical pathway management for medical quality improvement–based on a semiotically inspired systems architecture. *European Journal of Information Systems*, 23(4), 400–417.

Limbuwala, H., 2006, Retail – Customer Is King – RFID & CRM Based Customer Loyalty Program (CLP), Skandsoft Technologies, Pvt. Ltd. http://www.homilimbu.com/pdf/retail_customer_is_king-homi_limbuwala.pdf.

Lindgreen, P. (Ed.), 1990, A Framework of Information System Concepts, Interim Report of the IFIP WG 8.1 Task Group FRISCO.

Liu, K., 1993, Semiotics Applied to Information Systems Development. PhD Thesis, University of Twente, Enschede.

Liu, K., Benfell, A., 2011, Pragmatic web services: A semiotic viewpoint. software and data technologies. *Communications in Computer and Information Science*, 50, 18–32.

Liu, K., Dix, A., 1997, Norm Governed Agents in CSCW. The First International Workshop On Computational Semiotics. Paris.

Liu, K., Gao, Z. L., 1997, A Problem Articulation Method for Information Systems: Planning for Responsive Information Management Infrastructure. In Avison, D. (Ed.), *Key Issues in Information Systems*. McGraw Hill.

Liu, K., Ades, Y., Stamper, R., 1994, Simplicity, Uniformity and Quality: The Role of Semantic Analysis in Systems Development. In Ross, M., Brebbia, C. A., Staples, G., Stapleton, J. (Eds.), *Software Quality Management*, Vol. 2. Computational Mechanics Publications.

Liu, K., Alderson, A., Qureshi, Z., 1999a, Requirements Recovery of Legacy Systems by Analysing and Modelling Behaviour. In *Proceedings of the International Conference of Software Maintenance*, Oxford.

Liu, K., Alderson, A., Shah, H., Sharp B., Dix, A., 1999b, Applying Semiotic Methods to Requirements Recovery. In Jayaratna, N. (Ed.), *Methodologies for Developing and Managing Emerging Technology-Based Information Systems*. Springer, London.

Liu, K., Clarke, R. J., Andersen, P. B., Stamper, R. K., 2001, *Information, Organisation and Technology: Studies in Organisational Semiotics*. Kluwer Academic Publishers, Boston.

Liu, K., Clarke, R. J., Andersen, P. B., Stamper, R. K., 2002, *Organizational Semiotics: Evolving A Science of Information Systems*. Kluwer Academic Publishers, Boston.

Liu, K., Sun, L., Barjis, J., Dietz, J. L. G., 2003, Modelling dynamic behaviour of business organisations-extension of demo from a semiotic perspective. *Knowledge-based Systems*, 16, 101–111.

Liu, K., Sun, L., Tan, S., 2006, Modelling complex systems for project planning: A semiotics motivated method. *International Journal of General Systems*, 35(3), 313–327.

Liu, K., Sun, L., Rong, W., 2009, Semiotic Modelling for Complex Enterprise Systems. *The 11th International Conference on Informatics and Semiotics in Organisations, IFIP WG8.1 Working Conference*. Aussino Academic Publishing House, Australia.

Liu, K., Sun, L., Jambari, D., Mitchell, V., Chong, S., 2011, A Design of Business-Technology Alignment Consulting Framework. In *Proceedings Of International Conference on Advanced Information Systems Engineering (CAiSE)*, 422–435. Springer, Heidelberg.

Liu, K., Li, W., Gulliver, S. R., (Eds), 2013, Web of Things, People and Information Systems, *Proceeding of the 14th International Conference on Organisational Semiotics in Organisations*. Science and Technology Publications, Portugal.

Long, S. (Ed.), 2013, *Socioanalytic Methods: Discovering the Hidden in Organisations and Social Systems*. Karnac, London.

Loomis, M. E. S., 1990, OODBMS Vs. Relational. *Journal of Object Oriented Programming*, July/August, 79–82.

Loux, M. J., 1978, *Substance And Attribute – A Study in Ontology*. Reidel, Dordrecht.

Lundeberg, M., Goldkuhl, G., Nilsson, A., 1981, *Information Systems Development: A Systematic Approach*. Prentice-Hall, Englewood Cliffs, NJ.

Lyons, J., 1977, *Semantics*, Vol. I. Cambridge University Press, Cambridge.

Lyytinen, K., 1987, Two views of information modeling. *Information and Management*, 12, 9–19.

Lyytinen, K., Lehtinen, E., 1986, Action based model of information system. *Information Systems*, 11(4), 299–317.

Ma, L., Nuseibeh, B., Piwek, P., De Roeck, A., Willis, A., 2009, On Presuppositions in Requirements. In *2nd International Workshop On Managing Requirements Knowledge, Mark'09*. IEEE, Atlanta, GA.

Maalej, W., Thurimella, A. K., 2013, An Introduction to Requirements Knowledge. In *Managing Requirements Knowledge*. Springer, Berlin.

Machlup, F., 1980, *Knowledge: Its Creation, Distribution, and Economic Significance*, Vol. I, *Knowledge and Knowledge Production*. Princeton University Press, Princeton, NJ.

Macro, A., Buxton, J., 1987, *The Craft of Software Engineering*. Addison-Wesley, Wokingham.

Masterman, M., 1970, The Nature of a Paradigm. In Lakatos, I., Musgrave, A. (Eds.), *Criticism and the Growth of Knowledge*. Cambridge University Press, Cambridge.

McCarty, L. T., 1986, Permissions and Obligations: An Informal Introduction. In Martino, A. A., Natali, F. S. (Eds.), *Automated Analysis of Legal Texts: Logic, Informatics, Law*. Elsevier Science, Amsterdam.

McDavid, D., 1998, A Standard for Business Architecture Description. *IBM Systems Journal*, 38, 12–31.

McMahon, M., 1997, Social Constructivism and the World Wide Web – A Paradigm for Learning. *ASCILITE Proceedings*. Perth, Australia.

Menzel, C., 2013, "Actualism". In Zalta, N. (Ed.), The Stanford Encyclopedia of Philosophy. http://plato.stanford.edu/archives/win2013/entries/actualism.

Meyer, J. J. C., 1988, A different approach to deontic logic: Deontic logic viewed as a variant of dynamic logic. *Notre Dame Journal of Formal Logic*, 29(1), 109–136.

Meyer, J. J. C., Wieringa, R. J., 1993, Deontic Logic: A Concise Overview. In Meyer, J. J. C., Wieringa, R. J. (Eds.), *Deontic Logic in Computer Science*. John Wiley, Chichester.

Micallef, J., 1988, Encapsulation, reusability and extensibility in object-oriented programming languages. *Journal of Object-oriented Programming*, April/May, 12–34.

Michaels, C. F., Carello, C., 1981, *Direct Perception*. Prentice-Hall, Englewood Cliffs, NJ.

Minker, J. (Ed.), 1988, *Foundations of Deductive Databases and Logic Programming*. Morgan Kaufmann, San Francisco.

Mintzberg, H., 1988, *Mintzberg on Management*. Free Press, New York.

Mintzberg. H., 1973, *The Nature of Managerial Work*. Harper & Row, New York.

Mishra, G. N., 1982, *Ontology*. Shri Maheshwari, Varanasi.

Morris, C. W., 1938, *Foundations of the Theory of Signs*. International Encyclopedia of Unified Sciences, 1(2).

Morris, C. W., 1946, *Signs, Language and Behaviour*. Braziller, New York.

Müller-Veerse, F., 2000, Mobile Commerce Report. http://www.dad.be/library/pdf/durlacher1.pdf.

Mumford, E., Weir, M., 1979, *Computer Systems in Work Design – The ETHICS Method*. Associated Business Press, London.

Muscholl, M., 2005, Integrated Clinical Pathways in Health Information Systems – An Architectural Concept. Professional Knowledge Management, *Lecture Notes In Computer Science*. Springer 3782, 349–359.

Nachmias, C., Nachmias, D., 1981, *Research Methods in the Social Sciences*. St Martin's Press, London.

Nadin, M., 1987, *Pragmatics in the Semiotic Frame*. Versión Digital.

Nauta, D., 1972, *The Meaning of Information*. Mouton, The Hague.

National Office for the Information Economy, Canberra, 2003, E-Government Benefits Study, Commonwealth of Australia, Canberra.

Nijssen, G. M., 1986, *Knowledge Engineering, Conceptual Schemas, SQL and Expert Systems: A Unifying Point Of View*. University of Queensland, Brisbane.

Nuseibeh, B., Easterbrook, S., 2000, *Requirements Engineering: A Roadmap, Proceedings of the Conference on the Future of Software Engineering*, 4–11 June, Limerick, Ireland. ACM, USA.

Office of Management and Budget (OMB), 2010, Executive Summary for E-Government Benefits Report to Congress 2010, United States. http://www.whitehouse.gov/sites/default/files/omb/assets/egov_docs/fy10_e-gov_benefits_report.pdf.

Olle, T. W., Sol, H. G., Verrijn-Stuart, A. A. (Eds.), 1982, *Information Systems Design Methodologies: A Comparative Review*. Elsevier Science, Amsterdam.

Olle, T. W., Hagelstein, J., Macdonald, I. G., Rolland, C., Sol, H. G., Assche, F. J. M. V. *et al.*, 1991, *Information Systems Methodologies: A Framework for Understanding*. Addison-Wesley, Wokingham.

Open Group, 2009, *The SOA Source Book*. Van Haren, Zaltbommel, Netherlands.

Open Group, 2011, An Introduction to TOGAF® Version 9.1. https://www2.opengroup.org/ogsys/catalog/w118.

Organisation for Economic Co-operation and Development (OECD), 2003, *The E-Government Imperative*. OECD E-Government Flagship Report. Public Management Committee, Paris.

Organisational Semiotics Workshop, 1995, *The Circulation Document*. Organisational Semiotics Workshop, Enschede.

Ould, M.A., 1995, *Business Processes: Modelling and Analysis for Re-engineering and Improvement*. Wiley, New York.

Pacific Council for International Policy, 2002, *Roadmap for e-Government in the Developing World*. PCIP, Los Angeles.

Parsons-Hann, H. 2003, Information Infrastructure for e-Policing. BSc Thesis, Computer Science Department, University of Reading, Reading.

Paul, R. J., 2010, Loose change. *European Journal Of Information Systems*, 19, 379–381.

Pavelin, C., 1988, Logic in Knowledge Representation. In Ringland, G. A., Duce, D. A. (Eds.), *Approaches to Knowledge Representation: An Introduction*. Research Studies Press, Taunton.

Peirce, C. S., 1958a, *Collected Papers*, Vols. 1–8. Hartshorne, C., Weiss, P. (Eds.), 1960, Harvard University Press, Cambridge, MA.

Peirce, C. S., 1958b, Nomenclature and Divisions of Triadic Relations, as far as They are Determined, Collected Papers, Vol. 2 Reprinted: In Essential Peirce, V. 2, Pp. 289–99.

Peirce, C. S., Welby-Gregory, V., 1977, *Semiotic and Significs: The Correspondence Between C. S. Peirce and Victoria Lady Welby, edited by Charles S. Hardwick with the assistance of James Cook*, Indiana University Press, Bloomington, IN.

Perez, C., 1983, Structural change and the assimilation of new technologies in the economic and social system. *Futures*, 15(5), 370–375.

Perez, C., 2010, Technological revolutions and techno-economic paradigms. *Cambridge Journal of Economics*, 34(1), 185–202.

Pohl, K., 2010, *Requirements Engineering: Fundamentals, Principles, and Techniques*. Springer.

Police Information Technology Organisation (PITO), 2002. *e-Policing Strategic Framework*. PITO, London.

Police Information Technology Organisation (PITO), 2003. *Forward Plan 2003 to 2008.* PITO, London.
Polovina, A., Heaton, J., 1992, An introduction to conceptual graphs. *AI Expert*, 7(5), 36–43.
Popper, K., 1970, Normal Science and its Dangers. In Lakatos, I., Musgrave, A., (Eds.), *Criticism and the Growth of Knowledge.* Cambridge University Press, Cambridge.
Porat, M. U., 1977, *The Information Economy: Definition and Measurement.* US Department of Commerce, Washington, DC.
Porter, M. E., 1985, *Competitive Advantage: Creating and Sustaining Superior Performance.* Free Press, New York.
Porter, M. E., 1996, What is Strategy? *Harvard Business Review*, November–December, 61–78.
Prates, R. O., Souza, C. S. D., Barbosa, S. D. J., 2000, Methods and Tools: A Method for Evaluating the Communicability of User Interfaces. *ACM Interactions*, January–February, 31–38.
Prawat, R. S., Floden, R. E., 1994, Philosophical perspectives on constructivist views of learning. *Educational Psychologist*, 29(1), 37–48.
Pwc, 2013, The 2013 Top Ten Technology Trends for Business. Pwc's 5th Annual Digital IQ Survey Digital Conversations and the C-Suite, http://www.pwc.com/us/digitaliq.
Queiroz, J., Gudwin, R., 2003, Computational Intelligence and Semiotics – On the Synthesis of Semiosis in Artificial Systems and Creatures. *Semiotics, Evolution, Energy, and Development*, 3(3) (Special Issue).
Randal, D. M., 1988, Semantic Networks. In Ringland, G. A., Duce, D. A., (Eds.), *Approaches to Knowledge Representation: An Introduction.* Research Studies Press, Taunton.
Reiter, R., 1984, Towards a Logical Reconstruction of Relational Database Theory. In Brodie, M. L., Mylopoulos, J., Schmidt, J. W., (Eds.), *On Conceptual Modelling: Perspectives from Artificial Intelligence, Databases, and Programming Languages.* Springer-Verlag, New York.
Ringland, G. A., Duce, D. A. (Eds.), 1988, *Approaches to Knowledge Representation: An Introduction.* Research Studies Press, Taunton.
Rogoff, B., 1990, *Apprenticeship in Thinking: Cognitive Development in Social Context.* Oxford University Press, New York.
Rolland, C., Achour, C. B., Cauvet, C., Ralyte, J., Sutcliffe, A., Maiden, N., *et al.*, 1998, A Proposal for a Scenario Classification Framework. *Requirements Engineering*, 3(1), 23–47.
Russell, B., 2001, *The Problems of Philosophy.* Oxford University Press, Oxford.
Ryle, G., 1949, *The Concept of Mind.* Hutchinson, London.
Ryu, Y. U., Lee, R. M., 1993, Defeasible Deontic Reasoning: A Logic Programming Model. In Meyer, J. J. C., Wieringa, R. J. (Eds.), *Deontic Logic in Computer Science.* John Wiley, Chichester.
Sabri, E. H., Shaikh, S. N., 2010, *Lean and Agile Value Chain Management: A Guide to the Next Level of Improvement.* J. Ross, Plantation, FL.
Sadeghi, R., Samson, W. B., Deen, S. M., 1988, HQL – A Historical Query Language. In *Proceedings of the South British National Conference On Databases (BNCOD6).* University College, Cardiff.
Sarda, N. L., 1990, Algebra and query language for a historical data model. *Computer Journal*, 33(1), 11–18.
Schank, R. C., 1972, Conceptual dependency: A theory of natural language understanding. *Cognitive Psychology*, 3(4), 552–631.
Schank, R. C., 1975, Conceptual Information Processing. Elsevier Science, New York.
Schueler, B., 1977, Update Reconsidered. In G. M. Nijssen (Ed.), *Architecture and Models in Data Base Management Systems.* North-Holland, Amsterdam.

Scitepress, R. J., Liu, K., Jiang, G., Nakata, K., Sun, L., (Eds.), 2010, *Pervasive Informatics in the Digital Economy, Proceeding of the 12th Conference on Organisational Semiotics*. Aussino Academic Publishing House; Australia.

Scott, D., Souza, C. S. D., 1990, Getting the message across in RST-based text generation. *Current Research in Natural Language Generation*, 4, 47–73.

Seacord, R. C., Plakosh, D., Lewis, G. A., 2003, *Modernizing Legacy Systems: Software Technologies, Engineering Processes, and Business Practices*. Addison-Wesley Professional.

Searle, J. R., 1969, *Speech Acts – An Essay in the Philosophy of Language*. Cambridge University Press, Cambridge.

Searle, J. R., 1979, *Expression and Meaning*. Cambridge University Press, Cambridge.

Searle, J. R., 1983, *Intentionality – An Essay in the Philosophy of Mind*. Cambridge University Press, Cambridge.

Searle, J. R., D. Vanderveken, 1985, *Foundations of Illocutionary Logic*. Cambridge University Press, Cambridge.

Shannon, C. E., Weaver W., 1949, *The Motsky Mathematical Theory Of Communication*. University of Illinois Press, Urbana.

Shearer, I., 1992, Retrospective update: Data as it was believed to be. *Computer Journal*, 35(2), 184–186.

Shlaer, S., Mellor, S. J., 1988, *Object Oriented Analysis, Modelling the World in Data*. Yourdon Press, Englewood Cliffs, NJ.

Shlaer, S., Mellor, S. J., 1992, *Object Lifecycles, Modelling the World in States*. Yourdon Press, Englewood Cliffs, NJ.

Simon, H. A., 1960, *The New Science of Management Decision*. New York, Harper.

Smit, H. J., 1991, Consistency and Robustness of Knowledge Graphs. Doctoral Thesis, University of Twente, Enschede.

Snodgrass, R., 1985, A Taxonomy of Time in Databases. In *Proceedings Of ACM-SIGMOD, International Conference On Management Of Data (SIGMOD '85)*. ACM, New York.

Snodgrass, R., 1987, The temporal query language TQUEL. *TODS*, 12(2), 247–298.

Souza, C. S. D., 1993, The semiotics engineering of user interface. *International Journal Of Man-Machine Studies*, 39, 753–773.

Souza, C. S. D, 1997, Supporting End-User Programming with Explanatory Discourse. In *Proceedings of ISAS'97. Intelligent Systems and Semiotics – A Learning Perspective* NIST, Gaithersburg, MD.

Souza, C. S. D., 2005, Semiotic engineering: Bringing designers and users together at interaction time. *Interacting With Computers*, 17, 317–341.

Souza, C. S. D., 2006, Semiotic Engineering – A New Paradigm for Designing Interactive Systems. In *IFIP 19th World Computer Congress, TC-8*. Information System Stream, Santiago, Chile.

Souza, C. S. D., Barbosa, S. D. J., 2001, Semiotic engineering principles for evaluating end-user programming environments. *Interacting With Computers*, 13(4), 467–495.

Sowa, J., 1984, Conceptual Structures: Information Processing in Mind and Machine. Addison-Wesley, Reading, MA.

Ssr, A., 2008, Healthcare Knowledge Management: The Art of the Possible. In *Proceedings of the Conference on Knowledge Management for Health Care Procedures*. Springer-Verlag, Berlin.

Stamper, R. K., 1973, *Information in Business and Administrative Systems*. John Wiley, New York.

Stamper, R. K., 1980, LEGOL: Modelling Legal Rules by Computer. In Niblett, B. (Ed.), *Computer Science and Law: An Advanced Course*. Cambridge University Press, Cambridge.

Stamper, R. K., 1985, Knowledge as Action: A Logic of Social Norms and Individual Affordances. In Gilbert, G. N., Heath, C., (Eds.), *Social Action and Artificial Intelligence*. Grower Press, Aldershot.

Stamper, R. K., 1987. Semantics. In Boland, R. J., Hirschheim, R. A. (Eds), *Critical Issues In Information System Systems Research.* John Wiley, Chichester.

Stamper, R. K., 1992, Language and Computer in Organised Behaviour. In Riet, R. P. V. D., Meersman, R. A., (Eds.), *Linguistic Instruments in Knowledge Engineering.* Elsevier Science, Amsterdam.

Stamper, R. K., 1993, Social Norms in Requirements Analysis – An Outline of MEASUR. In Jirotka, M., Goguen, J., Bickerton, M. (Eds.), *Requirements Engineering, Technical and Social Aspects.* Academic Press, New York.

Stamper, R.K., 1996, Signs, Information, Norms and Systems. In Holmqvist, P., Andersen, P.B., Klein, H., Posner, R. (Eds.), *Signs of Work: Semiotics and Information Processing in Organisations.* Walter de Gruyter, Amsterdam.

Stamper, R.K., 2000, Information Systems as a Social Science: An Alternative to the FRISCO Formalism. In Falkenberg, E. D., Lyytinen, K., Verrijn-Stuart, A. A. (Eds.), *Information Systems Concepts: An Integrated Discipline Emerging.* Kluwer Academic Publishers, Boston.

Stamper, R. K., Nauta, D., 1990, *Information in a Semiotic Framework.* FRISCO Task Group Of IFIP WG 8.1.

Stamper, R. K., Liu, K., Kolkman, M., Klarenberg, P., Slooten, V. F., Ades, Y. *et al.*, 1991, From Database to Normbase. *International Journal of Information Management,* 11, 62–79.

Stamper, R. K., Liu, K., Huang, K., 1994, Organizational Morphology in Re-engineering. In *Proceedings of the Second European Conference of Information Systems.* Nijenrode University, Breukelen.

Stamper, R. K., Liu, K., Hafkamp, M., Ades, Y., 1997, Signs Plus Norms – One Paradigm for Organisational Semiotics. In *The First International Workshop On Computational Semiotics,* Paris.

Stamper, R. K., Althaus, K., Backhouse, J., 1988, MEASUR: Method for Eliciting, Analyzing and Specifying User Requirements. In Olle, T. W., Verrijn-Stuart, A. A. And Bhabuts, L., (Eds.), *Computerized Assistance During the Information Systems Life Cycle.* Elsevier Science, Amsterdam.

Stamper, R., Liu, K., Hafkamp, M., Ades, Y., 2000, understanding the role of signs and norms in organisations: A semiotic approach to information systems design. *Journal of Behaviour and Information Technology,* 19(1), 15–27.

Stonebraker, M., Rowe, L. A., Lindsay, B., Gray, J., Carey, M., Brodie, M. *et al.*, 1990, Third Generation Data Base System Manifesto. The Committee For Advanced DBMS Function, Memorandum No. UCB/ERL M90/29. College of Engineering, University of California, Berkeley, CA.

Stowell, F. (Ed.), 1995, *Information Systems Provision.* McGraw-Hill, London.

Strassmann, P., 1980, The office of the future: information management for the new age. *Technology Review,* December/January, 54–65.

Strassmann, P., 1990, *The Business Value of Computers: An Executive's Guide.* Information Economics Press, New Canaan, CT.

Strassmann, P. A., 2004, Six rules for finding IT value. *Cutter IT Journal,* 17, 5–9.

Systä, T., 1999, On the Relationships Between Static and Dynamic Models in Reverse Engineering Java Software. *Proceedings of the 6th Working Conference on Reverse Engineering,* Atlanta, GA.

Thayse, A. (Ed.), 1989, *From Modal Logic to Deductive Databases.* John Wiley, Chichester.

Thoenissen, K., 1990, Semantic Analysis: A Study and Comparison. MSc Thesis, University of Twente, Enschede.

Thomas, R., Cullen, P., 2001, Building an enterprise architecture framework. *US Customs Today,* 1(4), 31–39.

Tiwari, R., Buse, S., Herstatt, C., 2006, From electronic to mobile commerce: Opportunities through technology convergence for business services, *Asia Pacific Tech Monitor*, 23(5), 38–45.

Tomberlin, J. E., 1996, Actualism or possibilism? *Philosophical Studies*, 84(2), 263–281.

Tomberlin, J. E., 1998, Naturalism, actualism, and ontology. *Noûs*, 32(S12), 489–498.

UK Academy For Information Systems (UKAIS), 2014, Definition of Information Systems. http://www.ukais.org.uk/about/definitionis.aspx.

United Nations Public Administration Network UNPAN, 2012, Expanding Usage to Realize the Full Benefit. United Nations E-Government Survey. http://unpan1.un.org/intradoc/groups/public/documents/un/unpan048065.pdf.

Verheijen, G., Bekkum, J., 1982, NIAM: An Information Analysis Method. In Olle, W., Sol, H., Verrijn-Stuart, A. (Eds.), *Information Systems Design Methodologies: A Comparative Review*. Elsevier Science, Amsterdam.

Wagenaar, J., 2012, The Impact of the Internet of Things on Revenue in Supply Chains. Know What's in Store With RFID. White Paper.

Waters, J. K., 2008, Agile Lands Role in Games and Business Software. *Register*. http://www.theregister.co.uk/2008/02/28/agile_crossing_chasm/.

Way, E. C., 1991, *Knowledge Representation and Metaphor*. Kluwer Academic Publishers, Dordrecht.

Weg, R. V. D., Engmann, R., 1992, A Framework and Method for Object-Oriented Information Systems Analysis and Design. In Falkenberg, E. D., Rolland, C., El-Sayer, E. N. (Eds.), *Information System Concepts: Improving the Understanding*. Elsevier Science, Amsterdam.

Weigand, H., 1990, *Linguistically Motivated Principles of Knowledge Base Systems*. Foris, Dordrecht.

Weigand, H., 1993, Deontic Aspects of Communication. In Meyer, J. J. Ch., Wieringa, R. J. (Eds.), *Deontic Logic in Computer Science*. John Wiley, Chichester.

Welty, B., Becerra-Fernandez, I., 2001, Managing trust and commitment in collaborative supply chain relationships. *Communications of the ACM*, 44(6), 67–73.

Wieringa, R. J., Meyer, J. J. C., 1991, Applications of Deontic Logic to Computer Science: A Concise Overview. In Meyer, J. J. Ch., Wieringa, R. J. (Eds.), *Deontic Logic in Computer Science*. John Wiley, Chichester.

Wieringa, R., Meyer, J. J. C., Weigand, H., 1989, Specifying dynamic and deontic integrity constraints. *Data and Knowledge Engineering*, 4, 157–190.

Wilks, Y. A., 1978, Primitives. In Shapiro, S. C. (Ed.), *The Encyclopedia of Artificial Intelligence*, Vol. 1 John Wiley, New York.

Wilson, B., 1984, *Systems: Concepts, Methodologies, and Applications*. John Wiley A, Chichester.

Winograd, T., 1975, Frame Representations and the Declarative/Procedural Controversy. In Bobrow, D. G., Collins, A. M. (Eds.), *Representation and Understanding: Studies in Cognitive Science*. Academic Press, New York.

Winograd, T., 1983, *Language as a Cognitive Process*, Vol. I, *Syntax*. Addison-Wesley, Reading, MA.

Winograd, T., Flores C. F., 1987, *Understanding Computers and Cognition*. Addison-Wesley, Reading, MA.

Wright, G. H. V., 1951, *An Essay in Modal Logic*. North-Holland, Amsterdam.

Wright, G. H. V., 1963, *Norms and Action – A Logical Enquiry*. Routledge & Kegan Paul, New York.

Yang, H., De Roeck, A., Gervasi, V., Willis, A., Nuseibeh, B., 2010, Extending Nocuous Ambiguity Analysis for Anaphora in Natural Language Requirements. In *Proceedings Of The 18th IEEE International Conference On Requirements Engineering*, Sydney.

Yourdon, E., 1989, *Modern Structured Analysis*. Prentice-Hall, Englewood Cliffs, NJ.

Yourdon, E., Constantine, L., 1979, *Structured Design*. Prentice-Hall, Englewood Cliffs, NJ.

Yu, C. H., 1994, Abduction? Deduction? Induction? Is There a Logic Of Exploratory Data Analysis? The Annual Meeting of American Educational Research Association, New Orleans, Louisiana, http://seamonkey.ed.asu.edu/~behrens/asu/reports/peirce/logic_of_eda.html.

Zachman, J., 2008, *John Zachman's Concise Definition of the Zachman Framework*. Zachman International, USA.

Zachman, J., 2009, *The Zachman Framework: The Official Concise Definition*. Zachman International, USA.

Zorayda, R. A., 2003, *e-Commerce and e-Business*. e-ASEAN Task Force, Jakarta.

INDEX